FRITZ

Perls

Key Figures in Counselling and Psychotherapy

Series editor: Windy Dryden

The *Key Figures in Counselling and Psychotherapy* series of books provides a concise, accessible introduction to the lives, contributions and influence of the leading innovators whose theoretical and practical work has had a profound impact on counselling and psychotherapy. The series includes comprehensive overviews of:

Fritz Perls
Petrŭska Clarkson and Jennifer Mackewn

Sigmund Freud
by Michael Jacobs

Melanie Klein
by Julia Segal

Eric Berne
by Ian Stewart

Carl Rogers
by Brian Thorne

FRITZ Perls

Petrūska Clarkson
Jennifer Mackewn

SAGE Publications
London • Newbury Park • New Delhi

First published 1993

SAGE Publications Ltd
6 Bonhill Street
London EC2A 4PU

SAGE Publications Inc
2455 Teller Road
Newbury Park, California 91320

SAGE Publications India Pvt Ltd
32, M-Block Market
Greater Kailash – I
New Delhi 110 048

British Library Cataloguing in Publication Data

A catalogue record for this book is available from the
British Library.

ISBN 0–8039–8452–9
ISBN 0–8039–8453–7 (pbk)

Library of Congress catalog card number 93–083562

Typeset by Mayhew Typesetting, Rhayader, Powys
Printed in Great Britain by Biddles Ltd, Guildford, Surrey

Contents

ACD 2031

Gift de Bellack 8/19/93

Acknowledgements

The authors and the publishers would like to thank the following for permission to reproduce figures from the sources shown:

Figure 2.3 (*Gestalt Completion Test*) is reprinted by permission from Teachers College Press from Street, R.F. (1931) *Gestalt Completion Test*, Teachers College Press, Columbia University, New York. All rights reserved.

Figure 2.4 (*Illustration of Figure and Ground*) is reprinted by permission from Gyldendalske Boghandel, from Rubin, E. (1921) *Visuell Wahrgenommene Figuren*, Gyldendalske Boghandel, Köbenhaven. All rights reserved.

Figure 2.5 (*Wu Gi and Tai Gi*) is reprinted by permission from Vintage Books (a division of Random House), from Perls, F.S. (1969) *Ego, Hunger and Aggression*, Vintage Books, New York, (first published 1947). All rights reserved.

Figure 5.1 (*Awareness-Excitement-Contact Cycle*) is reprinted by permission from Vintage Books (a division of Random House) from Zinker, J. (1978) *Creative Process in Gestalt Therapy*, Vintage Books, New York, (first published 1977). All rights reserved.

Figure 5.2 (*The Cycle of Gestalt Formation and Destruction*) is reprinted by permission from Sage Publications from Clarkson, P. (1989) *Gestalt Counselling in Action*, Sage, London. All rights reserved.

Every effort has been made to obtain permission to reproduce copyright material throughout the book. If any proper acknowledgement has not been made, or permission not received, we would invite any copyright holder to inform us of this oversight and the necessary arrangements will be made at the first opportunity.

Preface

Fritz Perls is well-known as the founder or co-founder of Gestalt therapy. He was a popular but very controversial psychotherapist, teacher and writer. Beginning his professional life as a German Jewish doctor and neuropsychiatrist with a passion for the theatre, he swiftly developed an interest in psychoanalysis, Gestalt psychology, existential phenomenology, holism and the work of innovative psychoanalysts, such as Karen Horney, Wilhelm Reich and Stack Sullivan. He synthesized ideas from these and many other sources to co-create (with his wife Laura Perls) a new branch of psychotherapy, which he and his colleagues later named Gestalt therapy. In the 1960s he became world famous as a prominent leader of the growth and humanistic psychotherapy movements in America – putting on frequent workshops and seminars to demonstrate the practical application of some of his later ideas.

Fritz Perls' work has had both a positive and negative influence upon the subsequent development of Gestalt therapy. On the positive side, he wrote the first theoretical text, *Ego, Hunger and Aggression* (Perls, 1947/1969a), which would form the basis for Gestalt psychotherapy and he collaboratively co-authored the major theoretical work of Gestalt psychotherapy – *Gestalt Therapy: Excitement and Growth in the Human Personality* (Perls, Hefferline and Goodman, 1951/1973). He undoubtedly did much to promote Gestalt psychotherapy and to ensure that it became established as a major alternative to traditional psychoanalysis. His demonstrations, together with the transcripts and films that he made of himself at work, did much to demystify psychotherapy, to make the psychotherapist accountable and to render the psychotherapist's work available for public scrutiny in a way that was hitherto virtually unknown and which has been to the benefit of generations of later clients.

On the other hand, Fritz Perls was also showy, charismatic and attention-seeking. He often demonstrated a very active and dramatic style of psychotherapy. Many mistook this style for Gestalt therapy and copied his more obvious therapeutic tools and methods without either his clinical expertise or his creative flair. Some of his emulators thus reduced Perls' individually designed therapeutic experiments to mere gimmicks or repetitive techniques and thus missed the very essence of Gestalt therapy as Perls and his colleagues had originally conceived and developed it. For a central aspect of Gestalt therapy is its open exploratory attitude that avoids imitations, mechanical assumptions or sterile repetitions and seeks the unique creative resolution of this unique situation for this unique person, in this relationship, in this field, at this moment in time. Thus as well as co-founding and popularizing Gestalt psychotherapy, Fritz Perls also contributed to a widespread misunderstanding of Gestalt psychotherapy which frequently reduces it to a set of active techniques.

In this book we describe Fritz Perls' seminal and positive contribution to the theoretical foundation of Gestalt psychotherapy and his tremendously vital demonstration of one style of applying theory to practice, while at the same time indicating the ways in which he undermined his own major contribution by presenting his personal style as though it *was* Gestalt therapy and by damaging the reputation of Gestalt therapy through some of his personal conduct. We explore the influence which Fritz Perls has had upon the subsequent development of Gestalt therapy and the impact (frequently underestimated) which his work has made upon the overall field of counselling.

Fritz Perls died over twenty years ago. Since then Gestalt psychotherapists have continued to evolve and change, building upon and reacting to the root contribution made by Perls and his colleagues; while at the same time introducing and developing new emphases and synthesizing ideas and approaches from other schools of thought. This generation of Gestalt practitioners has abjured unethical behaviour and established ethical codes and accountability procedures in the interests of the safety of the client. By clarifying the nature of Perls' contribution, exploring the 'ambiguous shadow' (Miller, 1989) which he has cast upon the ranks of his followers and indicating both the rich diversity and the drawbacks of his work, we hope to make the evolution of Gestalt therapy and the concepts of current Gestalt psychotherapy more accessible *both* to Gestalt practitioners and trainees *and* to counsellors and psychotherapists of other disciplines.

Layout of this book

The sequence of the chapters in the book is the same as in the other volumes in the *Key Figures in Counselling and Psychotherapy* series. Chapter 1 is an overview of Fritz Perls' life and career. We have especially paid attention to the experiences, ideas and people which had the most important influence upon him and the therapeutic approach he evolved. Chapter 2 describes Perls' major contributions to theory and identifies which movements and writers influenced specific aspects of his theoretical contributions. Chapter 3 summarizes the main contributions which Perls made to the practice of psychotherapy and counselling and illustrates each contribution described by one or two detailed examples of Perls working with clients. It thus capitalizes upon the rich fund of filmed and transcribed demonstration sessions, which was in itself one of Perls' major legacies and brings his work and ideas alive in a very tangible way. As we have indicated, Perls and his work have attracted a good deal of criticism and misunderstanding as well as praise. Chapter 4 examines these criticisms, as expressed by widely-read authors and makes an honest attempt to evaluate the degree of justification for each. Finally, Chapter 5 appraises Perls' influence upon some of the subsequent developments and innovations in Gestalt psychotherapy and examines the impact which Perls' work has had upon the overall field of counselling and psychotherapy, discussing how many of the ideas which he popularized have now been absorbed as though by osmosis into the mainstream of psychotherapy.

Perls' professional career as a psychotherapist spanned approximately thirty-five years. He wrote or co-authored six books, delivered many public talks, published numerous papers and wrote many more which as yet remain unpublished. During the course of this prolific output, he often described his ideas in slightly different ways and with different emphases. We chose to include in this book those aspects of Perls' theory and practice which we believed had retained importance in current Gestalt and would contribute to the reader's understanding of Gestalt psychotherapy. Where several different versions of a theory or approach exist, we have *either* given a short historical synopsis of the development of a concept; *or* we have exercised our own judgement to choose that version which to us seemed the clearest and most useful in the practice of Gestalt psychotherapy; or we have given a composite description of a concept, summarizing what we have understood from the body of Perls' work. Throughout we have included references to specific books and papers by Perls; so that the reader may refer back to Perls' original with ease.

Style of writing in this book

We have varied the gender of the third person pronouns in each chapter. Thus we have used 'she' and 'her' to mean 'he' or 'she' and 'his' or 'her' in Chapter 1; 'he' and 'him' to mean 'he' or 'she' and 'his' or 'her' in Chapter 2 and so on. In quotations from Perls' work, we have retained his use of the pronoun 'he' to mean 'he or she' except when this upsets the flow of the sentence and then we have indicated any change to the pronoun used in the original quotation by the use of square brackets.

A discussion of the distinction between counselling and psycho-therapy lies beyond the scope of this book (see Clarkson and Carroll, 1993) and therefore for the purposes of the present publication we have accepted the arguments of Nelson-Jones (1982) that attempts to distinguish between counselling and psychotherapy are not generally wholly satisfactory and have followed the example of Truax and Carkhuff (1967) who use the terms interchangeably.

In our own discussions of Perls' work, we have used the current widely employed term 'client' to describe those who come for psychotherapy; while retaining Perls' usage of the word 'patient' in direct quotes.

We have chosen to capitalize the initial letter of the word 'Gestalt' whenever it refers to a movement or discipline, such as Gestalt psychotherapy, the Gestalt approach, Gestalt psychology and so on. We have on the other hand used 'gestalt', whenever the word denotes a common noun or verb, such as in the phrase 'in the formation and destruction of gestalts'; 'fixed gestalt' 'fixing the gestalt', on the grounds that the word 'gestalt' in this sense has now been integrated into English and can therefore be used in a normal English idiom and does not need to follow the German usage of capitalizing all nouns.

Thanks

Many people have generously supported us in the writing of this book. We would like particularly to appreciate the late Laura Perls, Erving and Miriam Polster, Isadore From, Gary Yontef, Ed Nevis, Joe Wysong, Robert Posner, Rae Perls, Renate Gold, Gilles Delisle, who helped us by being interviewed, by responding to question-naires, by supplying us with anecdotes, reminiscences, unpublished papers and by contributing to the collection and collating of the information for the publication. We are also most grateful to the many theorists of the Gestalt and other approaches, whom we consulted. Irving Polster, Gary Yontef, Ed Nevis, Bob Resnick and Hunter Beaumont read the complete draft manuscript and made many necessary corrections and invaluable suggestions. Lee McLeod, Malcolm Parlett and Peter Philippson gave the same manuscript a most meticulous reading and made line by line improvements. Sue Fish, Philip Raby, Patricia Shaw, Derry Watkins, Judy Ryde, Jenifer Elton Wilson, Anne Kearns, Charlotte Sills, Phil Joyce, Caro Kelly, Audrey Vollans, amongst many others, read various parts and stages of the manuscript and suggested modifications. All are warmly appreciated. We would like to thank friends and colleagues at the **metanoia** Psychotherapy Training Institute, especially editorial assistants Katherine Pierpoint and Camilla Sim. The Series Editor, Windy Dryden, commented on the manuscript and made many perceptive comments and suggestions and offered us invaluable encouragement throughout the process of writing. The Editor at Sage, Susan Worsey, has been both efficient and warmly supportive. There are of course others who made their own particular contribution, who should consider themselves gratefully acknowledged.

Finally we would like to acknowledge and appreciate the profound personal support and considerable patience of Petrūska's husband, Vincent Keyter, and Jenny's partner, Philip Raby, whose lives were often inconvenienced by our project.

1

The Life of Fritz Perls

Introduction

This chapter provides an overview of Perls' life. It tells his life
story and pays particular attention to the movements, people and
experiences which influenced him and the therapeutic approach –
Gestalt psychotherapy – which he co-founded, along with Laura
Perls and Paul Goodman. The life story thus includes brief
detours which explore some of the influences upon that life story.
These influences include: the theatre, dance, movement and
psychodrama; Freud and orthodox psychoanalysis, as well as
various innovators in psychoanalysis; Reich and body therapy;
Gestalt psychology, Goldstein's organismic theory, Wertheimer's
field orientation and Kurt Lewin's field theory; existentialism,
phenomenology and Buber; holism, especially Smuts; interpersonal psychoanalysis (e.g. Horney, Sullivan); and Eastern
religion. In addition, numerous political upheavals had a singular
impact upon Perls' life: the First World War; the rise of Fascism
and anti-Semitism in Germany in the 1930s; his flight as a refugee
to Holland and then to South Africa; a change in allegiance from
Germany to England in his active service in South Africa during
the Second World War; and a further change of continent and
culture from South Africa to the USA in 1946. Finally, there are
various important individuals (especially Laura Perls and Paul
Goodman) whose life stories interweave with Perls' and who
contributed to the founding of Gestalt psychotherapy.

Chapter 1 thus offers a context for the discussions of Perls'
theoretical and practical contributions which follow in Chapters 2
and 3 respectively, for the evaluation of the criticisms of his work
which forms the basis of Chapter 4, and for the exploration of
his overall influence upon the field of psychotherapy and counselling in Chapter 5.[1]

Childhood in Berlin

Fritz Perls was born Friedrich Saloman Perls on 8 July 1893 in a
Jewish neighbourhood on the outskirts of Berlin, the youngest of
the three children of Amelia Rund and Nathan Perls. His birth was
difficult, and shortly afterwards he fell seriously ill when his
mother had problems feeding him. Fritz's father Nathan was a
wine merchant who travelled away from home a great deal and
showed little interest in his children. Although Nathan was witty,
handsome and entertaining, by the time of Fritz's birth Amelia was
disillusioned by her husband's dominant manner and repeated
affairs. The middle child Grete said that her father wanted to rule
everyone in the house, just like he ruled the Freemasons' Lodge
where he was Grand Master (Perls, 1969c: 250). With Fritz,
Nathan developed a particularly harsh and acrimonious relationship, alternately ignoring, bullying and despising him.

When Fritz was three years old, the family moved from the
Jewish neighbourhood to the more fashionable centre of Berlin.
Nathan was a modern Jew who wanted to break out of the narrow
confines of the Jewish world in order to enter the larger German
community. He was anti-religious and imposed his views on the
rest of the family. Jews like Nathan who wanted to integrate into
the non-Jewish community were not accepted fully at the time by
German Aryans; so they never quite belonged to either community
but often continued searching for a home, forever open to new
ideas and new people, much as Fritz was to be in his adult life.
Fritz was not brought up completely without religious beliefs,
however, for he attended Hebrew classes and had a bar mitzvah,
while the family continued to attend the synagogue for major
festivals. By the time he was a teenager, Fritz declared himself an
atheist – which he remained throughout his life.

During his early years Fritz seems to have had an easier relationship with his mother. Amelia lavished attention on her children and
ran around picking up after Fritz, who developed a lifelong expec-
tation that others would clear up his mess. Many of the people
who knew him in later life found his habits deplorable and on
several occasions quarrelled with him quite bitterly about the way
he took their hospitality for granted (Posner, 1991). Amelia was
passionately interested in the arts and communicated her love for
the theatre to Fritz, who wrote warmly of this legacy: 'Mama . . .
was very ambitious for me and not at all the "Jewish mother"
type. . . Her father was a tailor and considering her background,
her interest in art – especially in the theatre – was amazing' (Perls,
1969c: 182).

The eldest daughter of the family, Else, was three when Fritz was born. She was partially sighted and clung to her mother. Fritz may have resented Else, for he certainly disliked her, writing many years later that when he heard of her death in a concentration camp, he mourned little. In contrast he got on well with the second daughter, Grete, who was one and a half years older than him: 'I was close to my sister Grete. She was a tomboy, a wildcat with stubborn curly hair' (Perls, 1969c: 181). When she grew up, Grete maintained contact with Fritz and eventually followed him to New York, where she cared for him and his family for ten years and was proud and delighted when Fritz became famous.

As a young child, Fritz seems to have been reasonably happy and came top of the class at his elementary school. However, from the age of ten onwards, Fritz's relationship both with his parents and with his school deteriorated. He wrote later (1969c) that his parents began to think of him as bad at the age of ten, when he broke into his father's room, stole a gold coin that was being saved for Else and spent it on stamps for a Christian boy whose friendship he was trying to cultivate (pp. 249–51). On another occasion, his mother became so infuriated with him, that she chased him with a carpet beater intending to hit him. To get away from her, Fritz threw a glass at her and slammed the door in her face. 'He was a wild child – wild, wild' (Grete Gutfreund in Gaines, 1979: 1). Despite her rages with her son, Amelia hid his misbehaviour from her husband. This, along with Nathan's continued affairs and reluctance to support his family financially, contributed to the growing alienation of the couple and the ever-worsening relationship between Fritz and his father.

The teachers at his secondary school – the Mommsen Gymnasium – were anti-Semitic disciplinarians and most unsympathetic to Fritz. Refusing to do any work, Fritz played truant and then intercepted the notes which the school sent to his parents reporting his behaviour. Eventually after failing grades through negligence, Fritz was expelled. Following a short and miserable spell in business, he and his friend Ferdinand Knopf, also a dropout from the Mommsen Gymnasium, enrolled themselves in the liberal Askanasische Gymnasium, where the teachers were interested in the children and affirmed Fritz's independent ways, intelligence and interest in the theatre. By his mid adolescence, he was getting parts as an extra at the Royal Theatre in Berlin. Although he only played non-speaking roles, he relished the glamour of performing on a professional stage.

Fritz met and studied with the director of the Deutsche Theater, Max Reinhardt. Reinhardt was a challenging teacher, who insisted that his students closely observe how people express emotion through tone of voice and gesture. Reinhardt's teachings first awakened Fritz's interest in process, and his realization that the means by which a person expresses herself are as important for her overall message as the words she speaks. This emphasis upon non-verbal communication was an important influence upon Perls. He developed a genius for reading people's body language and in later life astonished his audiences by the amount of personal information he could pick up just by watching how they spoke, sat or walked. With Reinhardt, Perls developed his taste and talent for performing, his mastery of dramatic technique, his flair for timing and the buildup of creative tension, which were later features of his therapeutic work. Perls (1969c) acknowledged his debt to Reinhardt, describing him as 'The first creative genius I ever met' (p. 282).

Fritz reconciled himself with his mother and redeemed himself scholastically, graduating top of the class from the Askanasische Gymnasium. He remained estranged from his father who denigrated and insulted him, frequently calling him 'ein Stuck Scheisse' or a piece of shit. Although Fritz understandably disliked his father, he was most probably profoundly influenced by him despite himself. Fritz Perls' own style of fathering was to be surprisingly similar to Nathan's: he too was often away from home during his children's early years and he was often uncaring to them (Shepard, 1975). In a broader sense, his sometimes harshly confrontative style as a therapist and deliberate use of language that shocked may have been legacies of his formative years with his father.

Medical Studies in Berlin and the First World War

On graduating from high school, Perls started medical studies at Berlin University. The beginning of the First World War made relatively little impact on his life and studies, because at his army medical he was classified as unfit due to a stoop, an elongated heart and asthma. By 1916, the fighting had escalated enormously and the unprecedented death toll led to a sharp decline in the standards of fitness required for active service in the German army. Fritz Perls and his best friend Ferdinand Knopf enlisted, and Perls became a medical officer in the 36 Pioneer Battalion, a unit trained for gas attacks.

From 1916 to 1917 Perls spent months living in the squalor and filth of the trenches, and was wounded, gassed and decorated for bravery. He was often anguished by the choices that he had to make when as medical officer there were too many injured to treat.

On one particularly awful occasion, the wind shifted just after the Germans made a gas attack on their enemies; so that the gas drifted back over the German trenches and many German soldiers were gassed because their gas masks failed or were inadequate. Perls had only four oxygen tanks for such emergencies and arbitrarily had to rip the oxygen away from men who were begging for air, in order to help others: 'I have to tear the flask away to give some comfort to another soldier. More than once was I tempted to tear my mask off my sweating face' (Perls, 1969c: 154). In 1917 when he was promoted to the position of medical sub-lieutenant, his conditions of service improved somewhat. However, at the end of the war his battalion was ordered to return home by forced marches of twenty hours a day. Under this new stress, Perls started his lifelong habit of smoking.

His wartime suffering had a deep effect upon Perls. Ferdinand Knopf had been killed; he had witnessed wholesale slaughter; he had been decorated for bravery and humiliated by the contemptuous and prejudiced attitude of many of his superior officers. His conviction that the destruction he had witnessed had been of no value, except perhaps to a few rich individuals, influenced his politics for the rest of his life. After the war he became active in left-wing politics and was henceforth to be associated with anti-establishment movements.

In 1918 he returned to his interrupted medical studies in Berlin and Freiburg, and qualified as an MD on 3 April 1920.

Practice as a Neuropsychiatrist, Mainly in Berlin, 1921 to 1926

After qualifying, Perls set up practice in Berlin as a neuropsychiatrist, prescribing medical cures for a variety of psychological and neurological complaints.

Socially, Perls joined Berlin's Bohemian community and thus associated himself with the artists, poets, architects, writers, actors, and left-wing intellectuals of his time, including members of the Bauhaus group. In this set, Perls met the philosopher Sigmund Friedlander (1918), who introduced him to the idea that opposites define each other and that there is a resting point in the middle – the point of creative indifference – which embraces both polarities. Friedlander's concepts made a big impact upon Perls, who drew on them extensively in his first book (1947/1969a). Around the same time and through the same group of people, Perls became acquainted with an innovative dancer named Palucca, a disciple of Mary Wigman, the innovative German expressionist dancer and choreographer of large chorale performances. Palucca inspired in Perls an interest in dance and movement as a means of spontaneous self-expression and creativity.

In 1923 Perls went to New York, where he worked in the Department of Neurology in the Hospital for Joint Diseases, while simultaneously preparing for certification as a doctor in the United States. He was not happy in America. Homesick and hampered by his poor English, he greatly missed the creative exchange of ideas with his Bauhaus friends.

After only six months, in April 1924, he returned to Berlin and re-established his practice as a neuropsychiatrist. He continued to live in his mother's house although he was by now 31 years old. According to Shepard (1975) he was physically, sexually, socially and professionally unsure of himself. Looking for some personal help, Perls decided to try psychoanalysis and chose Karen Horney, an innovative psychoanalyst, who established her own psychoanalytic approach (1937; 1939). Although Perls' analysis with Horney was truncated before it really got going because he soon moved away from Berlin, he often turned to her for advice and supervision over the next decade; later, when he moved to the USA, he had a friendly professional relationship with her. He was considerably influenced by her – both in the fundamental sense that she was his first contact with psychoanalysis and therefore she affected his choice of career, and also by her innovations and questioning of orthodox psychoanalysis (Cavaleri, 1992). At the time, Perls was sufficiently enthusiastic about this first contact with psychoanalysis to start training as a psychoanalyst himself.

Frankfurt, 1926 to 1927

In 1926 Perls moved to Frankfurt where he continued his analysis with Clara Happel, a student of Horney. At the time Frankfurt was a very exciting intellectual environment: the Gestalt psychologists Gelb and Goldstein were living and working there, as were the existentialists Martin Buber and Paul Tillich. Perls attended lectures on Gestalt psychology but had little time personally to study existential philosophy. He deepened his understanding of Gestalt psychology and existential ideas through his friendship with a young psychology graduate, Lore Posner, who later became his wife and was to be known as Laura Perls (see p. 11).

The Influence of Gestalt Psychology
In Frankfurt, Perls learnt about the discoveries of the Gestalt psychologists Wertheimer (1938; 1944), Koffka (1935) and Köhler

(1970), becoming familiar with the main Gestalt principles of perception and the work of Zeigarnik (1927) and Ovsiankina (1928).

The German word *gestalt* means a whole or a complete pattern, form or configuration. A gestalt or whole includes the whole thing or person being considered, its context and the relationship between the two. For example a single snowflake on a dark surface is perceived quite differently from the same snowflake in the context of many other snowflakes falling during a blizzard. The meaning and significance of the snowflake depend on and cannot be separated from the context in which it is seen. The gestalt or whole of the snowflake consists of the thing itself and of its relationship to the environment. Its meaning derives from its relationship to its background. See pp. 38–9 and 40–7 for further discussion of the Gestalt principles of perception.

Basic principles of Gestalt psychology that Perls later integrated into Gestalt therapy include the notion that people structure their perceptual experience, organizing the totality of what they perceive into things which are currently interesting to them and things which are not. They see the things which are currently interesting as perceptual wholes (gestalts or figures) which they endow with meaning. People tend to remember unfinished experiences better than finished ones (Zeigarnik, 1927). They have a natural tendency to resume and complete unfinished tasks (Ovsiankina, 1928) and make meaning out of incomplete information and situations.

Although Gestalt psychology and Gestalt psychotherapy share a name, they are distinct disciplines. Gestalt psychology was academic and experimental. It described perception. The Gestalt psychologists had no thought of using their research in any therapeutic way. Some have even gone so far as to raise doubts as to whether the Gestalt therapy system has much to do with Gestalt psychology. However Yontef (1982) has demonstrated that the basic methodology of Gestalt therapy is descended philosophically from Gestalt psychology and Wheeler (1991) has explored the Gestalt psychology background to Gestalt therapy in depth.

Perls was influenced by the field orientation of Wertheimer and by the field theory of Kurt Lewin (1935; 1952), a social psychologist who was associated with the Gestalt psychologists Koffka and Köhler in the early 1920s. Although it is unclear how much of Lewin's published texts Fritz had actually read, he certainly mentioned Lewin (1952) and incorporated some of his ideas (see p. 47).

While in Frankfurt, Perls worked at the Institute for Brain-Damaged Soldiers as assistant to Kurt Goldstein, who was interested in extending the relatively academic studies and discoveries of the school of Gestalt psychology and seeing how he could apply their principles of perception to living human beings. In his work with soldiers suffering from brain lesions, Goldstein discovered that damage to one part of a human being affects the whole organism. Goldstein (1939) later discussed the human being as a whole organism and proposed that the overriding human drive is to actualize as a complete person. Professional contact with Goldstein, as well as familiarity with his published organismic theory, influenced Perls considerably (Perls, 1979 for example) in his later development of the concept of a human being as a whole system in which all the different aspects interconnect and inter-relate, and in his views of self-actualization.[2]

The Influence of Existentialism and Phenomenology

Laura Perls has suggested that she shared with Fritz her knowledge of, and enthusiasm for, existential ideas and phenomenological methods. She had studied the phenomenologist, Husserl (1931: 68). When she lived in Frankfurt, Laura, unlike Fritz, actually met the existential theologian, Buber, personally and worked with Tillich for some years (Laura Perls in Rosenblatt, 1991). This fact was to have a considerable impact upon the future development of Gestalt psychotherapy; for it seems probable, at least initially, that Laura was the main channel through which Fritz learnt of many of the existential concepts which became integral to Gestalt therapy. Directly or indirectly, Perls was moulded by the basic themes of existentialism, which include existential isolation, being-with-others, freedom within strict human limitations, authenticity, and individual responsibility for creating personal meaning in a world which is without universal meaning. Each individual is ultimately alone: no matter how many friends we may have, each one of us must enter and leave this life alone. We exist now but one day we shall die. Thus a fundamental conflict of human existence is the tension between the awareness of our mortality and the wish to continue to exist.

Perls (1969b; 1976) especially emphasized the existential concepts of freedom, responsibility, authenticity and anxiety. In its existential sense, freedom refers to an absence of external structure or obligation in which the individual is responsible for her choices and actions. This notion of our responsibility and therefore of our freedom to choose who we make ourselves from moment to moment has terrifying implications. Most of us try to escape the truth of our freedom and personal responsibility by imagining obligations to other people or institutions or by blaming others for our fate. Closely related to the idea of personal freedom is the existential concept of authenticity; living authentically means choosing to live with integrity, to face, without self-deception or game-playing, the fact that we are free and responsible and yet at the same time condemned to die. Authenticity provokes continual insecurity, existential anxiety or dread. Anxiety is not, then, a symptom to be relieved or suppressed but an intrinsic factor in living existence authentically (see p. 80 for a discussion of Perls' view of anxiety in this context).

Human beings are meaning-seeking and yet they are destined to live out their existence in a world that has no ultimate meaning. Phenomenological existentialism – which Perls adopted as the philosophical foundation to his Gestalt therapy – emphasizes that human beings have an urge to make meaning and therefore to construct meaning in their own lives. Our experience of the world is open to a range of interpretations – there is no single indisputable truth – so the meaning that each person constructs is unique to that person. Phenomenology therefore emphasizes the importance of subjective as well as objective data of experience, describes what is perceived while bracketing previous assumptions about the significance of what is described; in order to reach a direct grasp of the essence of the thing or experience itself (see pp. 46, 92 and 113).

Vienna and Berlin, 1927 to 1933

The Influence of Freud and Psychoanalysis
In 1927 Fritz Perls' savings ran out and Clara Happel abruptly announced that his analysis was now complete. She advised him to continue his training as a psychoanalyst by taking clients under supervision. Perls himself felt far from complete and was still looking for some more satisfactory means of self-knowledge. However he followed Happel's advice in one respect, in that he moved to Vienna, the centre of psychoanalytic training, and lived there for about a year. He started seeing clients and had supervision from the psychoanalysts Helene Deutsch and Edward Hitschmann, as well as studying with Paul Federn.

In 1928, having completed his final training as a psychoanalyst in Vienna, Perls returned to Berlin. Here he set up his own psychoanalytic practice. From 1928 to 1933 Perls worked in Germany, mainly in Berlin, as a certified Freudian psychoanalyst.

Freud's influence upon Perls was considerable. Freudian theory and orthodox psychoanalysis were the essential background to the new system of psychotherapy which Perls was to devise. It was Perls' belief (1948; 1976) that Freud's ideas were extremely valuable but that much of the philosophy and methods of psycho-analysis were obsolete. Although Perls eventually criticized, modified, added to and rejected many of Freud's ideas, he also integrated many of Freud's contributions as the foundation upon which he built Gestalt therapy. For example he accepted and developed Freud's revolutionary ideas that there is some underlying meaning to neurotic and psychotic behaviour and that childhood experiences influence adult behaviour. His views on homeostatic balance owe much to Freud's constancy principle. Although he worked with dreams differently, he agreed with Freud's evaluation of their great importance.

Perls was, of course, also influenced by many innovative psycho-analysts and by people who had started out as psychoanalysts but who later broke away from orthodox psychoanalysis. For example he was most probably aware of Ferenczi's active techniques and emphasis upon mutuality, of Jung's creative imagination and of Adler's holistic view of the individual as an integral part of a social system (Perls, 1948). Isadore From has suggested (1991) that Perls adapted the idea of the dream as projection and the concept of the here-and-now from Otto Rank. Perls was directly influenced by Horney's innovations in psychoanalysis both in Europe and later in America (Perls, 1948; 1978a; Cavaleri, 1992). Her emphasis upon the importance of the cultural and sociological background of the individual, of interpersonal factors both in child development and in the therapeutic relationship, as well as her holistic philosophy and exploration of the reciprocal influence of organism and environment made a great impact upon Perls, who later integrated these concepts into Gestalt therapy. (Reich's important impact upon Perls is discussed on p. 12, while Sullivan's is described on p. 17.)

Altogether, Perls underwent three or four analyses (with Horney – so briefly that that analysis is often discounted – and with Happel, Harnik and Reich) and was in supervision with various analysts including Horney, Deutsch, Hitschmann, Fenichel and Landauer. Perls' earlier writings (1947/1969a; Perls, Hefferline and Goodman, 1951/1973)[3] assume that the reader has a background knowledge of psychoanalysis, which make some parts of these books hard to follow for those who do not.

Perls sought his second analysis with Eugen J. Harnik in Berlin in 1928. This was a terrible experience. Harnik believed in an extreme form of detached passive analysis. During the one and a half years that Perls worked with Harnik, Harnik said almost nothing:

> I once had an analyst who did not open his mouth for weeks; to indicate that the session was finished he merely scraped the floor with his foot . . . Only after I had heard, many years later, that he was suffering from paranoia, the truth struck me forcibly. I stopped blaming myself for my inability to understand and to appreciate his remarks and directed the blame on to his inability to make himself understood and to appreciate my situation. (Perls, 1947/1969a: 231)

This negative experience of psychoanalysis profoundly influenced Perls' professional and philosophical development. It led him to question and then to reject many aspects of psychoanalysis – especially those aspects of the analysis with Harnik which he had found so unhelpful and painful. For example he later challenged what he saw as psychoanalysis' exclusion of ordinary human relationship and its insistence on the analyst's interpretation. Instead he emphasized the opposite: real contact and relationship between therapist and client in the here-and-now, and the phenomenological method of description.

Marriage to Laura

As mentioned above, Fritz Perls had met Laura Posner in one of Goldstein's seminars on Gestalt psychology at the University of Frankfurt in 1926, and had soon become her friend and lover.[4] Laura was a clever and talented woman who came from a cultured family and was an accomplished pianist. A gifted and hardworking academic, she was a graduate student of Gestalt psychology, had studied the development of existential ideas in the writings of Kierkegaard, Heidegger, Buber and Tillich, and was familiar with the work of the phenomenologists Husserl and Scheler. Overall Laura had a great influence upon the development of Fritz Perls' ideas from 1926 until the end of his life and was to become one of the three co-founders of Gestalt psychotherapy (Humphrey, 1986).

When Fritz left Frankfurt in 1927 to move to Vienna and then Berlin, he had continued to develop his relationship with Laura, seeing her at intervals and holidaying with her. In 1928, Perls returned briefly to Frankfurt, partly because Laura was there. The nature of their relationship after this date is controversial. Fritz later claimed (1969c) that Laura pressed him to marry her, and Shepard (1975) has reiterated this as though it were historical fact: 'Laura, by then, was pressing for marriage' (p. 39). Laura herself remembered this period differently:

> In *Garbage Pail* Fritz writes that I was pressing for marriage. It simply was not true. I never expected that he would marry me . . . Actually, it was the other way around. Fritz wanted to have a child. For a long

time he had the fear that he was sterile. I think he got married to a
great extent to find out if he *could* have a child. (Laura Perls in Gaines,
1979)

Fritz and Laura married on 23 August 1929. For a few years after
their marriage, the Perls led a comfortable life in Berlin. Perls'
practice was successful; Laura's father continued to pay her an
allowance to help with their living expenses; they had a comfortable apartment and modern furniture especially designed by the
Bauhaus group. Their apartment with its fashionable furnishings
was even photographed for Germany's leading architectural
magazine. Fritz and Laura became parents on 23 July 1931 when
their first child, Renate, was born.

The Influence of Wilhelm Reich
After the unsatisfactory analysis with Harnik, Fritz still felt
unfinished in his quest for self-knowledge. He therefore turned
once more to Karen Horney, who advised him to see Wilhelm
Reich, saying: 'The only analyst that I think could get through to
you would be Wilhelm Reich' (Perls, 1969c: 49). This for Perls
was a happy suggestion: years later he told the innovative art
teacher, Fritz Faiss, that Reich was the first man he had been able
to trust. Perls was in analysis with Wilhelm Reich from 1931 until
just before Reich had to leave Germany for political reasons in
1933. Perls' analysis with Reich was as positive an experience as
that with Harnik had been negative. Again the analysis had an
important influence upon Perls and caused him to question
orthodox psychoanalysis.

Reich related personally to Perls and entered into lively
exchanges with him about a wide variety of topics. At last Perls
had met someone who was willing to engage with him, to become
involved with him and his process. Reich was himself challenging
the methods and precepts of current psychoanalysis; his theoretical
ideas (1945; 1952; 1968), methods and techniques of therapy
were active and radically different. They appealed to Perls as
much as his personal style of relating. Reich questioned the value
of working with verbal memories and maintained that the life
energy can become blocked or distorted because of life experience.
Life energy and its repression is physical as well as psychological.[5] People's bodies store their emotional memories as well
as their defences against those memories in the form of muscular
contractions and body armour. Reich's knowledge of body
language and his 'body armour theory' are both acknowledged in
positive terms by Perls.

The Rise of Fascism

In the economic crisis of the late 1920s and early 1930s, Hitler and the Nazi Party gained increasing support. In 1933 Hitler was offered the Chancellorship. During these years both Fritz and Laura were politically very active in left-wing, anti-Fascist movements. Fritz taught at the Workers' College and contributed to attempts to bring about a conciliation between communists and socialists, in order to stop the rise of Hitler.

The Nazis introduced increasingly harsh anti-Jewish measures, and when the Perls applied for passports they received a racially abusive, anonymous letter. Although anti-Semitism was thus already virulent, Laura Perls has said (Gaines, 1979) that it was primarily because of their political activities, rather than because they were Jews, that she and Fritz had to leave Berlin in the spring of 1933: 'Our last few nights in Berlin we slept in a different place every night. People were getting pulled out of their beds between two and four in the morning – not only Jews but also people who were active in any leftist or communist movement' (p. 14). On 25 March Laura's father died. The Perls escaped, abandoning all their possessions. Laura and Renate stayed with Laura's mother in her home town of Pforzheim in south Germany, while Fritz crossed the border into Holland with 100 marks hidden in a cigarette lighter.

Holland, 1933

If Perls hoped to be safer in Holland it was a fragile and temporary safety that he found there. He was unable to get work because he had no permit and it was difficult to find anywhere to live. He survived on charity and lived in a home packed with other Jewish refugees. In September 1933 Laura and Renate joined Fritz in Amsterdam and they managed to find a freezing attic apartment, where they lived in utter misery.

These were very hard months for Laura and Fritz, as for the other Jews who lived or sought refuge in Amsterdam. They had nothing, they lived from day to day. Laura became pregnant and had an illegal abortion, suffering depression after the termination. Fritz and Laura tried to get work permits but were refused because there were already too many refugees in Holland. The fact that their failure to do so actually turned to their advantage only highlights the grimness of their situation, 'because the ones who stayed all perished. My sister, her family who lived in Holland, all died' (Laura Perls in Gaines, 1979: 17). For financial, professional, political and survival reasons, Fritz, Laura and Renate urgently needed to move country once more. Perls made enquiries and learnt from Ernest Jones (Freud's biographer) in London of a request for a training analyst in South Africa. Fritz and Laura sailed to South Africa, arriving there at the beginning of 1934.

Johannesburg, South Africa

Fritz and Laura set up psychoanalytic practices in Johannesburg and were instantly successful. Within a year they were able to build a luxurious Bauhaus-style house with swimming pool, tennis courts and spacious grounds. Fritz learnt to ice-skate and took flying lessons, becoming a proficient pilot. He tried to buy a plane of his own and to fly to Europe but was outbid on the price. Fritz and Laura seem also to have been happy together for a while: 'We were terribly in love with each other and the baby – those were very good years. He acknowledged then that I was his wife, his lover, and the mother of his child' (Laura Perls in Gaines, 1979: 19). Fritz was devoted to his daughter Renate for the first three or four years of her life.

However, Laura soon became pregnant again. Fritz, already 41 years old, was becoming increasingly irritable with children. He tried to persuade Laura to have another abortion, but she was adamant: 'If you don't want the child, I'll have it. It will be my child' (Laura Perls in Gaines, 1979: 23). On 23 August 1935 their second child, Steve, was born. Laura maintained (Gaines, 1979) that when four-year-old Renate got jealous of the new baby, Fritz 'simply dropped' his daughter (p. 23). Fritz on the other hand implied that he felt excluded from the relationship between Laura and Renate. Whatever the truth, Fritz and Laura were both by their own admission extremely busy with their work and Renate seems to have suffered. In her adult life, she has spoken at length (Shepard, 1975; Gaines, 1979; R. Perls, 1992) about the difficulties of her childhood and the misunderstandings with her father, as well as of occasional moments of tenderness between the two of them.

Fritz and Laura founded the South African Institute for Psychoanalysis and began training a few people as psychoanalysts. In 1936, Perls decided to return to Europe to attend the International Psychoanalytic Conference in Czechoslovakia. For this event, he prepared a paper entitled 'Oral Resistances' which (drawing extensively upon Laura's observations of feeding her first child) stressed that the baby relates to the world through the intake of food and drew a parallel between people's eating habits and their interactions with the rest of their environment. Perls hoped to make a valuable contribution to existing psychoanalytic theory of resistance – by proposing that resistance can be associated with the period when the angry child refuses to take in nourishment from the mother. Perls was also keen to meet Freud while in Europe and report to him his successful establishment of psychoanalysis in South Africa.

Perls' hopes for his European trip were all disappointed. Freud barely spoke to him. Perls' paper was received coldly by the other analysts at the conference, most of whom did not understand it or considered it suspect because it was clearly influenced by Reich. Perls was also dismayed by Reich himself: his former analyst was now withdrawn and uncommunicative. A year or two later, the International Psychoanalytic Association decided that psychoanalysts who had not previously acted as trainers in Europe could not do so in other parts of the world. So the Perlses' position as trainers in South Africa was revoked. These experiences of rejection made a considerable impact upon Perls. He had wanted to be an innovative member of the psychoanalytic community: after 1936 he became progressively more aggressive towards Freud and psychoanalysis.

The Influence of Jan Smuts

Perls became familiar with the work of Jan Smuts, the prime minister of South Africa at that time. Smuts was a great general and a philosopher, who catalysed the formation of the League of Nations and the Pan-African Congress. Although Perls only met Smuts once, he was deeply influenced by his *Holism and Evolution* (1987, first published 1926), which had a pervasive impact upon the intellectual climate in South Africa (Clarkson, 1991b; Laura Perls in Gaines, 1979: 31). In Smuts' book, it is possible to find the seeds of an extraordinarily large number of Perls' later ideas, including some which are usually thought to derive solely from Gestalt psychology and field theory. For instance, Smuts introduced from physics the idea that everything has a field and that things and organisms are unintelligible if considered without these fields. He criticized the nineteenth-century sciences for trying to study individual entities in isolation in too narrow and rigid a fashion. He emphasized process, stating that all things are in an incessant process of creative change, and proposed that it is characteristic of organisms to form structured wholes. Smuts emphasized the holistic nature of people and of the universe and the interconnectedness of all things, living and non-living, and spoke of the way in which the individual and the universe are actively 'whole-making'. Perls may also have found the idea for his cycle of interdependency of organism and environment in Smuts.

Ego, Hunger and Aggression
During the same period, Perls revised and enlarged his paper on oral resistances and turned it into his first book, *Ego, Hunger and Aggression* (1947/1969a). The text for this book was written in 1941–2. It was published in South Africa in the early 1940s and in Britain in 1947, with the subtitle 'A Revision of Freud's Theory and Method'. Although the book fiercely attacks certain aspects of psychoanalysis, the original subtitle may have represented a hesitation to break completely with psychoanalysis.

There is some controversy about the extent of Perls' cooperation with his wife Laura on the book. Shepard (1975) barely mentions any cooperation, but Laura herself (Gaines, 1979: 28–9) points out that her original interest in infant feeding and weaning inspired the paper and the book. She also says that she and Fritz sat and worked on the book together at weekends when Fritz was an army psychiatrist during the Second World War (see below). It is certainly true that in the British edition Fritz acknowledged that Laura made a major contribution to the book, whereas later in the American edition (1969a) the original Preface and all mention of Laura were deleted.

Ego, Hunger and Aggression was an innovative blend of Freudian psychoanalysis, Friedlander's differential thinking, Smuts' holism, Reich's ideas, organismic theory, Gestalt psychology, Wertheimer's and Lewin's field theories, phenomenology, existential thoughts and original contributions. Perls called his new approach to therapy 'concentration therapy'. In this book Perls introduces, sometimes in a rudimentary form, many of the ideas which later became central to Gestalt psychotherapy. The book is divided into three parts: the first two parts are devoted to a theoretical discussion, while the third part is a series of exercises intended to help the reader explore and assess the practicality of some of the ideas presented in the previous parts.

The Second World War
In January 1942, Fritz Perls volunteered for service in the South African army joining the Allied Forces in the war against the Germans. He worked as a medical officer and army psychiatrist from 1942 to 1945 near Pretoria, returning home only infrequently. He and Laura inevitably led independent lives and his children Renate and Steve both remember him as being absent in these years. Towards Steve he seems to have maintained a cool detachment, whereas his relationship with Renate continued to be stormy.

After the war, Fritz and Laura decided to leave South Africa, which they experienced increasingly as a cultural desert as other intellectuals emigrated in the changing political climate. Smuts was to retire as Prime Minister in 1948 and to be replaced by the Nationalist Party, which introduced apartheid. Karen Horney was by now in America and was willing to act as Perls' sponsor for immigration.

New York

Perls arrived in the United States in 1946. At first, he was so miserable that he seriously considered returning to Johannesburg where Laura had stayed with the children. At this point, however, Perls met Erich Fromm who, having read and appreciated *Ego, Hunger and Aggression*, encouraged him to stay and establish a practice in New York, which Perls did.

In New York, Perls became friendly with Clara Thompson, one of the leading faculty members of the William Alanson White Institute – New York's primary psychoanalytic training institute at the time. He presented at least one paper (Perls, 1979) at the White Institute in late 1946 or early 1947 in which he spoke warmly of having found in the members of the Institute people who spoke the same language and saw the world in a similar way. He associated with Clara Thompson, Erich Fromm, Karen Horney, and the followers of Harry Stack Sullivan who were key figures in a movement which has been called 'interpersonal psychoanalysis' (Greenberg and Mitchell, 1983). Perls was influenced by Horney and Sullivan in particular in a number of important ways. (We have discussed some of Horney's contributions on p. 10.) Sullivan's insistence upon existence as process almost certainly contributed to Perls' view of experiences, behaviour, symptoms, thoughts and of the self itself as process and to Perls' objections to language that 'reifies' or turns processes into structures (Perls, 1969b). Sullivan's emphasis upon mental illness as a reaction to events taking place between the individual and his environment probably influenced Perls, Hefferline and Goodman's (1951/1973) emphasis upon the background of the individual being treated; while Sullivan's belief that the interpersonal relationship between patient and therapist is the most important determining factor in the outcome of the therapy may have contributed to Perls' emphasis upon the human here-and-now relationship. Sullivan's deep respect for the uniqueness of individual experience is echoed throughout Perls, Hefferline and Goodman's book.

Picking up Perls' life story once again – Laura and their children arrived in New York in the autumn of 1947. In January 1948,

Fritz Perls read a paper entitled 'Theory and Technique of Personality Integration' to the Association for the Advancement of Psychotherapy. This paper was published in the *American Journal of Psychotherapy* later the same year and has been described as 'arguably his best early work' (Yontef, 1992b: 101).

Within a couple of years of Laura's arrival, Fritz and Laura started a weekly experiential training/therapy group, which included the innovative educationalist Elliot Shapiro, the physician Paul Weisz, Isadore From, Ralph Hefferline, Professor of Psychology at Columbia University, and the philosopher and creative writer Paul Goodman. Laura Perls and Paul Goodman became co-founders, along with Fritz Perls, of the Gestalt therapy approach; while many other members of this group made substantial contributions to the early development of Gestalt therapy (Laura Perls in Rosenblatt, 1991).[6]

The Influence of Eastern Religion

Around this time, Perls became better acquainted with Eastern religion, especially Zen Buddhism, largely through his friendship with Paul Weisz (Laura Perls in Rosenblatt, 1991). Weisz was a doctor and a serious student of Zen, who trained with Fritz and Laura Perls and became a gifted Gestalt therapist. Weisz explained Zen ideas to Perls, who sought to integrate them into his philosophy and methods. Perls was delighted with the wisdom and non-moral attitude of Zen which reinforced his rejection of what he had already called 'shouldistic' behaviour. In particular, the Zen notion of mindfulness had some similarity with Perls' view of present awareness; while the Zen concept of paradox was compatible with Perls' paradoxical notion of the change which happens when we cease to try to change ourselves (see p. 90). Perls remained fascinated by Zen and believed that his awareness exercises offered a Zen kind of self-transformation for Westerners. Perls later studied Zen in Kyoto in Japan and was influenced by Alan Watts (1951; 1957), who was lecturing on the West Coast in the 1960s when Perls was living there. Although Perls frequently voiced scepticism about spiritual disciplines, he continued to interweave Zen concepts and paradoxes in his teaching.

Paul Goodman (1911–72)

Goodman was a man of great and varied talent. While a number of the members of the New York training group made a significant contribution to the establishment and development of Gestalt therapy, Paul Goodman is generally acknowledged, along with Fritz and Laura Perls, as one of the three main co-founders of the

Gestalt therapeutic approach. He was a social philosopher and critic as well as a writer of plays and novels and a hero of the counterculture in the sixties (Laura Perls in Rosenblatt, 1991: 21). He was politically and philosophically interested in anarchy as a movement, and both in his life and in his writing he was committed to exploring anarchism as a basis for community, believing that individuals generating their own living structures and regulations would be more to the advantage of both individuals and society than regulation by government (Goodman, 1947; 1960; 1962).

Goodman's lasting cultural impact is illustrated by the fact that his books are currently being republished (Goodman, 1991), that a new biography is currently in preparation (Stoehr, in press) and that his plays are once more being performed. For example, he wrote five Noh plays in 1941. By a curious synchronicity, one of us attended these plays on the same day as the memorial service held for Laura Perls in New York (Clarkson, 1991a). The programme note on these plays bears witness to Goodman's range of talents and commitment to holism: 'Novelist, poet, psychologist, expert on city planning and literary critic, Mr Goodman described himself as "really a playwright and novelist". He "insisted on keeping all the parts together, freedom and power, sexuality and adulthood, poetry and citizenship"' (Goodman, 1990: 3).

Perls and Goodman exercised considerable influence upon each other. Goodman's intelligent and radical challenging of established convention in many fields and his uninhibited behaviour supported and encouraged Perls' naturally subversive stance. An intrinsic part of their challenge to established societal norms was their open flouting of sexual convention. Goodman was an avowed bisexual, Isadore From was an open homosexual and Perls was well known for his wide-ranging sexual exploration, both with and without Laura (Shepard, 1975). The breaking down of moral and psychological assumptions and clichéd forms of relationship was an intrinsic and significant part of the *Zeitgeist*, which Perls and Goodman were instrumental in creating. A questioning spirit and willingness to risk was a necessary component of moving further and further away from the institution of Freudian psychoanalysis which, Perls believed, had become rigidified. However the rebellion of Paul Goodman and of Fritz and Laura Perls was not just rebellion for its own sake; it was for the sake of increasing human potential. Later Perls was to write:

> Gestalt therapy is one of the rebellious, humanistic, existential forces in psychology which seeks to stem the avalanche of self-defeating, self-destructive forces among some members of society. . . Our aim as therapists is to increase human potential through the process of

integration. We do this by supporting the individual's genuine interests, desires and needs. (Perls in Stevens, 1975: 1)

Through Goodman, Perls became associated with a group of anarchic and revolutionary intellectuals and artists, including Julian Beck and his wife Judith Malina, directors of the Living Theater. This couple attempted to involve actors and audience in an 'I and Thou' relationship (Julian Beck in Shepard, 1975). Their practical interpretation of Buber's existential concept of dialogue influenced Perls, who expressed an interest in doing something that was halfway between living performances and therapeutic sessions – an ambition that Perls was to fulfil in his public demonstrations of Gestalt therapy in the 1960s which were very much a synthesis of drama and therapy.

Influence of Moreno

In the 1950s Perls became familiar with psychodrama, which had had an enormous impact upon the intellectual and radical circles which he frequented in New York, and he met its originator Moreno on at least one occasion in 1958. Moreno (1934; 1964) was extremely innovative, and is said to have coined the term 'group therapy' and to have launched the emphasis on spontaneity and here-and-now experience as early as the 1920s. He introduced psychodrama in America in 1925. Psychodrama emphasizes the roles – child, parent, friend, teacher, lover, boss etc. – which each of us plays in the course of our lives. An individual may play a fixed and inflexible role with regard to other individuals in his life or may find the different roles he plays to be in conflict with each other. Moreno devised a therapeutic approach which allowed the individual to re-create the conflict of these roles in the here-and-now, controlled therapeutic setting. The client becomes the 'protagonist' and plays one of the roles in his story, while other members of the group take up and play the other roles. From time to time the protagonist switches roles with the other group members and thus he fully explores the problem situation.

Perls adopted some aspects of psychodrama in the active approach to therapy which he was to demonstrate in the 1960s, and he has acknowledged (1976) the influence of Moreno upon his later work. Eric Berne, the founder of Transactional Analysis, has highlighted Perls' debt to Moreno: 'Dr Perls is a learned man. . . In his selection of specific techniques, he shares with other "active" psychotherapists the "Moreno" problem: the fact that nearly all known "active" techniques were first tried out by Dr J.R. Moreno in psychodrama so that it is difficult to come up with an original idea in this regard' (Berne, 1970: 163–4). In fact Perls did make substantial and original modifications to psychodrama (see p. 103).

Gestalt Therapy: Excitement and Growth in the Human Personality

Perls asked Ralph Hefferline and Paul Goodman to co-author a book he had been planning. Perls provided some sort of initial manuscript for the book (Isadore From in Wysong and Rosenfeld, 1982). He intended to develop it further with his colleagues. In fact, Hefferline tried out the practical exercises with his Columbia students and therefore added much to the first half; while Paul Goodman collaborated with Perls upon the second half and was probably the primary writer of many sections. 'In Paul Goodman's writings on Gestalt therapy, one finds Perls' inspirations reconstructed into far-reaching concepts' (Miller, 1989: 21).[7] The exact nature and extent of Perls' contribution to the book remains, and will probably always remain, highly controversial. Seeds of many of the ideas developed in *Gestalt Therapy* can be found not only in *Ego, Hunger and Aggression* (Perls, 1947/1969a) but also in papers (Perls, 1948; 1979) which Perls presented in 1946–7 and in 1948 before the collaboration with Goodman. Traditionally *Gestalt Therapy* is referred to as the work of Perls, Hefferline and Goodman. Despite a recent trend to acknowledge the theoretical section as the work of Goodman and Perls (Wheeler, 1991), we have followed the established means of referring to it, honouring the major contribution of Goodman and Hefferline, by giving all three names throughout our text, rather than the common abbreviation of Perls et al.

This is the foundation text of Gestalt therapy and really launched the new school of therapy. After some disagreement regarding the name of the new approach, Fritz Perls decided on the title of Gestalt therapy. This choice was opposed by Laura and was later objected to by those who find Gestalt therapy and Gestalt psychology contradictory (e.g. Sherrill, 1974; Henle, 1978). However Yontef (1982) has demonstrated that Gestalt therapy is descended philosophically, if not historically, from Gestalt psychology.

Gestalt Therapy is divided into two books. Book One, written by Hefferline and Perls, is devoted to practical exercises designed to increase the individual's awareness of her present functioning. Book Two (probably initiated or drafted by Perls and widely acknowledged as the collaborative work of Perls and Goodman) is a theoretical discussion of Gestalt therapy. Originally the 'books' were intended to be presented in the reverse order but the publisher advised putting the exercises first because he thought the do-it-yourself nature of this part would have more popular appeal. Book Two is further divided into three parts. Part One starts with a chapter called 'The Structure of Growth' which provides a synopsis of the theoretical portion of the book and is an invaluable orientation to the reader. The first-time reader may wish to jump directly from the end of this chapter to the beginning of Part Three, which contains some of the best known theoretical aspects of Gestalt therapy, as described in Chapter 2 of this book. Perls wrote a new Authors' Note in 1969 for a reprinting of the book and the *Gestalt Journal* is currently publishing a new edition (Perls, Hefferline and Goodman, 1951/1993) with an introduction by Isadore From and Michael Miller, in which the order of two 'books' will be in the order originally planned.

Shortly after the publication of *Gestalt Therapy*, Fritz and Laura Perls founded the Gestalt Institute of New York. Meantime, news of the innovative therapeutic approach was spreading outside New York and Perls was invited to present and share his ideas. He travelled regularly to Cleveland, Detroit, Toronto and Miami, running small groups for professionals and lay people interested in Gestalt therapy, and in 1954 he, Laura, Paul Goodman and Isadore From supported the foundation of the Gestalt Institute of Cleveland. Fritz Perls continued to visit Cleveland and provided an influential model by working as an occasional and brilliant visiting therapist with the Cleveland group (Polster, 1992). His friend and colleague Isadore From, however, had a more extended and consistent impact upon the early development of Gestalt therapy in Cleveland, because he went there regularly for several days, first twice a month for five years and then once a month for another five years (From in Wysong and Rosenfeld, 1982). From saw members of the Cleveland group for group and individual therapy and also offered a theory group, in which participants discussed the theoretical section of *Gestalt Therapy* in great detail.

At home in New York between 1952 and 1956, there was increasing rivalry between Fritz on the one hand and Paul Goodman and Laura Perls on the other. Fritz felt that they criticized and put him down, while Laura and Paul accused Fritz of being oversensitive to criticism and lacking in intellectual rigour. In 1956 Perls was diagnosed as having a heart condition. Feeling ill and disillusioned with the situation in New York, he left Laura and moved to Miami, seeking milder winters. He was already 63 years old. Although Fritz and Laura never again lived together for any length of time, she has claimed that he did not really leave but just stayed away from home for longer and longer periods. They never divorced and Fritz continued to visit Laura in New York from time to time. Their daughter-in-law Rae Perls has described how each would visit her in turn, complaining about the other.

Miami, Florida

In Miami, Perls met Marty Fromm, whom he later called the most significant woman in his life. Shepard (1975) sees theirs as an attraction between two very similar people, who reflected each other's extreme, wide-ranging and contradictory personalities, despite their considerable age difference (she was 32; he was 64). They met once socially, then Marty started individual therapy with him. They became and remained lovers and friends for several years, while she continued to be in therapy with him. Anarchistic and radically questioning, Perls often defied established convention – even the prohibition upon sexual contact between psychotherapist and client. Although Marty Fromm has sometimes justified their sexual relationship as a means of development for her, we believe that Perls' attitude towards sexual contact between therapist and client was irresponsible and unethical, and it would not be tolerated in the current Gestalt field which has established specific codes of ethics for Gestalt psychotherapists to safeguard the safety of the client and forbid the sexual exploitation of clients by therapists.

In 1958 Perls moved briefly to Ohio in order to train psychiatric residents at the Columbus State Hospital, but by the end of the year he was back in Miami, having missed Marty Fromm more than he expected. Gradually, his therapeutic support of her development and freedom as a person came into direct conflict with his personal neediness and sexual jealousy. At the same time, Marty Fromm related, he was using a lot of drugs, particularly LSD, and became increasingly paranoid. Perls' health failed and he was rushed to hospital twice, first for a haemorrhoidectomy and then for a prostatectomy. He was 67.

During the period that he spent with Marty Fromm, Perls continued to write – Marty Fromm has recently given substantial unpublished manuscripts to the editor of the *Gestalt Journal* (Joe Wysong, 1992).

Mendocino, San Francisco, Los Angeles and a World Tour

In 1959 Wilson Van Dusen, the Chief Psychologist at Mendocino State Hospital, on the West Coast, invited Perls to act as consultant.

Here Perls worked with many groups of professional social workers, psychologists and psychiatrists, astonishing these groups with his ability to observe people and read the significance of surface mannerisms, looks and behaviour. On one occasion he entered a room where he knew no one except Van Dusen. Indicating that they should not speak, he went round the room observing what he saw in the body posture, self-presentation and facial expression of each member. His description of what he saw reflected each person's life and character to a degree that shocked the participants. Between two periods of consultancy at Mendocino, Perls lived and practised in San Francisco.

In late 1960, Perls grew restless and moved to Los Angeles to work with Jim Simkin, a friend and former student, who was to have an independent influence upon the development of Gestalt therapy (Simkin, 1974). They soon had two training groups. In addition Perls developed a practice and set up what he and Simkin called the freeway routes. He would set out on weekly trips along the San Bernardino Freeway and the Santa Ana Freeway, running groups in one or two hospitals and with private individuals.

By 1962, his work in Los Angeles had palled. Again disillusioned and seeking some reorientation in his life, Perls set out on a tour of the world, visiting the Orient, the Middle East and Europe. Highlights of the trip for Perls were Kyoto in Japan and Elath and Ein Hod in Israel. In Kyoto, Perls studied Zen Buddhism with intermingled pleasure and cynicism. He spent two months in Ein Hod, an artist's community near Tel Aviv, learning to paint.

Perls returned refreshed to Los Angeles in 1963. At Christmas time he was invited by the psychologist Gene Sagan to attend a conference for leaders of humanistic, existential and body healing at the Esalen Institute, Big Sur. In the summer of 1964 Perls ran the first residential training course in Gestalt therapy at Esalen. From then on Perls became enthusiastic about Esalen and has written warmly of how he found a home there: 'The target Esalen scored a bull's-eye with the arrow Fritz Perls' (1969c).

The Esalen Institute, Big Sur, California

Perls moved to live at Esalen in 1964, remaining there as resident trainer of Gestalt until he left the Institute in 1969. Here at last he was able to make Gestalt psychotherapy known to thousands of people and to gain the personal respect, affection and appreciation that he had longed for. Esalen is situated on the cliffs of the West Coast of America, a third of the way from San Francisco to Los Angeles. It has the most magnificent views of the Pacific Ocean and natural hot sulphur springs, which are used for bathing. Perls loved the position and within a year he had a specially designed semi-circular house built there, facing the ocean.

When Perls arrived at Esalen, his heart condition had deteriorated, he was in pain and consequently he was frequently mean and bad-tempered. Ida Rolf (1977) was at that time developing her system of profound muscle massage – structural integration or Rolfing – inspired by Reich's theory of body armour which was designed to break up habitual chronic tension. In 1965 she came to Esalen and worked on Perls. By the end of a week he was out of pain. Absolutely delighted, he expressed his appreciation and gratitude to her in his autobiography (1969c). He believed that Ida Rolf, along with the good climate at Esalen, gave him the last six years of his life.

In the mid 1960s the Esalen Institute became very successful. The programme was varied – including all aspects of the new growth and human potential movement. Resident trainers included Perls, the masseur Bernard Gunther, and William Schutz, one of the main founders of the encounter group movement and author of several books on group work, ecstasy, honesty, encounter and simplicity.[8] Esalen appealed to many people who sought to enrich their lives and wanted to get to know themselves better emotionally, physically and sensually as well as cognitively. It also had a huge popular impact on many who never visited Esalen itself, through a film about a fictional centre which was based on Esalen (*Bob and Carol and Ted and Alice*); through the best-selling book *Joy* (Schutz, 1967); and through the videos, films and books that Perls made of his own work there.

Between 1964 and 1969, Perls worked with many future therapists, trainers, artists and other professionals. He influenced their styles and through them spread his philosophy, his ideas and his techniques. Among the many people that Perls influenced in this way were Robert Hall, Claudio Naranjo, Abe Levitsky, Janet Lederman, Anna Halprin, John Stevens, Barry Stevens, Joe Wysong, Stanley Keleman, Janie Rhyne, George and Judith Brown, Gabrielle Roth, Edward Rosenfeld, and Sam Keen (Gaines, 1979). Many of the Esalen trainers, including William Schutz, Virginia Satir and Rollo May, sat in on Perls' workshops or became his friend and were also influenced by him. Abraham Maslow, pioneer of the human potential movement, attended or led at least one event in which Perls participated, but seems to have remained impervious to Perls. The story goes that Perls got bored with Maslow's serious contribution and started crawling around on his belly. Maslow dismissed him as crazy.

Perls began doing larger and larger groups, both at Esalen and on his frequent trips. He launched a new style of event which he called his 'circuses', where he gave demonstrations of Gestalt therapy upon a stage in front of a hundred or more people. For these larger events he developed the now famous *hot seat technique*. He would invite members of the audience who wished to work with him to come and work in the empty chair beside him in front of all the others. This was a dramatic way of demonstrating his methods, his keen power of observation and his unique intuition. The method allowed Perls to maximize upon his lifelong and practical knowledge of the theatre and theatrical methods: 'Every time he worked with somebody, it was like a performance . . . Fritz loved being the theater director. He loved it' (Anna Halprin in Gaines, 1979: 200). In between demonstrations, Perls made brief remarks about the thinking or theory behind how he had worked.

In 1968, a 75th birthday celebration was organized for Perls at the Miyako Hotel in San Francisco. At least 200 people attended the celebration dinner and congratulatory speeches were made. As Perls' popularity became established, he apparently mellowed in mood. He could still be – and often was – rude, brash and deliberately socially outrageous, but many people speak of his vitality and his affection to both staff and visitors to Esalen during that time.

Gestalt Therapy Verbatim

John Stevens edited transcriptions of Perls' demonstration workshops and of his short talks on theory, turning them into a book, which was published as *Gestalt Therapy Verbatim* in July 1969 (Perls, 1969b). The book thus produced is lively and easy to read but there is no consistent overall development of a theoretical context for the transcripts. The workshops represented in the book are mainly dream workshops and illustrate Perls' methods of working with dreams (see p. 120). Some editions of the book claim that these are verbatim transcripts of complete *therapy* sessions. Perls himself took the trouble (1969b: 74) to differentiate between therapy and large demonstration seminars and stressed that these demonstrations were *not* therapy.

One of the distinctive features of this book is that it is packed full of the clever, catchy phrases – such as 'Anxiety is the gap between the now and the later' (p. 30), 'Very few people go into therapy to be cured, but rather to improve their neurosis' (p. 39), 'Lose more and more of your mind and come to your senses' (p. 50) – which became Perls' hallmark in the 1960s. These catchy phrases caught people's attention and were easy to repeat so they certainly helped to popularize Gestalt therapy; and yet they also made it accessible to people who would trivialize and misunderstand it. In that free and easy period people attended a workshop or two, learnt the slogans, picked up a few techniques and called themselves Gestalt therapists, with little or no theoretical orientation or clinical experience to support their claim. By 1969 Perls had become aware of the dangers to Gestalt therapy inherent in his own sloganeering style of teaching, and he used the preface of *Gestalt Therapy Verbatim* to deplore and disassociate himself from those who offer instant cure or use gimmicky techniques.

Cowichan, 1969

After five years at Esalen, Perls was restless again, partly because of his political fears that with the election of Richard Nixon, America would become Fascist; partly because he was growing dissatisfied with Esalen itself and he probably disliked the competition to his own work from other disciplines and leaders such as Schutz. Above all, Perls had come to believe that the next step in the growth movement was some form of community living where people could integrate their growth.

Perls bought an old motel at Cowichan Lake, Vancouver Island, Canada and moved up there in 1969 to start a Gestalt community. Perls ran residential training workshops at Cowichan, first alone and then supported by Teddy Lyon, Barry Stevens and Janet Lederman. Later that summer Perls experimented with another style or structure for the training at Cowichan. He stopped actually leading any of the groups. Instead he wandered from group to group, following his emerging interest and intervening when he wished:

> That was the way he did things, changing all the time. As soon as he saw that we were getting our feet anchored in any situation, he'd pull the rug out by switching the situation; . . . It is so easy to get into a pattern (which is another name for rut) and live according to the pattern instead of by observation and awareness, which is Gestalt. (Barry Stevens in Gaines, 1979: 360)

Cowichan was Perls' home and he was very proud of what he had created there. He loved welcoming old friends and students as well as meeting new enthusiasts: 'The summer that Fritz went to Canada, we visited him for a few days. He walked out of the house and down the lawn like a king. Happy. He was just really happy' (Ilana Rubenfeld in Gaines, 1979: 369). Indeed at Cowichan, Perls seems to have been happier than at any other time in his life. He confided to Barry Stevens, 'For the first time in my life, I am at peace. Not fighting with the world' (Gaines, 1979: 369). With his work also he was content: 'I have arrived. I can't do any better.' Overall, he felt he had created a family and was experienced by many of those around him as a valued and beloved family member, as well as a brilliant therapist and trainer.

In and Out the Garbage Pail

In 1968 while still at Esalen, Perls had decided to write an autobiography, which was published as *In and Out the Garbage Pail* in December 1969 (Perls, 1969c). This book is a *mélange* of reflections, memories, theoretical exposition, verse and discussion, all written in a lively, highly spontaneous and personal fashion, which mirrored Perls' current emphasis upon the unfolding moment. There is little structure and sadly (from the practical point of view) the original versions lacked an index.

Other Books and Manuscripts

Perls worked on two other books while at Lake Cowichan which were published posthumously. *The Gestalt Approach, and Eye Witness to Therapy* (1976, originally published 1973) is two separate volumes. In *The Gestalt Approach*, Perls attempted to formulate a simple outline to Gestalt therapy theory which would be comprehensible to the intelligent layman. Although it was mainly written in the 1950s, Perls worked on it again in 1969 at Lake Cowichan and integrated some of his experiences of the intervening twenty years regarding Eastern religion, meditation and body work. *Eye Witness to Therapy* is a book of transcripts of films of Perls at work. He had intended to produce transcripts, films and theory as teaching materials which would help people understand his approach.

Legacy from Fritz (Baumgardner and Perls, 1975) again consists of two volumes. *Legacy from Fritz* contains a theoretical statement – 'The Teachings' – and further transcripts of Perls at work at Esalen and at Cowichan – 'The Therapy'. Volume II, *Gifts from Lake Cowichan*, is a description and integration of the experiences of one of Perls' trainees, Patricia Baumgardner.

In addition to these two posthumous books, Perls left numerous unpublished manuscripts in the home of Marty Fromm and in the apartment of his wife Laura Perls. The *Gestalt Journal* hopes eventually to publish a selection of these unpublished papers (Joe Wysong, 1992).

Illness and Death

Throughout 1969, Fritz Perls continued to make trips to promote Gestalt and to invite people back to Cowichan. Some say he was indefatigable; others mention that he tired very easily and seemed to realize that his time was now limited. In December 1969, Perls set off for Europe. But he was not well and wrote to his sister Grete that his beloved opera was no longer the same. On his return from Europe, Perls was very ill. He was at first determined to carry on his intensive schedule of workshops, but upon his arrival in Chicago he saw Dr William Shlaes, who told him that he was possibly suffering from cancer of the pancreas.

Fritz phoned Laura to tell her, but when Laura said that she would fly to join him, he grumbled that he didn't want her. Fritz and Laura Perls continued their ambivalent relationship to the end. She did arrive a few days later and sat by his bedside during his last illness while he alternately confided in her, wished her elsewhere, shouted at her and ignored her.

Following his consultation with the doctor, Perls was admitted to the Weiss Memorial Hospital, where he underwent an exploratory operation. Although Perls survived the operation, he was in great pain and discomfort after it and died of a heart attack on 14 March 1970. The autopsy later showed that he was indeed suffering from cancer of the pancreas.

Funeral services were held on the East and West Coasts. At the funeral service in Manhattan, Paul Goodman delivered a rather ambivalent oration which described the contributions to Gestalt therapy made by both Fritz and Laura and was deeply resented by many of Fritz Perls' West Coast trainees and colleagues. The funeral service in San Francisco was attended by between 1200 and 1500 people. Anna Halprin choreographed a dance and Abe Levitsky gave a witty appreciation of Fritz which, while it did not ignore his weaknesses, was filled with respect and love:

> Fritz, you were very definitely not a good boy, and frankly, it's a bit puzzling to know exactly where to send this farewell note. You could be most anywhere. I imagine that typically you are shuttling back and forth between both polarities. You wouldn't want to get stuck in either place. . . We, gathered here tonight, appreciate that you were with us, that we met and touched each other. And we say to you, farewell, Fritz, and thank you for being. (Shepard, 1975: 196)

Fritz Perls, the Man

The flavour of Fritz Perls the man is hard to capture; as though he is evading definition, he shifts and changes with each description.

Who Perls was depends upon whom you speak with, and when. To some he was a hero, to others a bastard; to some cruel, to others tender; to some generous, to others the world's biggest taker; to some a genius, to others a near-illiterate non-intellectual; to some he seemed sociable and happy, to others lonely and poor at making genuine contact with the people around him; to some he was a beautiful sensuous man, to others an ugly toad, a dirty lecherous old man; to some a narcissistic exhibitionist, to others a shy, withdrawn introvert too proud to ask for love.

He prided himself on being genuine, authentic and true to himself. So he behaved, spoke and felt exactly as he wanted to, not as others expected him to. Descriptions of Perls are almost always extreme and paradoxical. He generally flouted social and professional conventions, ignored ordinary politeness and loved to outrage. Yet even in this, his most consistent quality, he was unpredictable, for when he chose to be so, he could be courteous and gracious. He seemed generally not to care what anyone thought of him; yet most agree that he yearned for recognition and respect from the psychiatric profession.

Theorists often develop the theory that best describes themselves. Perls' theory of the self conveys the best sense of the man he was: 'Thus the self is various. It manifests differently in different situations, according to the . . . environmental stimuli. It is always changing' (Perls, Hefferline and Goodman, 1951/1973: 281).

Notes

1. We have drawn extensively on Shepard's (1975) biography, on Gaines' (1979) collection of anecdotes and upon the personal communications of those who knew Fritz Perls as well as Fritz Perls' own autobiographies (1969c; unpublished ms) for the biographical details in this chapter.

2. Maslow (1954; 1968) was also influenced by Goldstein.

3. Perls, F.S., Hefferline, R.F. and Goodman, P. *Gestalt Therapy: Excitement and Growth in the Human Personality* (1951/1973) was originally published in New York by Julian Press in 1951 and reprinted by Penguin books in 1973. The Penguin edition is the one referenced and referred to throughout this book.

4. Laura Perls was called Lore Posner before her marriage and later Anglicized her first name to Laura.

5. Alexander Lowen (1975) later developed bioenergetics from Reich's innovations. A force similar to Reich's 'life energy' is described as *élan vital* by Bergson (1965) and is explored by Clarkson (1991c; 1992) as the principle of Physis.

6. Of course, many others also had a seminal influence upon the essential nature of Gestalt therapy, as for example Erving and Miriam Polster (1974), Joseph Zinker (1978) and James Simkin (1974) (see Yontef, 1982).

7. 'For example, there is an intricate definition of the contact boundary as the meeting place between the self and the world where all psychological growth occurs,

a careful delineation of the resistances to contact as building blocks of neurotic character, and a phenomenological account of Gestalt (figure/ground) formation as a powerful explanatory principle in understanding human experience' (Miller, 1989: 21).

8. See John Rowan's *Ordinary Ecstasy* (1988) for a discussion of the origins of the humanistic psychology movement and the role of Esalen and individuals such as Schutz and Maslow, as well as Perls, in its development.

2

Major Contributions to Theory

All of Perls' ideas are interwoven and cannot be understood in isolation from each other. The very essence of Perls' contribution to the theory of psychotherapy is the holistic notion that everything is related to everything else; that all things and beings are mutually dependent upon one another; and that a whole theory is more than the sum of its individual parts. Describing Perls' theoretical position therefore poses a challenge which is intrinsic and peculiar to the position itself. An understanding of any single aspect of his theory requires and presupposes a simultaneous understanding of the other aspects, and indeed of the whole.

Perls and his colleagues seem to have faced a similar challenge when trying to organize *Gestalt Therapy* (1951/1973) for they say: 'Indispensable – both for the writing and the thorough understanding of this book – is an attitude which as a theory actually permeates the content and method of the book. Thus the reader is apparently confronted with an impossible task: to understand the book he must have the "Gestaltist" mentality, and to acquire it he must understand the book' (p. 14). Luckily for their readers (and for ours), however, the Gestalt outlook is not hard to acquire, for it is a unitary, harmonious approach to life which Perls believed is natural to each one of us if we will only let go our acquired habit of thinking in terms of dualistic and divisive contrasts and categories.

To catch this spirit of interconnectedness, we have grouped Perls' theories as six clusters of interrelated concepts. Since one of Perls' most important innovations was to propose that people have the innate capacity to be healthy and self-regulating, we have chosen to build up a picture of Perls' theory of the human being as a whole person, interacting in a spontaneous, responsible, self-regulating manner with his environment, before introducing his theories of psychological disturbance. Thus the first five clusters in this chapter deal with holism, field theory, cycles and sequences of experience, contact, and theory of the self; while the sixth and much longer cluster deals with psychological disturbance (see Figures 2.1 and 2.2).

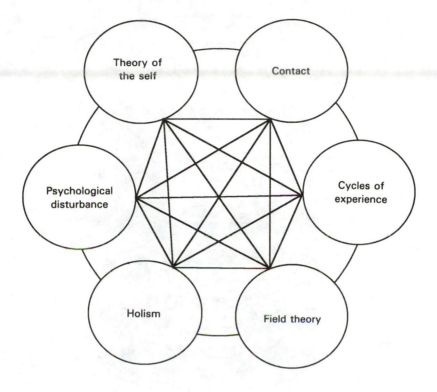

Figure 2.1 *Diagrammatic synopsis of the six clusters of interrelated concepts*

Cluster One: Holism

The most important theoretical concept permeating all of Gestalt therapy is the notion of the whole. Indeed *gestalt* means a whole that cannot be broken without destroying its nature. Perls (1976) gave the example of a triangle which is made up of three bits of wood: if you take them apart, the triangle disappears and that particular gestalt is destroyed. The English translations of the word *gestalt* do not capture the full sense that the whole precedes the parts and *that the whole is always more than and different from the sum of its parts.*

The Whole Person
A fundamental principle of holism is that nature is a unified and coherent whole made up of lesser wholes. All the elements of the

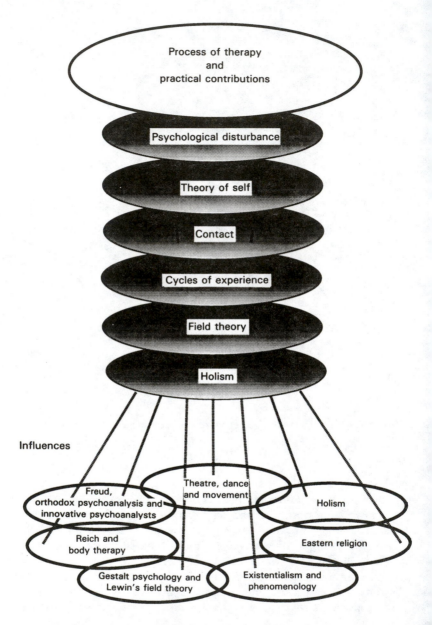

Figure 2.2 *Diagrammatic representation of how the influences of the field working upon Perls contributed to his ideas and how all his ideas are interrelated and interwoven and cannot be understood in isolation*

universe – things, plants, animals, human beings – coexist in a changing process of coordinated activity. Existentially, human beings are not the centre of the universe but one active element in the complex ecological system of the cosmos.

Perls was especially concerned with the holism of the human organism (or person) in his surroundings. Perls' holistic approach to the individual embraces and affirms complexity, inclusion and diversity and resists any attempt at reductionism.

From his earliest writing Perls emphasized his holistic understanding of humankind. His approach is based upon the inseparable unity of bodily, emotional and mental experience, upon the integrity of language, thought and behaviour. He believed that the body, mind and soul all naturally function as one whole process. All parts of the human being are coordinated and arranged to function with complete collaboration in support of each other and the whole organism: 'Body and soul are identical in "re" though not "in verbo"; the words "body" and "soul" denote two aspects of the same thing' (Perls, 1947/1969a: 33), and 'We believe further that the "mental–physical" or "mind–body" split is a totally artificial one, and that to concentrate on either term in this false dichotomy is to preserve neurosis, not to cure it' (Perls, 1976: 53).

Thus when a person experiences a feeling say of sadness or of anxiety, there will always be an accompanying physiological sensation and psychological component. An anxiety attack without breathing difficulties, quickening of the pulse or similar symptoms does not exist. A feeling of grief without heaviness, heartache, tearfulness or muscular restriction to inhibit such responses is equally impossible. The mind or emotions do not cause the body to respond in this way – as is often thought – nor does the body cause the mind to operate. Body and mind cooperate simultaneously. So if a person is thirsty, the need exists in the body as a deficiency (dehydration), as a sensation of thirst, and in the mind as a complementary image – say of a glass of water or of a bubbling stream. If the person is able to quench his thirst, the deficiency, the sensation and the images of water all disappear spontaneously in one unitary, holistic and synchronistic process.

In his writing, Perls came back to the holistic nature of human beings again and again, expressing in different words the idea that people are unitary creatures, in which body and mind are essentially cooperative and harmonious: 'Where there is good contact, one can always show the cooperation of sense and movement (and also feeling)' (Perls, Hefferline and Goodman, 1973: 274), and 'The true nature of man, like the true nature of any other animal, is integrity' (Perls, 1976: 49).

Modern people, according to Perls (1948; 1976), have learnt to separate body and mind artificially and the aim of Gestalt therapy is to re-establish the intrinsic holistic harmony of the individual: 'We are as we are today – fractionalized people – people who are split up into bits and pieces. And it's no use to analyze these bits and pieces and cut them up still more. What we want to do in Gestalt therapy is to integrate all the dispersed and disowned parts of the self and make the person whole again' (1976: 181).

In keeping with his holistic attitude, Perls valued human qualities and activities associated with both the left and right hemispheres of the brain (Perls, 1948; 1976; 1978a; Ornstein, 1972). The kind of psychological theory which was permeating the field of psychotherapy when Perls commenced his work was primarily psychoanalytic on the one hand, or behaviouristic on the other. Both these emphasize rationality, causality and analysis – all activities associated with the left hemisphere of the brain. Perls believed that the overvaluing of these rational, causal activities had created a split between deliberate behaviour on the one hand and spontaneous being on the other, a split which was the cause of much malaise both in the individual and in modern society. Perls was particularly gifted in his immediate intuitive knowledge and his feel for fantasy, imaginative playfulness and spontaneity (right-hemispheric activities). Drawing upon the innovations of Moreno, Ferenczi and Jung, Perls emphasized the creative aspects of clients and therapist and popularized all sorts of experimental, playful and active approaches to psychotherapy (see Chapter 3). This is not to say that he excluded analytic understanding, but that he affirmed and valued all sides of the human being: 'This includes the harmonizing of both deliberate and spontaneous attitudes' (Perls, 1948: 572).

Perls thus synthesized body and mind, left- and right-brain into his concept of the whole person and developed a unitary method of therapy which integrated different approaches and techniques in order to work more effectively with the client: 'We candidly accept as powerful approaches a number of different theories and techniques: they are relevant in the total field and, however incompatible they may seem to their several proponents, they must nevertheless be compatible if one allows the synthesis among them to emerge' (Perls, Hefferline and Goodman, 1951/1973: 292).

Interdependence of the Person and his Environment
A person forms an interactive whole with his environment. The gestalt of an individual includes the whole person, *together with* his context and the relationship between the two. For example, a

lonely soldier on the run is perceived quite differently from the same soldier in the midst of many other soldiers marching towards the observer in battle order. His significance for the observer depends upon the context and cannot be understood in isolation from it. We are relationship, for we exist and define ourselves in connection to our surroundings, to other people, other creatures, other ideas (see p. 59).

Perls, Hefferline and Goodman (1951/1973) called the relationship of the person and his environment the organism/environment field. They were insistent that it never makes sense to think of a person out of context. Human beings are always a part of the holistic universe and participate in the unity formed of their relationship to other human beings, plants, objects and events. The person survives in his environment by means of a creative exchange, which Perls called contact and assimilation (see p. 55). The exchange may be physical or emotional, literal or metaphoric, but it is essential.

The unitary nature of man and his environment has recently been brought forcibly to our attention by the ecological devastation which we ourselves have precipitated through ignoring their interrelationship. Perls was an early and vociferous exponent of the holistic interdependence of human beings with their environment: 'The safeguard against such a danger [one-sided approaches] is the concept and experience of the human personality as being an indivisible whole and as always embedded in, and related to, an environmental personal and social field' (Perls, 1979: 21, originally delivered in 1946–7).

Criticism of Scientific Analytical Techniques
Drawing upon the work of modern physicists such as Planck and Heisenberg, Perls (1947/1969a) criticized the late-nineteenth-century experimental psychologists and scientists for being reductionistic, analytical and causal rather than holistic. Perls, Hefferline and Goodman (1951/1973: 287) believed that academic psychologists had little to contribute to the understanding of emotion and personality, or to practising psychotherapists who from the beginning need to meet with the full complexity of a whole human being. The scrutiny of isolated parts of the organism leads only to an understanding of those isolated parts. The essence of the whole can never be captured by an analysis of the parts: phenomena which appear as unitary wholes must have their wholeness respected and can be analytically broken into bits only at the price of 'annihilating the thing that it was intended to study'.

Instead Perls, Hefferline and Goodman (1951/1973) proposed a radically different approach in which they fused experimental technique with clinical situations. Through a series of practical experiments, the individual is enabled to experience himself by becoming aware of and describing to himself various aspects of himself – so that he comes to a fuller understanding of how he functions as a whole organism and as a whole person.

Innate Drive towards Wholeness and Self-Actualization

Underlying and informing his holistic philosophy is Perls' belief that all living things have an innate drive towards growth and self-actualization. Our early education and socialization on the other hand almost always lead us to deny, suppress or feel ashamed of many aspects of our authentic natures. We learn to be what we are taught we ought to be. As a result people often feel guilty when they behave the way they 'want' to rather than the way they 'should'. Only human beings want to become something they are not. Existentially, at any given moment an adult person *is* his full potential. All that is needed is for him to accept himself as he is and face up to life and the situations around him authentically: *'Man transcends himself only via his true nature, not through ambition and artificial goals'* (Perls, 1976: 99).

Forcing our natures to behave in a 'shouldistic' way is an attempt to actualize a self-image rather than the self (Perls, 1969c). It is an attempt to create an inauthentic image of the self rather than to know, accept and be an authentic self. Such an attempt leads people to pretend, to play at and to adopt roles, which result in all sorts of phoney behaviour and mental torture. Human beings do not need to coerce themselves in this way. With awareness, self-acceptance and the knowledge of the right to exist *as they currently are*, they will naturally grow and change in ways that are supportive to the whole person fulfilling their life force energy.

Urge to Complete

The Gestalt psychologists (see pp. 6–8) had demonstrated that an individual organizes his perceptions into meaningful wholes. They also showed that if the whole is incomplete, the individual will tend to see the whole anyway, supplying or guessing at the missing parts in order to complete or make meaning of the partial form. Perls, Hefferline and Goodman (1951/1973) adopted this principle of perception as fundamental to their way of conceiving the individual and the world. They illustrated the human being's innate tendency to complete by showing the reader a series of incomplete pictures.

Seeing pictures such as those in Figure 2.3 for the first time,

Figure 2.3 *Gestalt completion test (from* Gestalt Completion Test *by Roy Street, Bureau of Publications, Teachers College, Columbia University, 1931, reprinted by permission of the publisher and the author)*

people 'complete' them so that they make sense to them. The left and centre pictures are usually completed instantly and in a similar way. The right picture gives rise to more uncertainty and discussion because it provides less information – so people have to puzzle over different possible ways of completing it, often coming up with different solutions according to their own experiences.

Building upon the Gestalt psychologists' discoveries regarding people's innate tendency to complete incomplete forms, Zeigarnik (1927) experimentally demonstrated that people remember unfinished tasks better than finished ones, while Ovsiankina (1928) extended her work to show that people spontaneously resume interrupted activities. Thus we have a nagging memory of the unfinished tax forms that await our attention on our desk. Only when we have completed such tasks can we truly forget them.

Because people tend to make wholes of their experience they also try to complete any emotional situations which remain unresolved from their past. Perls called such situations unfinished business (see p. 68). Perls applied the tendency to seek closure in a practical and innovative way to psychotherapy. He invented therapy techniques which help the individual to surface unfinished situations from the past and resolve them in the present, as is illustrated in Chapter 3.

Influences upon Perls' Holism

Perls was extensively influenced by the holistic ideas of Jan Smuts (1987) (see p. 15) and by the discoveries of the Gestalt psychologists (p. 6): that human beings tend to make meaningful wholes of their experience (Wertheimer, 1959; Koffka, 1935); that the whole configuration, not the individual parts, stimulates perception, so that the whole precedes the parts (Koffka, 1935); and that if the whole thing perceived is broken or incomplete, the individual will tend to see the whole anyway, supplying the missing parts as needed (Wertheimer, 1925).

Perls' emphasis upon the interrelationship between the individual and his environment was also influenced by Sullivan's concept of the interpersonal field and by Horney's interest in the cultural background of the individual.

From his analysis with Reich, as well as from his studies with the theatre director Max Reinhardt and his association with the innovative dancer Palucca, Perls had developed an abiding interest in bodily expression and a belief in the authenticity of the language of the body. Kurt Goldstein, with whom Perls worked in 1926, was another important influence upon Perls' holism and concept of self-actualization.

Perls' unique contribution to holism was that he gathered holistic notions from a wide range of sources, synthesized a number of different holistic principles and applied them to the field of psychotherapy, developing a holistic method of therapy which engages all aspects of the person. Different parts of the client may be emphasized at different times in the process of therapy but the Gestalt psychotherapist will always have as a guiding principle the integration of all the many facets of that unique individual.

Cluster Two: Field Theory

As discussed in Chapter 1, the German Gestalt psychologists were a school of academic and experimental psychologists who were concerned with perception. Cluster Two explains the Gestalt principle of figure and ground, by which the individual organizes his perception of himself and his surroundings; and then explores the field orientation which Perls adopted and adapted from the Gestalt psychologists, especially Wertheimer, and more indirectly from their associate Kurt Lewin (1935; 1952).

Gestalt Principle of Figure and Ground

The concept of figure and ground explains the process by which a person organizes his perceptions to form whole configurations which he endows with meaning: 'A man does not perceive things as unrelated isolates, but organizes them in the perceptual process into meaningful wholes' (Perls, 1976: 3). We do not see the whole of ourselves and our surroundings at the same time; we select and focus on something we are interested in and this thing then appears as a prominent figure against a dim background. As soon as we lose interest in that one particular aspect of ourselves or our environment, it recedes into the background and something else grabs our attention in its place. We are thus constantly organizing our perceptions of ourselves and our surroundings into meaningful figures or gestalten. Perls (1947/1969a) gives the everyday example that people do not usually notice post boxes but, as soon as they have an urgent letter to post, 'then out of an indifferently viewed background, a letterbox will jump into prominence . . . becoming a figure (gestalt) against an indifferent background' (p. 41).

To illustrate the basic principle of figure and ground formation, Perls, Hefferline and Goodman (1951/1973) used the now famous picture shown in Figure 2.4. Depending on whether you make the white or the black foreground, you see either a white chalice on a black background or two black heads in profile silhouette. You can switch your attention quickly from one to the other but you cannot see both at once. As you make one the focus of your attention, the other appears to recede and becomes the background.

Figure 2.4 *Illustration of the principle of figure and ground (originally from* Visuell wahrgenommene Figuren *by Edgar Rubin, Gyldendalske Boghandel, Köbenhaven, 1921)*

The Field Approach

Kurt Lewin took the discoveries of the Gestalt psychologists regarding perception out of the laboratory and into the realm of real life and personal relationships. He developed a theory of the individual within the environment in which the individual organizes his entire environment – figure and ground – in terms of both the prevailing conditions and his own dominant interests or needs in that environment or field. Perls assimilated aspects of Wertheimer's field orientation and Lewin's field approach.[1] Here we describe those adaptations of field theory which Perls (1947/1969a; 1976) and Perls, Hefferline and Goodman (1951/1973) made central to Gestalt therapy.

The field is all the coexisting, mutually interdependent factors of a person and his environment. In Perls' holistic field theory, a person's behaviour can only be understood in terms of his interdependence with his environment because his social, historical, cultural field is intrinsic to him. Understanding of human behaviour needs to begin with a sense of the situation or field as a whole and only then proceed to differentiation of the component parts.

All aspects of the person and of his field are interrelated, thus forming a whole or system. Any change in a part of that person or of that environment is manifested throughout the system. For example, if I am in pain because I pulled a muscle in my shoulder, other muscles in my body compensate by contracting and my overall posture is altered, while my mood becomes irritable and thus my relationship with the members of my family becomes more stressed than usual. Thus the family dynamic may be subtly or dramatically transformed because of one change in one part of one person in the whole family system.

All the phenomena of the field have potentially equal relevance. At any moment, the focus of attention may shift and the whole field take on a dramatic new meaning. So Gestaltists pay attention to all aspects of the field, confident that the meaning of this or that apparently 'irrelevant' detail or phenomenon may suddenly jump to the foreground and change the whole way that client and therapist understand the current situation – as for example when a person notices that his foot is twitching a little and, in the moment of noticing, he realizes he feels like kicking the friend he has been describing quite amicably. Perls had a genius for noticing all aspects of the current field, from a whining voice or a barely perceptible flutter of the hands to a quality or physical attribute that was missing (see Chapter 3).

For the background which is currently being ignored is as much part of the field as the person or aspect of the environment which is in focus. Therefore what is missing or appears to be missing from the overall situation may be as significant a comment regarding the individual's functioning as whatever he is focusing upon. (For an example of Perls' therapeutic application of paying close attention to what is missing from the field, see p. 113–15.)

Meaning, Organization and Differentiation of the Field

A person is active in the organization of his experiential field and in the creation of the meanings with which he endows it. Existentially, there is no ultimate or universal meaning to human experience. Yet human beings are meaning-seeking creatures; so individuals actively give meaning to various aspects of their fields of experience as well as to the overall field. The meaning that each individual assigns to his perceptual field is unique to that individual.

Perls (1947/1969a) gives an example of this principle by pointing out that a cornfield has a totally different significance for a farmer, a pilot, a painter, an agronomist, a merchant and a couple of lovers. The farmer sees corn to be harvested, the pilot observes an emergency landing place, the painter a composition to be painted, the lovers perceive a secluded spot to make love, the agronomist considers the likely chemical composition of the soil, while the merchant may calculate the financial benefit of handling the crop. Thus Perls illustrates the phenomenological view that objects exist in the way that they exist through the meaning that each person gives to them. The significance of the cornfield arises from the context, from the interests and previously established information and attitudes of each of the unique individuals concerned at the time.

When the person or his field is disturbed by some need or outside stimulus, he begins to distinguish aspects of the field into figure and ground, according to the prevailing conditions and his own needs or interests within those prevailing conditions. Thus in wartime, on the run from enemy troops, he may perceive a haystack as a potential shelter; while on a rainy day in peacetime he may not even notice the dank unappealing haystack, as he runs towards the warm and welcoming dryness of a barn. The need (or interest) organizes the field (Lewin, 1926). The individual differentiates his field into polar opposites – things which can meet his needs and things which cannot. Those things which can meet his needs or interests become more figural (the figure), while their opposites recede into the background (the ground). Phenomenologically we construct our meaningful perception of objects through selective attention to certain stimuli over others (Spinelli, 1989).

Differentiation of the Field into Polarities

From the undifferentiated background, two branches of differentiation develop, opposites are born. These opposites may seem irreconcilable. However, when they are illustrated as two polar extremes of a line with a zero point of pre-differentiation in the middle, they are seen to be essential aspects one of the other, as shown by Perls' examples (1947/1969a: 17–20):

zero point

beginning	middle	end
past	present	future
convexity	flatness	concavity

Contrast or polarities are needed in order to form clear, strong figures of interest against an indifferent background. Opposites coexist: the polar opposite of whatever is figure at the moment must inevitably be in the background. Light would not exist without dark, nor dark without light; they determine each other, they are two interconnected poles of a continuum of awareness. In the same way, black and white, night and day, warm and cold, desire and aversion, love and hate determine and define each other.

This way of thinking of polarities is a holistic and existential conception of difference. Gestalt is interested in both the qualities that separate and the qualities that bring together the polar aspects of the field. Both the differences and the interdependence of polar opposites within the organism/environment field are explored. Examples of Perls' working with clients to explore the significance of polarities within the individual/environment field are given in Chapter 3 (pp. 104–7).

Concept of Present Awareness

Awareness for Perls is your human ability to be in touch with your whole perceptual field. It is the capacity to be in touch with your own existence, to notice what is happening around or inside you, to connect with the environment, other people and yourself; to know what you are feeling or sensing or thinking; how you are reacting at this very moment. Awareness is not just a mental process: it involves all experiences, whether they be physical or mental, sensory or emotional. It is a whole process engaging the total organism: 'Awareness is like the glow of a coal which comes from its own combustion . . . In awareness a process is taking place in the coal (the total organism)' (Perls, Hefferline and Goodman, 1951/1973: 106).

Awareness is the experience of *right now*. You can only be aware of that which you contact at first hand, that is through your senses; you cannot experience or be aware of an event that is beyond the range of these receptors. You may imagine it but the imagining or picturing is *here* where you are *now*. Similarly, you may remember or reflect upon the past and you may plan for the future but the remembering, the reflecting and the planning are all actually happening in the present. Thus Perls differentiates phenomenologically between the process of experience *as it occurs* and reflections upon that experience which inevitably happen subsequent to the experience itself. Interpretation, reminiscing, explanations or 'talking about' are no substitutes for actual present experience as the vital essence of our existence, our means of learning and insight.

Perls insisted that the only psychological reality is the present: 'Laying the utmost stress on this sense of actuality – on the importance of realizing that there is no other reality than the present' (Perls, 1947/1969a: 208). A person's behaviour can only be explained in terms of the phenomena of the present field.

Perls does not deny that everything has its origin in the past and tends to further development in the future, but he emphasizes that past and future take their bearings continuously from the present field and have to be related to it: 'The actual situation is always, we must remember, an example of all the reality that there ever was or will be' (Perls, Hefferline and Goodman, 1951/1973: 508). (See p. 95 for a discussion of the place of the past in Gestalt psychotherapy.)

Perls criticizes Freud's view of the unconscious as an entity in which repressed feelings and experiences are located. He substitutes instead a more fluid concept of unaware and aware process:

> we use the word 'unaware' but give it a much wider scope than what was designated by Freud as the unconscious. The latter is identical with the Repressed, that is, with the once conscious material. Freud compares the Conscious and the Unconscious with an iceberg. Rather, we compare aware and unaware with the surface of the globe, and say that what we don't see must not necessarily have been on the surface before. (Perls, 1978a: 36)

Phenomenology as a Philosophical Method of Enquiry
Phenomenology emphasizes that ours is a phenomenal reality and as such it is open to a multiplicity of interpretations. The meaning that each individual assigns to his perception of his world is unique to that individual. A phenomenological method of enquiry therefore emphasizes that one individual cannot know the truth of another's reality. Thus, Perls believed the therapist must open himself to all the possibilities of the field and, instead of interpreting the client's behaviour, he must help the client to uncover his own unique sense of meaning and direction in life, through the phenomenological method, which consists of three interrelated steps (Spinelli, 1989):

1 *bracketing* or setting aside previous assumptions and biases so as to focus on immediate experience;
2 *describing* immediate and concrete impressions, rather than explaining or interpreting;
3 *equalizing* (or initially treating as equally significant) all aspects of the field thus described, rather than assuming any hierarchy of importance.

Perls' primary therapeutic method was developing awareness through phenomenological description of what is. Therapist and client describe what they experience or perceive without interpretation: 'I rely upon the patient's detailed descriptions of his experiences and my own observation, and try to use as little construction and guesswork – for instance interpretation – as possible' (Perls, 1979: 13). At least initially, the therapist avoids imposing any hierarchy of importance upon the items described by the client, suspending his own past assumptions about what is significant at any given moment. Phenomenology urges us to treat each bit of information regarding the perceptual field of another person, as if it is a bit of a jigsaw puzzle which we are trying to piece together without prior knowledge of what image the completed puzzle depicts. Phenomenology thus describes the surface of the object, behaviour or experience (trying to bracket the previous prejudices of the investigator), in order to grasp its very *essence*. Chapter 3 gives examples of Perls' use of phenomenological methods in practice (see pp. 92 and 113).

Influences upon Perls' Gestalt Field Theory
In developing his version of field theory in *Ego, Hunger and Aggression* (1947/1969a), Perls took over and used much of the vocabulary of Gestalt psychology – words such as gestalt, ground, figure, differentiation of the field and so on. These terms are

explained in this book as they are introduced. Perls (1947/1969a; 1976) and Perls, Hefferline and Goodman (1951/1973) adopted many of the principles of perception elucidated by the Gestalt psychologists, such as Wertheimer, Köhler, Koffka, Gelb and their students Zeigarnik and Ovsiankina. Yontef (1982) has said that, 'The Gestalt approach of both Gestalt movements is a form of phenomenological field theory. At its core is a mode of exploration (Wertheimer, 1938: 3) . . . [which] seeks insight into the functional interrelationships that form the intrinsic structure of the whole of any situation being studied (Köhler, 1969)' (p. 24).

Perls (1947/1969a; Perls, Hefferline and Goodman, 1951/1973) refers to Kurt Lewin, a social psychologist who was associated with Wertheimer and Köhler and 'took the Gestalt model out of the laboratory and into the much more complex realm of everyday life' (Wheeler, 1991: 27). Lewin developed the Gestalt psychologists' idea of the field into a complex theoretical approach known as field theory with its own specialized scientific constructs and vocabulary, which emphasized the interaction between needs and field. Perls was influenced by Lewin's ideas, although Wheeler (1991) has suggested that Perls and Goodman did not know Lewin's writings well and failed to understand essential aspects of Lewin's field theory, especially his rich concept of the differentiated ground.[2]

Perls was also familiar with Husserl's (1931; 1968) principles of phenomenology (Perls, 1948; Isadore From in Wysong and Rosenfeld, 1982) and believed that phenomenological methods provided a means of investigating or studying the overall perceptual field of the individual without reducing it through analytic interpretation. Perls' (1947/1969a) concept of the field was influenced by Jan Smuts (1987), who introduced from physics the idea that everything has a field and that things and organisms are unintelligible if considered without these fields. Perls acknowledged (1978a) the contribution of Harry Stack Sullivan and his interpersonal relations to his own emphasis upon the relatedness of the organism to its field.

Perls' unique contribution was that he took the Gestalt principles of perception and elements of Wertheimer's and Lewin's field theory and applied them to psychotherapy. He insisted that the general principles of field theory must be respected when attempting to understand human behaviour in the therapeutic setting. He extrapolated from field theory and Husserl's phenomenology a system of therapy which observed and described the structure and process of the present situation or field as its method of working.

Cluster Three: Cycles of Experience

Gestalt psychotherapy is based in the natural flow or cycles of nature. Its inspiration is biological functioning and structure, because man is a part of nature and obeys the laws of nature. Perls was fond of stressing that he had not discovered or invented Gestalt therapy but had found it or re-found it, because 'Gestalt is as ancient and old as the world itself' (Perls, 1969b: 15) and is a philosophy that tries to be in alignment or harmony with the natural universe, with what *is*. He emphasized that all life is process and flux, that nothing is static: 'Everything is in flux. Only after we have been stunned by the infinite diversity of processes constituting the universe can we understand the importance of the organizing principle that creates order from chaos; namely, the figure–background formation' (Perls, 1948: 571). On one occasion Perls acknowledged that his emphasis upon process dates back to Heraclitus: 'we have finally come back to the pre-Socratic philosopher, Heraclitus, who said that everything is flow, flux, process' (Perls, 1970: 19).

This cluster first explores the cyclical nature of self-regulation as Perls conceived it and then describes the Gestalt cycle, which is a crystallization or distillation of the process of self-regulation.

Organismic Self-Regulation
Perls believed that all living organisms are naturally self-regulating. They have needs that must be met if they are to live; and if they are not interfered with, human beings will spontaneously regulate themselves to meet those needs without any necessity 'deliberately to schedule, to encourage, or inhibit, the promptings of appetite, sexuality, and so forth, in the interests of health or morals' (Perls, Hefferline and Goodman, 1951/1973: 294). When deficiencies occur, the organic system spontaneously seeks to compensate. When excesses are present it equally spontaneously gets rids of them, in a constant cycle of attaining, losing and regaining homeostatic balance.

Thus a person experiences recurring disturbance in the form of needs (lacks or excesses, for example), together with a responding and equally recurrent automatic urge to re-establish his equilibrium. The lacks or needs may be created because of something which happens inside him (a need for affection or water, for instance) or because of some disturbance which happens outside him (for example a loud noise may irritate or create a need for silence). The individual is attracted alternately to both poles of a disturbance/balance continuum (the polarities of homeostasis and disturbance are further discussed on p. 52).

The person organizes his experience – his sensations, images, energy, interest and activity – around the need until he has met it. Once the need is met the person feels satisfied – so that particular need loses its interest for him and recedes. The person is then in a state of withdrawal, rest or equilibrium, before a new need emerges and the cycle starts all over again. In a healthy individual this sequence is self-regulating, dynamic and cyclical. Self-regulation does not, of course, necessarily ensure the satisfaction of the needs of the person. If the environment is deficient in one of the needed items – water in the desert or affection in a family – the person will not be able to quench his thirst or satisfy his need for love. Self-regulation implies that the individual will do his best to regulate himself in the environment given the actual resources of that environment.

If there is a conflict of needs, then the dominant need will take precedence. To illustrate that the dominant need of the moment takes precedence, Perls, Hefferline and Goodman (1951/1973) and Perls (1948) tell the story of a corporal who got lost in the desert and returned to camp exhausted and dehydrated. His friend greeted him with the news that he had been promoted, while the corporal rushed off to get some water. Later – to the friend's astonishment – the corporal claimed that he did not know he had been promoted. He had literally not heard his friend because at that moment he was oblivious to everything but his need for water. Yet shortly before the corporal got safely back to the camp, an enemy plane had attacked and the corporal had dived for cover, temporarily forgetful of his thirst. Here is a hierarchy of dominance: the acute threat of the enemy plane dominated the thirst; the thirst dominated the interest in promotion.

In his passionate defence of the principle of self-regulation, Perls did not deny the need for the individual sometimes to control his impulses. He recognized that sometimes self-regulation must be inhibited in the obvious interests of the self or of others – as for example when a person who feels murderous rage inhibits himself from killing. Nor does Perls deny the necessity for the individual to take into account the needs of others. As human beings are essentially social creatures, forming an interacting whole with their environment, it is an intrinsic aspect of self-regulation to consider the needs of others, who form part of the whole interrelated field: 'The Gestalt approach, which considers the individual as a function of the organism/environment, and which considers his behavior as reflecting his relatedness within that field, gives coherence to this conception of man as both an individual and a social creature', for 'man needs contact with other human beings' and his 'sense of relatedness to the group is as natural to him as his sense of relatedness to any one of his physiological survival impulses' (Perls, 1976: 25).

However Perls did feel that people's self-regulation is unnecessarily inhibited by the rules and institutions of current society: 'Let us remember that to the extent to which we agree to situations in which self-regulation rarely operates, to that extent we must be content to live with diminished energy and brightness' (Perls, Hefferline and Goodman, 1951/1973: 32).

The Gestalt Cycle

Perls crystallized the sequence of organismic self-regulation into what he variously called the 'disturbance cycle', the 'cycle of the inter-dependency of organism and environment' (1947/1969a: 44) and the 'cycle of organism/world metabolism'.[3] Perls originally proposed that the cycle consisted of six links. Although his description of these six links is written in language which now seems dated, we quote it in full because of its historical importance and to give the reader a chance to compare the first version with the second version later developed by Perls, Hefferline and Goodman (1951/1973):

1   the organism at rest
2   the disturbing factor, which may be (a) internal or (b) external
3   creation of image or reality (figure–background phenomenon)
4   the answer to the situation, aiming at
5   a decrease of tension, resulting in
6   return of the organismic balance. (Perls, 1947/1969a: 69)

Perls, Hefferline and Goodman (1951/1973) called their development of Perls' original cycle the 'process of contact'[4] or a 'continuous sequence of grounds and figures' (p. 459). They identified four phases in the process (or cycle) of contact – fore contact, contact, final contact and post contact – and emphasized that these different phases are not separate from each other but represent different foci in the process of gestalt formation and destruction. When one phase is in ascendance, the others are background. Below we summarize Perls, Hefferline and Goodman's description of the 'process of contacting' and give an illustrative example.

First Phase: Fore Contact   The individual experiences a need or is disturbed by an environmental stimulus. The body is the background, the sensation of need or the sensory stimulus from the environment is the figure. For example, a person experiences an ache in his chest. The person becomes aware and makes meaning of the sensation previously registered. He feels an emotion – for example he now experiences the ache as loneliness or a need for physical affection. Some object of desire or some means of meeting the need becomes figural for him.

Second Phase: Contacting Awareness of a need is followed by excitement and mobilization of self and resources to meet that need. The healthy person in this stage is energized and ready for movement. In our example, the individual who has just become aware of being lonely gets ready to contact a friend. He takes action, reaching out experimentally towards whatever possibilities exist in the present environment to fulfil his need. He needs to be active in overcoming any obstacles which get in his way as he identifies more and more with the chosen action and alienates the other options he was considering. The lonely individual may telephone one friend, get no reply, try another and go and visit him.

Third Phase: Final Contact Final contact is the stage when the' individual becomes fully engaged with whatever he has chosen to meet his need, while everything else temporarily recedes into an entirely unconcernful background. For a few moments the clear vivid figure is the only gestalt in existence, imbuing the here-and-now with a richness and clarity which unite perception, movement and emotion in unitary experience, whether it be the expression of grief, zestful eating or sexual climax. The lonely man hugs his friend, totally absorbed in his pleasure at meeting.

Fourth Phase: Post Contact If contact has been full and complete, the person experiences deep organismic satisfaction, like an afterglow or savouring of the exchange with the environment. The individual in our example has talked to his friend and felt close to him. No longer lonely, his need for human contact is satisfied for the moment. At this stage, digestion, assimilation and growth take place, even though the actual process of growth is out of awareness. Depending on the type of experience, the growth may be of differing forms, including increase in size, rejuvenation, re-creation, assimilation and learning. The figure which recently was so vivid and absorbing fades into the background. The gestalt is destroyed.

Withdrawal The person withdraws into a resting stage or a state of equilibrium between gestalt destruction and the formation of the next gestalt. There is no clear figure and the organism is in a state of perfect balance. He enters the fertile void from whence sensations heralding a new need will eventually emerge and the cycle of organismic self-regulation will recommence, for a person cannot remain at rest for an indefinite period.

Our example of loneliness is deliberately simple so as to provide a clear illustration. The Gestalt cycle applies to both emotional and biological needs and may take place over a long or a short time. Thus each day we go through the cycle many times, as we meet our emerging needs, to work, play, make love, differ from our friends, brush our teeth or weep in anguish. But at the same time we are going through longer-term cycles. A student, for example, experiences a three- or four-year cycle of study before he achieves his qualification, while a parent may engage in a twenty-year cycle of active parenting.

The Polarities of Homeostasis and Disturbance in the Gestalt Cycle

Perls (1947/1969a; Perls, Hefferline and Goodman, 1951/1973) frequently and overtly discussed the individual's organismic urge to regain homeostasis or equilibrium. Less overtly but still clearly, Perls also suggested that the individual has an equally strong urge to disturb his own balance, through spontaneously arising appetites and excitements: 'Appetite seems either to be stimulated by something in the environment or to *rise spontaneously from the organism*. But of course the environment would not excite, it would not be a stimulus, unless the organism were set to respond' (Perls, Hefferline and Goodman, 1951/1973: 460, italics added). Just as the biological and emotional organism cannot long remain *out of* homeostatic balance, so it cannot long remain *in* balance. Appetite, excitement, the urge to disturb the equilibrium are equally intrinsic. They are the impulse towards contact and growth and thus the means of self-actualization. Once balanced, the individual seeks disturbance, excitement, novelty and the assimilation of novelty. But when he is disturbed by need or excitement, he will equally naturally seek to meet his need and thus regain balance – at least temporarily. The urge for homeostatic balance and the urge for disturbance and excitement are complementary opposites that coexist. They are equally essential to the functioning and flourishing of the human being. It is in the nature of growing things to be *in* and *out of* alignment; to seek disturbance/excitement *and* to seek balance. Hence people are engaged in a fluctuating, alternating and meaningful dance between the poles of balance and disturbance.

Point of Creative Indifference or the Existential Void
Perls was particularly interested in the moment in the cycle when the person is in balance, which he called the zero point, the point of creative indifference (Friedlander, 1918) or the creative void. Although not aware of anything in particular, the person is alert and open to all possibilities. His interest could go in any direction, one way or another. He is balanced, centred. He simply is. The field is as yet undifferentiated: figure and ground are one. Perls (1947/1969a) used the Chinese symbol of the *Wu Gi* or empty circle to represent the pre-different state or non-beginning, in contrast to the *Tai Gi* which expresses the progressive differentiation into opposites (described on p. 44). These symbols are shown in Figure 2.5.

In Eastern religions 'nothingness' means there are no things: there is only process, happening, pure being. The phenomenological and existential philosophers (such as Husserl, 1931; 1968; Heidegger, 1962; Sartre, 1938; 1958) have also explored the creative concept of the 'nothingness' which arises from existential dread inspired by the realization that each individual is alone and that there is no ultimate meaning to life. Many ordinary people in the West fear and avoid the experience of nothingness. Influenced by the existential idea that people who deny the reality of anxiety, death and nothingness are living inauthentically, Perls proposed that facing the existential void can be a means of finding personal authenticity.

Instead of avoiding the void, Perls encouraged people to enter it and get to know it. In his first book (1947/1969a) he devoted a whole chapter to teaching the reader to listen to his internal silence – a practice similar to meditation. He believed that inner silence can help a person get in touch with the deeper, intuitive layers of

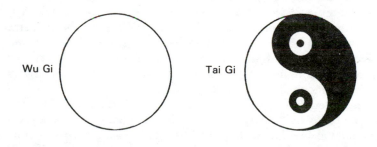

Figure 2.5 Wu Gi *and* Tai Gi *(in Perls, 1947/1969a)*

his existence. More than twenty years later Perls still spoke lyrically of the void: 'And we find when we accept and enter this nothingness, the void, then the desert starts to bloom. The empty void becomes alive, is being filled. The sterile void becomes the fertile void' (1969b: 57).

Influences upon the Gestalt Cycle

The original version of Perls' Gestalt 'disturbance cycle' or 'cycle of inter-dependency of organism and environment' is to be found in *Ego, Hunger and Aggression* (1947/1969a: 44 and 69). The existence of this early version is evidence that the first prototype of the Gestalt cycle was formulated by Perls *before* his collaboration with Hefferline and Goodman. The elaboration of the cycle (1951/1973) as described in this cluster owes much to Goodman.

The idea of living experience as cyclical, of ever-returning changes between the emergence of the gestalt and its disappearance, was not originated by Perls, of course (Clarkson, 1992a). It is intrinsic in the cycles of the seasons and of nature and Perls himself said that Gestalt is nothing but the natural way of apprehending things. As early as 500 BC Heraclitus was exploring the concept of being as a constant state of flux and he described the cyclical nature of change in words which prefigure those of Perls and other twentieth-century existentialists: 'The cycle is the compact experiential reconciliation of permanence and degeneration. Mythic man exists in the cycle or the whole' (Heraclitus in Guerriere, 1980: 88). On at least one occasion Perls (1978b) did refer to Heraclitus.

In the present age, Smuts (1987) described experience in terms which contain several of the elements of Perls' Gestalt cycle: 'It involves not only *sensations* and *perceptions*, but also concepts of a complex character, *feelings* and *desires* in respect of the end desired, and *volitions* in respect of the act intended; and all these elements are fused and blended into one unique purpose; which is then put into *action* or *execution*' (p. 258, author's italics). Harry Stack Sullivan's (1953; 1962; 1964) belief that life is process and flux was in tune with Perls' own thinking and almost certainly made an impact upon Perls in the late 1940s and early 1950s when he associated with followers of Sullivan.

For his interest in the point of creative indifference and the void, Perls was indebted to Friedlander (1918), whom he had known personally in Berlin in the 1920s and acknowledged fully (1947/1969a), as well as to the existentialists (Sartre, 1958, for instance).

Cluster Four: Contact

General Theory of Contact and Assimilation
Contact, as described by Perls, Hefferline and Goodman (1973), is the meeting between one person and another or the meeting between a person and his environment. It is the point at which I experience 'me' in relation to whatever is not 'me', when I experience 'me' as distinct from 'you'. Contact is what happens between us. Contact then involves not only a sense of one's self, but also a sense of the other person or thing with whom contact is made. Contact can only take place between two separate beings or entities: 'Instead of living in oscillation between a jelly-like confluence with, and complete isolation from, his environment, he knows now that "contact" means acknowledgement of differences' (Perls, 1948: 585–6).

Contact involves some kind of exchange, in which something is taken (literally or metaphorically) across the self's boundary and rendered usable. Contact is the creative exchange or adjustment between the organism and the environment. It is every kind of living relation that occurs in the interaction between the person and his surroundings, including, for example, approaching, eating, excreting, feeling, shouting, laughing, hugging, fighting and loving.

Essential aspects of the process of contact are: the maintenance of the difference of the person from the environment; the rejection of danger and toxicity; overcoming the obstacles which might prevent contact; and the selection and appropriation of assimilable novelty, such as food, love, learning, intellectual stimulus: 'the organism persists by assimilating the novel by change and growth. . . Primarily, contact is the awareness of, and behavior towards, the assimilable novelty; and the rejection of the unassimilable novelty' (Perls, Hefferline and Goodman, 1951/1973: 276).

One of the reasons that the concept of contact is so important in Gestalt therapy is that contact is the means by which people grow and change. When contact is vibrant and dynamic and assimilation is thorough, they automatically lead to change and growth.[5] The result of true contact and assimilation is never merely a rearrangement of the old elements but the creation of a fresh configuration containing aspects of the old personality and new materials from the environment. After each contactful experience a person has a new, enlarged or different sense of himself. The individual is necessarily active and creative in this process: he 'does not remember himself, merely reshuffling the cards, but "finds and makes" himself' (Perls, Hefferline and Goodman, 1951/1973: 281).

As contact leads to change, its outcome cannot be predicted. Each time a person ventures to the edge of his present limitations and takes new risks in the ways he is willing to make contact, his sense of who he is, and what he permits himself to do, grows. At the same time, he destroys part of his old habits (the old gestalt). To live authentically and vibrantly, he must risk his previously established identity in this way. Awareness and contact, as opposed to routine behaviour, are inevitably accompanied by existential anxiety. In health anxiety is tolerated because the disturbing energy soon flows into the new configuration and is thus engaged as excitement in the fresh adventure. For example, a man experienced acute anxiety and bouts of insomnia when he decided to move away from the home he had lived in for thirty years. Once he had actually purchased the new house, however, all his interrupted energy changed to excitement as he engaged in planning its garden.

Contact Boundary

The contact boundary consists of the sensitive skin and the means of making contact, that is the five senses, as well as proprioception and the ability to move around and to make sounds. The contact boundary contains and separates the person from his environment *while at the same time* being his point of contact with the environment. This is where he is in touch with the things and people he needs to live and also the potential dangers to his life. The contact boundary is changeable: it is sometimes experienced as being the skin but at other times it may be experienced as much further away from the individual. People harden and soften their musculature, their skin and themselves in order to open and close themselves – literally and metaphorically – to contact. They can make their contact boundary more or less permeable according to how safe or dangerous they perceive their environment or other people to be at any given moment (Kepner, 1987).

Perls proposed that people's experience occurs at the contact boundary between themselves and their environment. Experience is the functioning of the contact boundary of the organism and its environment: 'The study of the way the human being functions in his environment is the study of what goes on at the contact boundary between the individual and his environment. It is at this contact boundary that the psychological events take place. Our thoughts, our actions, our behavior, and our emotions are our way of experiencing and meeting these boundary events' (Perls, 1976: 17).

The Role of Aggression and Destructuring in Contact
Aggression and destructuring are an intrinsic phase of contact. Perls, Hefferline and Goodman (1951/1973) emphasized that they used the word 'aggression' to mean everything that the person does to reach out or initiate contact with the environment – *not* in its common sense of unprovoked attack. To assimilate and grow, an individual must actively approach aspects of the environment that he needs, lay hold of them, destructure them and make them his own:

> The psychological food with which the outside world presents us – the food of facts and attitudes on which our personalities are built – has to be assimilated in exactly the same way as is our actual food. It has to be destructured, taken apart, and then put together again in the form in which it will be of most value to us. (Perls, 1976: 33–4)

So true contact is always creative and dynamic. It cannot be routine or stereotyped and it cannot passively accept or merely adjust to novelty because novelty must be destructured in order to be assimilated.

Hunger Instinct
Perls (1947/1969a) criticized Freud for neglecting the hunger instinct in favour of the libido and death instincts. He maintained that an understanding of the hunger instinct was essential to an understanding of the human personality and used it as an underpinning metaphor for his concept of contact.

Perls divided the development of the hunger instinct into the prenatal, the suckling, the biting and the chewing periods. In the prenatal period, the embryo is nourished via the umbilical cord without any effort on its part. After birth the 'suckling' takes in his food by hanging on (to the nipple), sucking and swallowing. When he develops his first teeth – the incisors – the 'biteling' actively attacks his first solid nourishment, biting off bits from partially prepared food and spitting out food he doesn't want. With the arrival of the molars, the 'chewling' can destroy the lumps of food, grinding it up thoroughly before swallowing it.

Perls felt that the natural expression of the infant's hunger is often interfered with. In particular the biting of the biteling is frequently punished so that babies learn to inhibit their natural biological impulse to bite. Having learnt to suppress their biting impulse, many children and adults treat solid food – and other aspects of the environment – as if they were liquids, to be swallowed down like a baby swallows down his milk. Aggression and a tendency to destroy are natural, healthy impulses, which remain ungratified when people tear off their food and gulp it down without chewing it. The person who does not use his teeth to destroy his food thoroughly will be out of touch with his own capacity for aggression and will either project it on to others, imagining they are aggressive towards him, or will express it in dissociated ways such as waging wars or by turning it in on himself in self-torture.

Perls often repeated the notion that the way a person relates to his food reflects his whole attitude to life. When a person introjects authority figures or principles, for example, he is behaving like a new-born 'suckling', swallowing them down whole without discrimination (see p. 72 for a discussion of introjection). Perls also (1947/1969a) discussed the hanging-on attitude, which occurs when a person treats other people or theories like 'dummies' to which he hangs on, hoping through the mere act of hanging on to gain nourishment. He can never actually feel satisfied because he is afraid to question or destructure the objects of his interest.

Influences upon Perls' Theory of Contact

Perls extrapolated his concept of contact from ideas relating to the development of the hunger instinct in the human infant, and in this conceptualization he was greatly influenced by William Reich (1952) and his wife, Laura Perls. Laura Perls became interested in the hunger instinct and oral resistances when feeding their first child in the early 1930s. Fritz developed her research to produce a paper on oral resistances in 1936 and then the book *Ego, Hunger and Aggression* (1947/1969a, South African edition 1942, first British edition 1947). He and Laura collaborated on *Ego, Hunger and Aggression* and, for example, Laura contributed the chapter on the dummy complex. In this book, Perls was already suggesting that real contact between therapist and client is preferable to detachment and transference. Perls was also influenced by Smuts in his correlation of mental and physical metabolism: 'Just as organic assimilation is essential to animal growth, so intellectual, moral and social assimilation on the part of the Personality becomes the central fact in its development and self-realization' (Smuts in Perls, 1947/1969a: 105).

Although the importance of the hunger instinct, the development of dentation and the parallel between physical and mental metabolism are all explored in *Ego, Hunger and Aggression* (1947/1969a), the concept of contact is only introduced in a relatively rudimentary way. The elaboration of the theory and process of contact, as summarized here, was undertaken in *Gestalt Therapy* (Perls, Hefferline and Goodman, 1951/1973) and was therefore probably mainly devised by Paul Goodman (Wheeler, 1991). Goodman and Perls' concept of contact was probably informed also by the ideas of Harry Stack Sullivan (1964) concerning oral dynamics and the taking in of substance and by those of Buber (1965; 1987) concerning relationship (see pp. 59–60 and 65).

Cluster Five: Theory of the Self

Self as Process
For Perls, at least during the Goodman period, the self is not a thing or a structure or a fixed institution but a process. The self is an organizing process which is constantly changing. It is I-in-process. The self is the integrator, the artist of life; it plays the crucial role of finding and making the meanings that we live and grow by. Perls, Hefferline and Goodman (1951/1973) describe the activity or function of the self as gestalt formation and destruction – the forming of figures and ground. The self is thus the overall system of the person's contacts and responses, necessary for adjustment in the present field. As assimilation and growth are the inevitable result of contact, it follows that the self is the agent of growth.

Contact or creative adjustment takes place at the contact boundary between the person and his environment, and so the self was also described by Perls, Hefferline and Goodman as the contact boundary at work: 'Self may be regarded as at the boundary of the organism' (p. 427). Perls (1978b) suggested that the self exists only in the interaction between the person and his environment or in the interaction between one person and another. There is no 'self' without 'other'. Just as darkness is defined in contrast to light, so the self is defined and distinguished from that which is not-self. I only exist in so far as there are others (people or things) to distinguish myself from. A truly solitary self is illusory because if I was entirely alone, I would have no concept of 'I'; I know that I have a separate self because there are others (people or things) who are not me. Phenomenologically, the 'I' defines itself through its contacting and interactions with others or 'not-I':

> Or as Buber, a famous existentialist would say 'between the "I" and the "thous!"' . . . So what is the 'self'? Now the 'self' cannot be understood other than through the field, just like day cannot be understood other than by contrast with night. If there were eternal day, eternal lightness, not only would you not have the concept of a 'day', you would not even have the awareness of a 'day' because there is nothing to be aware of, there is no differentiation. So, the 'self' is to be found in the contrast with

otherness. There is a boundary between the self and the other and this boundary is the essence of psychology. (Perls, 1978b: 55)

In words that echo Buber's philosophy, Perls, Hefferline and Goodman say: 'The self is not aware of itself abstractly, but is aware of itself as contacting something. Its "I" is polar with a "You" and an "It"' (1951/1973: 432).

In moments of intense interaction or heightened contact, the person has a greater sense of self, while during periods when he is hardly interacting with the world around him, he will have much less sense of self. For example a woman gets a strong sense of who she is when she unexpectedly disagrees with her sister about their childhood experiences; conversely her sense of self diminishes when she is chatting comfortably with that same sister.

Thus Perls challenged the everyday assumption of the self as a fairly permanent entity and instead proposed that the self varies and changes according to the changing circumstances and the different people that it encounters. 'What concerns us as . . . psychotherapists in this ever-changing field, are the ever-changing constellations of the ever-changing individual. For he must change constantly if he is to survive' (Perls, 1976: 25). This is a phenomenological conception of the self which sees the self 'that we interpret and believe in at any given moment in time [as] both temporary and, at best, a partial expression of an infinity of potential interpreted selves' (Spinelli, 1989: 84).

Because the self is always changing to meet the requirements of each new contact with the environment, Perls, Hefferline and Goodman (1951/1973) differentiate different aspects of the self – the ego, the id, the middle and the personality functions. However, they stress that though they may talk in the psychoanalytic terms of id and ego functions, they are still talking about the self as process. There *is* no id or ego – only the processes of figure formation and destruction.

The Active Self and the Role of Responsibility

The fulfilment of our needs requires not only awareness of them but also deliberate choosing, action and organization of ourselves and our environment. Perls put tremendous emphasis on the fact that the self is active in these ways, not passive. He maintained that each mature person is therefore able to take existential responsibility for himself for most aspects of his life and, above all, for the meaning he gives his life. Perls (1969b; 1976) often spelt the word 'responsibility' as 'response-ability' to emphasize this point.

If one becomes intimately aware of events in one's own life, what they are and how they figure in one's functioning, 'Then one becomes responsible for them – not in the sense of now having to assume some burden that was not there before, but rather in the sense of now recognizing that it is oneself who determines in most instances whether they shall or shall not continue to exist' (Perls, Hefferline and Goodman, 1951/1973: 49). When we lose touch with the existential truth of our own responsibility, we become alienated from our existence; we seek to blame or praise others for what we do and credit or discredit ourselves for what others do.

Perls did not mean by this that the individual is personally responsible for all situations in which he finds himself. A person who is incarcerated in a concentration camp because of his race clearly did not bring about the terrible environmental conditions in which he now is. However, he is still actively responsible for how he lives out his life in this environment. For example Frankl[6] has described (1973) how his fellow prisoners in concentration camps remained active in the meaning they gave their lives, even though they were usually unable to change the bitter circumstances in which they existed.[7]

Language of Responsibility

A significant example of the denial of personal responsibility is embedded in our everyday language in such phrases as 'It makes me sad when you do that' or 'She made me hit her.' In the first phrase an abstract 'it' is made responsible for me, while in the second phrase someone other than 'I' is responsible for my actions. 'A man instead of raging is possessed by a "temper" that he cannot "control". Instead of thinking, a thought "occurs" to him. He is "haunted by" a problem. His troubles "worry" him – when indeed he is worrying himself and anybody else he can' (Perls, Hefferline and Goodman, 1951/1973: 259). When he speaks in this way, the individual projects initiative and responsibility and thus experiences himself in a permanently passive role. 'More specifically, this refers to the patient who is not willing to identify himself with his activities, who talks about his hard luck, about fate; who is the victim of circumstances. If his language is reorganized from an "it" language to an "I" language, considerable integration can be achieved with this single adjustment' (Perls, 1948: 583).

Perls' therapeutic attention to the language of his clients (see p. 109) was designed to help the individual explore the personal significance of the phrases he uses and re-establish the sense that he is actively at the centre of his own life and responsible for himself.

Concepts of Self-Support and Self-Sufficiency
Perls (1969b; 1976) defined the process of human maturation as the evolution from the environmental support needed in infancy to the self-support of adulthood. Child development initially involves a natural interdependence of infant and grown-up, in which the infant is not isolated and helpless because he is spontaneously cared for by the adult (the environmental support), who is an integral part of the same interconnected field. Gradually the infant grows in strength, knowledge and technique and becomes more mobile and articulate. As he does so, a new whole is created in which the infant needs the adult less and less and delights in his growing independence. Physically and psychologically, he lets go his dependency upon outside support in progressive and spontaneously occurring stages, until as a young adult he is largely self-supporting and able to stand on his own feet both literally and metaphorically.

A healthy mature person would thus rather generate self-support than depend (unnecessarily) upon the support of others. If an adult lacks self-support for some reason, he may manipulate others into providing the support which he lacks. For example, a healthy middle-aged parent sometimes manipulates one of the children into living on at home by making him or her feel guilty about leaving the parent alone. Perls saw this sort of manipulative strategy as a sign of neurosis, and suggested (1969b; 1976) that a neurotic will inevitably expect to manipulate the therapist into providing for his needs, using his habitual strategies or fixed patterns of behaviour (see pp. 107–9).[7]

Perls, Hefferline and Goodman had stressed that self-support does not mean self-reliance or isolation but includes a healthy mutual interdependency with other adults as 'a part in a social whole'. They also insisted that many needs for play or for bodily exploration, which the Freudians of the time might have dubbed 'childish', were a legitimate, indeed a vital part of a healthy adult. Supposedly childish feelings are important 'as some of the most beautiful powers of adult life that must be recovered: spontaneity, imagination, directness of awareness' (1951/1973: 348). The mature self-supporting adult can find some non-manipulative way to fulfil so-called childish needs. It is the goal of Gestalt therapy not to talk the client out of such needs, but rather to help him become aware of them, face them and seek to fulfil them honestly in the environment.

During the 1960s Perls took his concept of self-support to an extreme that seems more like insular self-sufficiency than the more humane self-support-within-the-environment envisaged by Perls, Hefferline and Goodman:

I do my thing and you do your thing.
I am not in this world to live up to your expectations
And you are not in this world to live up to mine,
You are you and I am I,
If by chance we find each other, it's beautiful.
If not, it can't be helped. (Perls, 1969b: 4)

Perls' intention in this oft-quoted piece was succinctly to challenge inauthenticity and pretended altruism. However, his 'prayer' has come to represent the uncaring polarity of Perlsian theory that makes individualism and responsibility for the self a higher priority than responsibility for the self-and-others-in-community. Erving Polster told us (1989) that he challenged Perls' emphasis upon individuality in the late 1960s. Having explored the polarity of self-sufficiency to the full, Perls recognized its limitations and started an experiment in communal living in Canada. The Polsters (1974), Elaine Kepner (1980) and Clarkson (1991c) amongst others have explored the themes of individuality and commonality in Gestalt, and Clarkson has pointed out that whenever Perls emphasizes individuality, commonality is inevitably background, and when the need for connectedness is figure, the need for individuation is background. Commonality and individuality are poles that coexist, determine and define each other:

> We have been at pains to show that in the organism before it can be called a personality at all, and in the formation of personality, the social factors are essential. . . The underlying social nature of the organism . . . fostering and dependency, communication, imitation and learning, love-choices and companionship, passions of sympathy and antipathy, mutual aid . . . all this is . . . repressible but ineradicable. (Perls, Hefferline and Goodman, 1951/1973: 386)

Self-Actualization
The concept of the self as process growing from environmental support through inadequate self-support and inauthentic manipulation towards authentic self-support is an essential aspect of Perls' belief in the innate human drive towards self-actualization. The neurotic person, having little sense of outgoing power to draw on, clings to the status quo, to his past achievements, his habits, his sense of security, indeed to an inauthentic, fixed sense of self. The healthy self, on the other hand, has and needs no sense of security. Having outgoing power, it accepts itself as constantly evolving. It has a sense of readiness, an acceptance of the excitement of reaching out to the novel and as yet unknown future and a feeling of its own potential to actualize itself authentically in each new situation which arises – as Perls, Hefferline and Goodman (1951/1973)

describe in delightfully fresh images:

> But where the self has power to draw on, it has precisely no sense of
> security. It has perhaps a sense of readiness: the acceptance of excite-
> ment, a certain foolish optimism about the alterability of reality, and an
> habitual memory that the organism regulates itself and does not in the
> end wear out or explode. . . The answer to the question 'Can you do
> it?' can be only, 'It's interesting.' (p. 472)

In one important but little known section, Perls, Hefferline and
Goodman actually define the 'Self as Actualization of the Potential',
describing the process in the poetic phrases which are typical of
Goodman's creative style of writing:

> The present is a passage out of the past towards the future, and these
> are the stages of an act of self as it contacts the actuality. . . In concen-
> trating awareness on the actual situation, this pastness of the situation
> is given as the state of the organism and the environment; but at once,
> at the very instant of concentration, the unchanging given is dissolving
> into many possibilities and is seen to be a potentiality. As concentration
> proceeds, these possibilities are reformed into a new figure emerging
> from the ground of the potentiality. . . The future, the coming, is the
> directedness of this process out of the many possibilities towards a new
> single figure. (p. 429)

The fullness of living is born not of inauthentic manipulation and
control of other people and the environment, but of authentic self-
realization. People actualize their full potential by knowing and
facing themselves in their wholeness.[8]

Influences upon Perls' Concepts of the Self

In his first book (1947/1969a) Perls barely discusses the self,
although his description of the ego functions includes a foretaste of
the terms in which he and his colleagues later describe the self
(p. 139). The concept of self as described in this cluster is largely
that of Goodman and Perls (Perls, Hefferline and Goodman,
1951/1973). They were influenced, either directly or indirectly, by
a number of overlapping sources, including the existential tradition
of Kierkegaard, Heidegger, Buber and Tillich, the ideas of Kurt
Goldstein, the approach of Harry Stack Sullivan, and the principles
of perception of Gestalt psychology.

Perls refers to Kierkegaard in *Ego, Hunger and Aggression*
(1947/1969a), while Laura Perls has stated that she studied
Kierkegaard and Heidegger and worked for years with Paul Tillich,
and has confirmed that both she and Fritz were interested in the
development of existential philosophy (Wysong and Rosenfeld,
1982).

From Heidegger (1962) come the ideas that a person is possibility; that he is free to choose from moment to moment from amongst his possibilities; and that he constructs himself through these choices. The choice is never final, and thus a person is not finally determined but is evolving and changing. Above all he is free to choose between an inauthentic and an authentic mode of existence. Kierkegaard (1939; 1941; 1944) introduced the idea of self-realization: he believed that it is the task of every person to become an entire person, by forming and renewing himself in the critical decisions of life. Kierkegaard also emphasized personal responsibility, the truth of subjective experience and individuality. Our choices are absolute ventures, personal decisions taken with the utmost responsibility. Each individual is alone and compelled to exist for himself. The phenomenologist Merleau-Ponty (1962) and the existentialist Marcel (1952) have particularly emphasized reciprocity and our simultaneous need for connectedness and individuation, including the notion that the self defines itself through contact with others: 'So far from being myself the ground of my certainty . . . *it is the existence of another that gives me my primary notion of existence* and it is in so far that I believe in the existence of others and act on that belief that I affirm my own existence' (1952: 66, italics added).

Harry Stack Sullivan's (1964) view that personality is not a concrete structure that can be known and measured but a 'temporal phenomenon, a patterning of experiences and interactions over time' (Greenberg and Mitchell, 1983: 90) almost certainly influenced Perls' and Goodman's view of the self as process. Perls' and Goodman's view of the self as defining itself in relation to others must surely have been inspired (directly or indirectly through Laura Perls) by Martin Buber's exploration of the I–Thou relationship. Buber contends that there is no 'I' without 'Thou' or 'It' and that to speak the word 'I' is already implicitly to recognize the 'Thou' from which 'I' distinguishes itself. On at least one occasion Perls (1978b) acknowledged his debt to Buber, and on another occasion (quoted on p. 59) Perls, Hefferline and Goodman (1951/ 1973) use words which seem reminiscent of Buber's 'I–Thou' treatise. In addition, Laura Perls met Buber and has related how she was much affected by his ideas; we can probably safely assume that her enthusiasm influenced Fritz.

Kurt Goldstein, with whom Perls worked in Frankfurt in 1926, coined the term 'self-actualization'. He believed that it is the primary motivation of each person to realize his unique potential – all of the many other apparent human drives being merely expressions of this sovereign motive. Self-actualization for Goldstein is the creative trend of human nature, whereby the person unfolds his potential into the world of the actual.[9] Moreno (1964, first published 1946), with whose work Perls became familiar in the 1950s in New York, also emphasized the individual's capacity to heal and actualize the self.

Perls was also influenced by Goldstein's and Sullivan's very different interest in and attention to language as an expression of the self. Goldstein emphasized the fact that our use of language represents our ways of thinking and experiencing and suggested that paying attention to the ways we habitually speak is an important way of developing insight into deeply embedded patterns of configuring the world. Sullivan, who believed passionately that life is process and flux, was suspicious of any language which described processes in terms of structures and criticized language which turns processes into entities (or 'reifies' them). Perls translated Goldstein's and Sullivan's ideas regarding the significance of everyday language into practical interventions and experiments, in which he suggested that individuals try using different turns of phrase (such as taking responsibility for their experience by using the pronoun 'I' or using verbs instead of nouns to avoid the reification of processes) and see how their changed use of language affected the way they configured themselves and their world.

Perls, Hefferline and Goodman's unique contribution to the theory of the self was that they linked Goldstein's concept of self-actualization to the existential concept of a self that chooses from moment to moment who he or she is, within the limitations of human existence. They then underpinned these two concepts with the Gestalt principle of figure/ground formation and thus provided a theoretical explanation for how the self actualizes.

Cluster Six: Psychological Disturbance

This relatively long cluster has been subdivided into the following sections:

1   an overview of Perls' descriptions of psychological disturbance;
2   an explanation of the key processes by which Perls proposed that an individual's development may become disturbed, i.e. unfinished business, fixed gestalt and repetition compulsion;
3   a description of the interruptions to contact, which are the mechanisms used by the individual to maintain the denial or displacement of a fixed gestalt
4   a discussion of Perls' five-level model of neurosis
5   an exploration of Perls' concepts of anxiety and excitement.

Perls' Descriptions of Psychological Disturbance

Perls' descriptions of psychological disturbance need to be understood against the background of his ideal of psychological health upon which this chapter has so far concentrated. In summary, pychologically healthy people (Perls, Hefferline and Goodman, 1951/1973; Perls, 1947/1969a; 1976) are self-regulating individuals, able to support themselves while accepting mutual interdependency with other people. They accept responsibility for the choices they make in life, including the meaning they give to those choices. They experience their ability to actualize themselves within the (sometimes difficult) circumstances of the environment. They are self-affirming and act in congruence with their own inner experience and set of values. They actively relate to their fellow human beings and their surroundings. They are potentially aware of and in touch with all the phenomena of themselves – their sensations, feelings, and thoughts – and their environment. They can thus recognize their needs and are continuously making creative adjustments at the contact boundary between themselves and the world, responding to, acting upon and withdrawing from the environment in order to meet their own needs, without either being swallowed up by society or impinging too heavily upon it (Perls, 1976).

The attributes of psychological health summarized in the preceding paragraph are of course an ideal and Perls often emphasized that all of us feature some disturbances or distortions of this ideal. It is these disturbances of the ideal which we will now consider.

During the course of his professional life, Perls described psychological disorder in a number of different interrelated ways, each with slightly different emphases. In *Ego, Hunger and Aggression* (1947/1969a), for example, under the influence of Reich, he stressed the role of excessive muscular control, stating that in neurosis a war is waged between the controlling body armour and the natural but unaccepted organismic impulses. Perls, Hefferline and Goodman (1951/1973) suggested that disturbance is the persistence of outdated attitudes and behaviours when the situation no longer warrants them.

In *Gestalt Therapy Verbatim* (1969b), Perls focused on the disturbed individual's inability to support himself in his field; whereas in *The Gestalt Approach* (1976), the emphasis is upon the balance of the individual's needs with the demands of society and the boundary between the two. The disturbed individual sees the social group to which he belongs as large and important and himself as small and insignificant in comparison. When the individual and the group have different needs, he will be incapable of distinguishing which of the conflicting demands (his own or the group's) is at the moment dominant. He will vacillate: 'When he cannot make a decision, or feel satisfied with the decision he has made, he can neither make a good contact nor a good withdrawal, and both he and the environment are affected' (Perls, 1976: 28).

For Perls psychological disturbance was not mental but organismic. He believed that the separation of mind and body is artificial and tends to create or contribute to neurosis. From the Gestalt perspective, organismic ill-health occurs when the person becomes overcontrolled, anxious or unable to engage and construct meaning in his life. Thus the individual's ability to grow through contact and assimilation of novel elements in his environment is disrupted and becomes fixed in outdated patterns of behaviour. Perls therefore suggested that the word 'neurosis' should be replaced by *growth disorder* (1969b), although he continued to use the terms 'neurosis' and 'neurotic'.

Unfinished Business, Fixed Gestalt and Repetition Compulsion

If the organism is flexibly and creatively self-regulating, how do the fixed patterns of behaviour (described above) arise? What is it in the organism/environment field that permits the distortion in balance between the individual and his environment to happen? Perls believed that these disturbances of the natural tendency to grow are the result of an accumulation of unresolved situations from the past and of premature solutions to problems which have become habitual and unaware (fixed gestalts). The concepts of unfinished business, fixed gestalt and repetition compulsion are now explained in more detail as they are the key processes by which the individual's development may become disturbed.

Unfinished Business   As discussed on pp. 38 and 50–2, the urge to complete the cycle of contact and withdrawal is natural and compelling. The healthy human being makes the fullest possible contact with whatever is currently interesting to him, whether it is a picture he is enthralled by or a meal he is hungry for. If he is able to be in full contact with the subject of his interest, he will be satisfied and will withdraw. If for some reason the individual is able to mobilize around some object of interest, but is *not* able to make contact with whatever is attracting him, the gestalt will be incomplete. An incomplete gestalt represents tremendous interrupted force or pent-up energy. Until he is able to complete the interrupted cycle, the individual is likely to interpret everything in his world in terms of the incomplete gestalt. 'The gestalt wants to be completed. If the gestalt is not completed, we are left with unfinished situations, and these unfinished situations press and press and press and want to be completed. Let's say if you had a fight, you really got angry at that guy, and you want to take revenge. This need for revenge will nag and nag and nag until you have become even with him' (Perls, 1976: 121).

Of course in everyday life, human beings do experience interruptions to the fulfilment of their needs and they are able to tolerate a considerable delay in the need fulfilment cycle. By bracketing off the need which cannot immediately be met, they are able to divert their attention to other things. However, as has been indicated, the incomplete gestalt of the interrupted need exerts a strong attraction; as long as it remains unfulfilled it is calling out for attention. So bracketing it off for later attention requires a good deal of energy from the individual. The more times an individual is forced to interrupt his needs, the more energy is required to bracket off the unfinished business which he is now accumulating. An individual who has to invest his energy in ignoring the urgency of a number of pressing unresolved situations does not have all his attention for his current situation. The accumulation of unfinished business is thus instrumental in the development of growth disturbance or neurosis in that individual. As long as the person remains in touch with the original need, however, there is still a possibility of it being resolved quite naturally some time in the future.

Fixed Gestalt   If on the other hand the delay becomes chronic, the need loses dynamism, is distorted or 'fixed': 'The unfinished situations cry for solutions, but if they are barred from awareness, neurotic symptoms and neurotic character formation will be the result' (Perls, 1948: 573). Initially the individual will strive with all his might to meet the unmet need, or close the incomplete gestalt. For instance, as a child, John spontaneously asked for cuddles, attention and appreciation of his everyday behaviour. When his requests brought no response, he first increased his efforts to attract his parents, then screamed his fury. Eventually when the denial of his need became chronic, he lost all hope, he gave up. He did not die physically, but there was a limited form of emotional death: to the best of his ability, he killed off or 'fixed' that particular need or gestalt.

Because people are holistic organisms, Perls stressed that the fixing of the gestalt involves the whole being of the person, that is the physical, emotional and cognitive (or meaning-making) processes. Physiologically the person may interrupt his breathing and harden his pectoral muscles so that he develops a rigid barrel chest as a way of cutting off from the sensation of pain that he experiences each time he longs for loving support. Cognitively he explains the lack of support as best he can with little information, so he may tell himself that he is not supported because 'There is something wrong with me' or because 'I have no Daddy' or because 'I am too much for my Mummy.' The original feeling of need is replaced by a substitute feeling, such as 'I don't need people' or 'I'll look after everyone else' which the child finds easier to tolerate and which protects him from the pain of rejection.

Being so young, the child often lacks the necessary information to make adequate judgements about what is happening to him. For example he is probably unaware his mother is an alcoholic or a young single parent, still in need of parental love herself. Yet he has this pressing need for loving support which is not being met. He must make sense of it somehow, so he does the best he can: he brings the incomplete gestalt to a physiological, emotional and cognitive closure but it is a premature closure, based on false or incomplete information. Fixing the gestalt in this way feels better than leaving it forever open, a gaping hole of aching need, and allows the organism to move on to the next emerging need: 'In any single experience, all of the powers of the self are mobilized to complete the situation as well as possible, either in a final contact or a fixation' (Perls, Hefferline and Goodman, 1951/1973: 520). However the premature closure can never really satisfy because the original need remains unmet.

When a natural need is not met but becomes fixed in the manner described, the need is distorted, it is denied or displaced: 'The desire was frustrated: there was a danger in satisfaction: and the tension of frustation was unbearable. One then deliberately inhibited the desire and awareness of the desire, in order not to suffer and to keep out of danger' (Perls, Hefferline and Goodman, 1951/1973: 345). If the original need is denied, it is pushed out of awareness and forgotten; so as an adult John (described above), who did not receive support as a child, still said 'I'm fine, I don't need support' even when his business went bankrupt and he and his family were reduced to poverty. Alternatively the original need may be displaced on to others and can then be 'met' by looking after and supporting them. In his therapy group, John said, 'I don't need any comfort, thank you. We cuddle a lot in my family: the children and my wife often seek me out to get a cuddle from me.' He gave rather than got support and was unaware of the difference.

Repetition Compulsion The individual, who has 'fixed' the unfinished situation, continues to make the same response he did as a child, even though the environment is now quite different – John continued to exclusively give support even when the members of his therapy group, instinctively feeling his buried need, offered to hold him. Though his disturbed functioning was acquired in the past, the perpetuation of the individual's disturbance occurs in the present. Over and over again he attempts to meet the original need, which is still unresolved in his background. John, for example, got himself into life situations where he needed support and he talked a lot about support, while refusing it. Support is a leitmotif for him, a charged and interesting subject.

This need to repeat is an organismically healthy urge, for it is the basic human need to seek closure and resolve the unfinished business that at some level still clamours for attention. 'Compulsory repetitions . . . are by no means automatic. On the contrary, they are vigorous attempts at solving relevant problems of life' (Perls, 1947/1969a: 102). However, because the original need has been interrupted, pushed out of awareness and fixed, each attempt carries the seeds of its own failure. The individual unawarely completes the distorted need cycle again and again, experiencing no satisfaction because the underlying need remains untouched:

> the neurotic tension is not completed; yet it is dominant, it *must* be completed before anything else is attended to; so the organism that has not grown by success and assimilation assumes the same attitude to make the same effort again. Unfortunately, the fixed attitude, which failed before, has become necessarily more inept in the changed circumstances; so that the completion is less and less likely. There is here a miserable circularity: it is only by assimilation, completion, that one learns anything and is prepared for a new situation; but what has failed of completion is ignorant and out-of-touch and therefore becomes more and more incomplete. (Perls, Hefferline and Goodman, 1951/1973: 344)

Each time the individual gets close to an experience, say in therapy, where he could loosen and reconsider the rigid fixed gestalt, he will experience acute anxiety – because if he undoes the fixed gestalt, he must feel again the pain or despair he felt when he first gave up on his need. This anxiety is typical of the client's stuck point where his need to keep the gestalt fixed (and thus protect himself from painful feelings) competes with his organismic desire to undo it and at last resolve it to his satisfaction. The art of Gestalt therapy is to help the client to reach and feel the stuck point or impasse and then to suggest experiences in which he may explore other options; Perls was particularly skilled at doing this (see Chapter 3, p. 117).

Interruptions to Contact

The process of maintaining a fixed gestalt or of denying or displacing a human need is an active disturbance at the contact boundary between the individual and his environment, requiring effort and energy even though the active effort, like the original need, is kept out of awareness. The mechanisms used by the individual to maintain the denial or displacement of a fixed gestalt are the interruptions to contact. 'The boundary disturbances operate primarily through four mechanisms which can be distinguished, one from the other: introjection, projection, confluence and retroflection' (Perls, 1976: 31). Although Perls (1976) only described four interruptions to contact, Perls, Hefferline and Goodman described six – the four already listed *and* desensitization and egotism.[10]

Introjection   Introjecting consists of taking into our system aspects of the environment without assimilating them. Things we swallow whole or introject are like foreign bodies. As they are not part of us, but still part of the environment, we cannot use them to grow. Food which is thoroughly assimilated nourishes; whereas food which is swallowed whole sits heavily on the stomach and is difficult to digest. The psychological process of assimilation is similar to the physical one: facts, ideas, moral standards and values, too, must be selected according to taste and chewed over, and the parts which seem good must be digested while other parts are discarded.

A person usually introjects when he is overwhelmed by environmental forces, such as parents, school and church or by experiences of physical and emotional deprivation. His individual needs are in opposition to the demands of the group. For example his parents may consistently give him the message that it is not all right to cry when he is hurt and they may withdraw love and contact if he does so. Then the child who experiences contact with his parents as a primary psychological survival need (Perls, 1976) subjugates his own needs and takes on the values of his parents. In the emergency of the conflict situation, the child makes the best adjustment he can: he introjects the belief that it is silly to cry and stops himself from crying.

Unfortunately the introjection interferes with his own functioning: he learns to side with his parents' wishes, controlling his own spontaneous behaviours. He can no longer cry: his natural cycle of contact and withdrawal has been interrupted and completed prematurely. The impulse to cry does not just go away, but remains as unfinished business which will naturally seek resolution and may pop up anytime. The introjector only succeeds in suppressing the forbidden impulse by maintaining a constant self-restraint. He may learn to hold his breath when he wants to cry and tighten his chest muscles while telling himself that big boys don't cry. He is divided and at war with himself and some of his life energy must henceforth go into restraining and forgetting his original wishes.

Introjection prevents the individual from developing his own personality and evolving his own values, for it 'makes us something like a house so jampacked with other people's possessions that there is no room for the owner's property. It turns us into waste baskets of extraneous and irrelevant information' (Perls, 1976: 34). It also destroys the individual's holistic functioning for he is internally split between the original impulse and the introject. Perls (1948) disagreed with Freud's view that only *total* introjection is a pathological phenomenon whereas *partial* introjection is a healthy process providing the building stones of the ego. Perls contended that every introject, partial or total, is a foreign body within the organism, which needs to be destructured and assimilated.

Typically the introjector identifies with the values of his social group; he is easily swayed by authoritative figures and may agree with the last person that he talked to. He is concerned with what he 'should' do and is often at a loss if asked what he wants. He swallows one method of self-improvement after another, moving on to another whenever the latest enthusiasm fails to satisfy – which it inevitably must because he has not destructured, assimilated and made it his own. 'He wants his solutions in liquid form, pre-prepared, so that he need but drink them down' (Perls, Hefferline and Goodman, 1951/1973: 235).

Projection Projection is a quality, feeling or behaviour which belongs to me but which I don't experience as such. Instead I attribute the quality, feeling or behaviour to other people or institutions around me. Projection, when chosen, may be a normal and healthy assumption based on observation and as such it is an essential part of human relating. Planning, anticipating and empathizing involve projections or assumptions based on observation about the outside world. When I empathize, I project myself into the other person's situation and imagine what it is like to be him. If I am in tune with my own shyness, for example, I project my knowledge, I assume that the other person experiences similar emotions and I feel understanding. The projection or assumption is recognized as an assumption and I realize that I may well be mistaken.

However if a person has learnt that certain traits or feelings or behaviours are unacceptable or dangerous, then he may project in a more unaware fashion. For example, he may have learnt not to reject others: if that is the case, when he feels rejecting, he may block this out of his awareness and instead believe that others are rejecting him. The process of unaware projection goes like this (adapted from Perls, Hefferline and Goodman, 1951/1973): the individual has some vague notion of the impulse involved, e.g. rejection; he interrupts his outgoing impulse because he excludes this particular impulse (e.g. rejection) from his self-image. Since he is aware that this impulse does exist, he believes it must come from somewhere – and experiences it as coming from the other person. 'In projection, then, we shift the boundary between ourselves and the rest of the world a little too much in our own favor – in a manner that makes it possible for us to disavow and disown those aspects of our personalities which we find difficult or offensive or unattractive' (Perls, 1976: 37). Perls, Hefferline and Goodman (1951/1973) suggest that if you continually suspect other people of rejecting you, you reverse the process and explore on what grounds you may in fact be rejecting the people you accuse. Similarly if you are prone to sexual jealousy and suspect your partner of infidelity, they propose that you consider whether you yourself are not suppressing the wish to be unfaithful in the very way that you assume your loved one is being unfaithful.

Unaware projection is an interruption to authentic contact and relating between people. It can lead to a great deal of misunderstanding and conflict. Once the projector has projected his denied feelings or attitudes on to other people, he can opt out of responsibility for the situation and regard himself as the passive victim of all sorts of unkind treatment. The chronic projector is often a suspicious or cautious personality, sometimes even paranoid and prejudiced. He tends to blame others or to use phrases in which he disowns and projects responsibility for his feelings. He is more likely to say 'It is a nuisance' than to clearly own his feelings by saying directly: 'I don't want to do that.'

Confluence   Confluence occurs when two people or two parts of the field flow together without a sense of differentiation. After a lively exchange, in which real contact has taken place, there is some natural and perfectly healthy merging or confluence of energy: '*After* contact has been achieved. . . At the end of any successful experience – one that is not interrupted but allowed to complete itself – there is always a confluence of energy or energy-producing materials' (Perls, Hefferline and Goodman, 1951/1973: 153). Perls (1976) gives an example of an individual taking part in choral singing: the person may feel his own boundaries disappear in the exalting and moving identification with the group. 'When the individual feels no boundary at all between himself and his environment, when he feels that he and it are one, he is in confluence with it' (Perls, 1976: 38).

Confluence is an interruption to contact when it is used unawarely as a means of avoiding or preventing contact. The chronically confluent person does not know where he ends and others begin. As he is unaware of the boundary between himself and others, he cannot make good contact; nor can he withdraw from them. A person who interrupts contact through confluence may not know when to finish a relationship or activity, for example; he hangs on to the situation, hoping to gain nourishment and enjoyment, even when none is forthcoming. He is afraid to let go because he does not feel secure about creating a new situation in which he will be able to meet his needs. He may frequently say 'we' instead of 'I'.

Unaware confluence has social consequences. Highly confluent people demand likeness and refuse to tolerate differences. Confluent parents, for example, consider their children merely to be extensions of themselves and expect them to follow in their footsteps. If the children fail to identify with their parents' expectations, the parents may reject their children verbally, or more subtly by withdrawing love and appreciation.

Retroflection Retroflection means doing to yourself what you originally did or wanted to do to other people or objects. Instead of creatively engaging with the environment and directing your energies outwards in attempts to contact the environment and meet your needs, you redirect your energy and activity inwards towards yourself: 'Retroflection means that some function which originally is directed from the individual towards the world, changes its direction and is bent back towards the originator' (Perls, 1947/1969a: 120). The retroflector splits his personality into doer and done to and treats himself as he originally wanted to treat other persons or objects.

Perls, Hefferline and Goodman (1951/1973) explain that retroflection is a habit usually acquired in childhood, when the child may have been punished or threatened with punishment if he expressed his needs or feelings freely:

However . . . punishment has the effect, not of annihilating the need to behave in the way that met with punishment, but of teaching the organism to *hold back* the punishable responses. . . The holding back is achieved by tensing muscles which are antagonistic to those which would be involved in expressing the punishable impulse. At this stage two parts of the personality struggling in diametrically opposite directions are in a clinch. What started as conflict between organism and environment has come to be an 'inner conflict' between one part of the personality and another part – between one kind of behaviour and its opposite. (pp. 183–4)

Obviously no human being can go through life giving full and immediate expression to all his outgoing impulses. It is essential that people are able to choose to restrain some of their impulses sometimes: for example, it is essential for an adult to restrain an impulse to hit a child or to stop himself from killing someone towards whom he is feeling murderous rage. When retroflection is aware, it is often sound and necessary behaviour.

Chronic unaware retroflection, however, is an interruption to contact and usually develops when the expression of aggressive or other outgoing feelings is perceived as dangerous. A child who is angry wishes to shout at the person he is angry with, but if he is punished for this behaviour he may give up and block even the desire to be angry out of his awareness. The need to express anger does not disappear, it has to go somewhere: so, without realizing what he is doing, the child may prematurely close the gestalt by turning the anger against himself. If he persists in this 'solution' even when the circumstances change and no one threatens him, his behaviour has become fixed, and retroflection may be chronic and unaware. So now when he starts to feel anger, he automatically stops the feeling, and tells himself off or hurts himself in some way.

A second form of retroflection involves doing to yourself what you originally wanted others to do to you. You treat a part of yourself as if it was the environment and do to yourself what you would like to have had done to you. Thus, yearning for affection, you may hug yourself. Seeking consolation when sorrowful, you may unawarely stroke your own hair: 'in passive retroflection, the "I" replaces the missing active object; I pity myself because nobody else does it; I punish myself in anticipation of someone else doing it to me' (Perls, 1948: 584).

An inflexible posture, shallow breathing, speaking in a choked voice, biting the lips or putting the hand over the mouth *may* all be signs of holding back and therefore of unaware retroflection. Perls was particularly skilled at bringing such non-verbal gestures to attention but he emphasized that the therapist must not interpret the gesture or *assume* that it implies retroflection. Instead he should encourage the individual to explore its personal significance to him.

Desensitization Desensitization is the process by which we numb ourselves to the sensation of our bodies. The existence of pain or discomfort is kept out of awareness. It is obviously useful to be able to do this sometimes: if you have a toothache, it is desirable to block out the ache or distract yourself until you can have the problem sorted out by the dentist. Desensitization may also be a creative adjustment for a child who is abused and has no other options.

Perls, Hefferline and Goodman believed people in the West have learnt to block out bodily sensation in a damaging fashion. Perls often gave the example of people who suffer from insomnia and habitually swallow sleeping tablets rather than stay with the experience of restlessness in order to discover its existential meaning or message. Desensitization anaesthetizes ourselves to our very existence and numbs our contact with others. 'Almost all persons in our society have lost the proprioception of large areas of their body' (1951/1973: 117).

Egotism Egotism is the slowing down of spontaneity by deliberate introspection and circumspection to make sure that there is no threat of danger, surprise or risk. Normally some degree of egotism is indispensable in any important decision or long-term process. If we are unable to slow down our spontaneous enthusiasm, for example, we may commit ourselves to actions which we later regret or have to laboriously undo. Healthy egotism allows us to stand back from ourselves or the opportunity offered and coolly review whether, in the light of what we know about our overall character and our present level of commitment, this is something we really want.

Egotism becomes a neurotic interruption to lively contact when the individual tries to control the uncontrollable and surprising elements in his life through persistent self-consciousness and non-committal vigilance. The example that Perls, Hefferline and Goodman (1951/1973) give is the man who maintains an erection and prevents the spontaneous development of an orgasm. He satisfies his need to prove himself but wards off spontaneity and letting go. The chronic 'egotist' may seem 'in control' of himself but he lacks the unselfconscious ease of being 'in tune' with himself and his surroundings.

Interrelationship of the Different Interruptions to Contact   The six interruptions to contact that we have described here do not occur in isolation. Perls indicated that although individuals may show a preference for one style of self-interruption, they inevitably use all of the interruptions to contact, and that any particular type of neurotic behaviour involves a combination of interrelated interruptions. Perls, Hefferline and Goodman (1951/1973) gave an example of a man who becomes anxious instead of satisfied when he has successfully completed some awareness exercises. They described how when the therapist draws attention to the way in which he is interrupting his own satisfaction, he first retroflects by blaming himself, then projects by assuming that the therapist is staring at him judgementally. When the therapist asks what he feels when he is stared at, he replies with the introject that 'naturally one has to love, or at least be well-disposed to, a person who is trying to help you' (p. 521). Then he is angry because the experiments are boring and sometimes painful. Falling silent, he gives up; the therapist must make the effort. He projects all the power on to the therapist and becomes confluent with his own helplessness.

Perls, Hefferline and Goodman also emphasized that the interruptions to contact are descriptions of processes and not of character types. This is a very important differentiation in Gestalt psychotherapy and is discussed more fully on p. 89 in the context of diagnosis.

Five-Level Model of Neurosis

In the latter part of his life, Perls developed a model of neurosis,[11] in which he proposed a five-level structure of neurotic disturbance (1969b; 1970), which applies some of the concepts of existential phenomenology to the practice of psychotherapy (Figure 2.6). This model of behaviour implies a relatively structured concept of the self and is thus in some important ways contradictory to the theories of the self evolved by Goodman and Perls (see p. 59).

The first layer of Perls' level model is the *cliché layer*. In this layer lie all the meaningless tokens of meeting, the clichéd greetings which often bear no relation at all to the true feelings of the individuals concerned. In this layer the person is often driven by introjects of expected, culturally accepted behaviour.

The second layer Perls called the *role layer*. Here we act as if we were whatever our role is – as if we were a helpless victim, or a powerful boss. We pretend to be better, tougher, more polite, more pathetic than we really feel. In the famous film of Perls working with Gloria (1964) he challenges her behaviour as phoney on several occasions: she acts 'as if' she were scared, backed into a

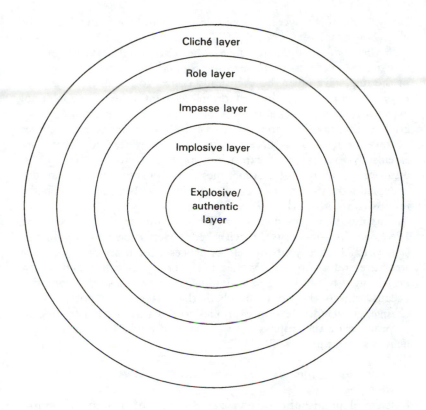

Figure 2.6 *Perls' five-level model of neurosis*

corner and so on. Many people relate to others and to their environment principally at the cliché or role levels. Existentially, they are living habitually or inauthentically.

If we drop the roles, we reach the third level or *impasse layer*. We may experience two aspects of ourselves locked in conflict: the healthy side which wants to complete the unfinished business, and the other side which wants to avoid the suffering. Many of us try to avoid experiencing the impasse because we want to avoid taking responsibility for our stuckness. We prefer to deny the existential dread or anxiety which is inevitably experienced when we realize both our freedom and our limitations. The impasse is characterized by feelings of stuckness, confusion and anxiety and is usually experienced as very uncomfortable.

Behind and contributing to the impasse layer lies the death layer or *implosive layer*. This layer is a paralysis of opposing forces. We pull ourselves together, we contract our muscles, we implode. We believe that if we were to explode, we would not survive or be loved anymore.

If the individual really faces the existential anxiety of the stuckness and confusion at the impasse and stays with the deadness of the implosive layer, he eventually comes to life in the *explosive layer*. In this layer, the person is authentic, he is capable of experiencing and expressing his real emotions. He explodes into grief, anger, joy, laughter, or orgasm. He acts. He lives: 'As I see it, this progression is necessary to become authentic. There are essentially four types of explosion: explosion into joy, into grief, into orgasm, into anger. Sometimes the explosions are very mild – it depends on the amount of energy that has been invested in the implosive layer' (Perls, 1970: 22).

This model informed much of Perls' demonstration work in the 1960s and is not consistent with Perls, Hefferline and Goodman's (1951/1973) theory of the self as process, for it seems to imply a structure and a core self (McLeod, 1991). Chapter 3 explains how Perls sought to work at the individual's impasse as soon as possible because this is the point at which there is greatest potential for change. It includes several examples to illustrate what Perls meant in practice by the impasse, implosive and explosive layers of the neurosis (see pp. 117–20).

Anxiety and Excitement in Healthy and Disturbed Functioning

Existential philosophy emphasizes the role of anxiety in human experience (Kierkegaard, 1944; Heidegger, 1962; Sartre, 1938; 1958; May, 1950; van Deurzen-Smith, 1988; Spinelli, 1989). The existential view of anxiety is that it is an inevitable part of authentic human living. *Angst* or anxiety is the fundamental malaise or dread which people experience when they face the fact that they will die, that there is no ultimate meaning to human life and that they, alone, have responsibility for choosing who they are and the meaning they give to their lives from moment to moment.

Perls viewed anxiety from a broadly existential standpoint, seeing it as a sign of the potential for authentic liveliness in the individual, a necessary first step in the quest for individual meaning. For example the individual who becomes aware of a previously 'fixed' or inauthentic way of being often feels anxiety, confusion or despair as he approaches the turning point (impasse) at which he may be able to review his earlier decision and change his behaviour. He feels anxiety because he must now experience again whatever feelings he suppressed or avoided in the original events – and because he becomes aware that he has the choice to behave differently from whatever has become his habit. He faces his existential freedom, which he had until now been avoiding by behaving in a fixed or rigid fashion. Rather than considering anxiety as a symptom to be treated or suppressed, Perls encouraged the client to face, explore and find its personal meaning:

> To be anxious is the basis of going forward. (Perls, 1978b: 59)

> The experience of confusion is very, very unpleasant and, like anxiety . . . we have a strong desire to annihilate it – by avoidance, by verbalism, or by any other kind of interruption. And yet a good deal of the fight against neurosis is won merely by helping the patient to become aware of, to tolerate, and to stay with his confusion. (Perls, 1976: 97)

In an original extension on the theme, Perls suggested that anxiety is in fact an expression of the interrupted excitement or vitality of full living. A healthy, self-regulating individual will automatically breathe more deeply to meet the increased need for oxygen which accompanies mobilization and contact. A neurotic or disturbed individual often tries to control himself and his spontaneity and thus interrupts the heightened energy and excitement which occur whenever there is strong concern or contact, by deliberately continuing to breathe evenly. Anxiety results from the constriction of the chest and the restricted intake of oxygen. However, if the interruption has become habitual, the individual who restricts his breathing and experiences anxiety is not usually able to make an immediate decision to exhale and inhale more deeply and transform anxiety to excitement. He must investigate himself and his field phenomenologically, exploring '*what* excitements [he] cannot at present accept as his own. . . [He must] find out just *how*, by various patterns of muscular contraction, [he] arrests full exhalation' (Perls, Hefferline and Goodman, 1951/1973: 167). Such an exploration is an essential facet of Perls' approach to therapy, which we discuss in detail in the next chapter.

Conclusion

This chapter has presented some of Fritz Perls' philosophical and theoretical ideas, which have formed a substantial part of the foundation of the subsequent development of Gestalt psychotherapy. The chapter has looked at Perls' holistic conception of the universe and of human beings, the interconnectedness of the overall organism/environment field and the cyclic nature of human experience within that field. It has explored Perls' theory of contact and his concept of the self. Finally it has outlined his views of psychological disturbance, explaining in some depth his concepts of unfinished business, fixed gestalts and interruptions to contact and his view of anxiety because these are essential for an understanding of his practical and clinical work, to which we now turn in Chapter 3.

Notes

1. Wheeler (1991) has argued that Perls probably had little or no first-hand knowledge of Lewin's work, and he has demonstrated the ways in which he believes Perls misunderstood Lewin. Yontef (1992b) on the other hand has suggested that Wheeler gives an inadequate account of Lewin and has not appreciated the impact of Wertheimer's field orientation upon Perls or the 'field theory that is clearly embedded in *Ego, Hunger and Aggression*' (p. 101).

2. Yontef (1992b) disagrees with Wheeler regarding Perls' understanding of field theory (see Note 1).

3. This cycle has also been called the cycle of experience; the process of contact and withdrawal; the cycle of need; the cycle of awareness; and the cycle of figure formation and destruction. The cycle is one of the best known and most influential aspects of Perls' work and has been redefined and illustrated in various diagrammatic forms by many subsequent Gestalt theorists (see Figures 5.1 and 5.2). The faculty of the Gestalt Institute of Cleveland, in particular Bill Warner, first labelled Perls' conceptual model the 'cycle of experience' (Nevis, 1992). This name for the cycle has become *much* more widely used than Perls' original terminology.

4. Perls, Hefferline and Goodman's (1951/1973) concept of contact is explained in cluster four in this chapter.

5. Perls (1969b: 178) believed that a person changes when he is most fully in contact with what he is, and not by trying to become what he is not (see p. 90).

6. Perls refers to Frankl in *In and Out the Garbage Pail* (1969c).

7. Such a fixed pattern of unaware behaviour is also called a fixed gestalt (see p. 69).

8. Clarkson (1992) has explored the phenomenon of the innate tendency towards growth and healing, drawing parallels between Smuts' holistic creative evolution, Perls' self-actualizing life force, Bergson's *élan vital* and the Greek concept of Physis or the force of nature. See chapter 5 for a more detailed discussion of Physis.

9. Maslow (1954; 1968) was also influenced by Goldstein's concept of self-actualization but there is no evidence that Maslow himself directly influenced Perls (1947/1969a) or Perls, Hefferline and Goodman (1951/1973), although Perls did encounter Maslow in the Esalen years.

10. Erving and Miriam Polster (1974) introduced and described an additional interruption to contact – deflection – which is now fully integrated into Gestalt theory.

11. Although Perls used the term 'neurosis' (1969b: 28), he believed that 'growth disorder' is a more accurate description.

3

Major Contributions to Practice

Fritz Perls' most original strokes of genius were the practical contributions that he made to the field of psychotherapy. 'As Alan Watts was a cultural hero at the intellectual level, Fritz was the same at the doing level of directly impinging on lives to an extent that is now being forgotten' (Claudio Naranjo in Gaines, 1979: 331). Perls brought the holistic conception of the human being fully alive in therapy through a unique and unprecedented blend of awareness, active experimentation, visualization, fantasy, enactment, attention to language and all aspects of non-verbal behaviour, bodywork, intuition and thinking. Some of Perls' practical contributions have been assimilated – as though by osmosis – into the overall field of psychotherapy, so that he is not always credited for innovatory methods and concepts which he introduced or popularized. Indeed, some of his contributions have now become so accepted that it is not easy for the modern reader to fully appreciate what fresh and creative leaps they were when they were introduced. Perls' practical contributions which have been assimilated or reinvented include his holistic synthesis of body and psychotherapies; his validation of the real or person-to-person relationship; his emphasis upon the here-and-now; his insistence upon the existential responsibility of the individual; his popularization of the phenomenological method of investigation; his application of field theory to psychotherapy; his active experimentation and dreamwork; and his emphasis upon health. The second part of Chapter 5 explores the parallels between these innovations and certain aspects of the practice and theory of humanistic, object relations and psychodynamic therapies which have evolved since Perls' time.

Perls was extraordinarily perceptive. Able to tune into people's voice tone or body gesture within moments, he could reach the nub of characters, highlight their stuck point, pretence or defence and help them to a genuine awakening or change within a remarkably short space of time. Participants in his workshops often thought that they had experienced or witnessed magical transformations, but in the last year of his life, Perls was preparing a multi-media textbook to teach people that his therapeutic methods were not magic but could be understood, assimilated, developed and used in their own way by others.

This chapter is divided into seven parts. The first part of the chapter describes Perls' view of psychotherapy and the process of change, including the role of the therapist, the nature of the therapeutic relationship, the place of diagnosis and Perls' criteria for success in therapy. The second part of the chapter outlines the methods of present awareness and phenomenological investigation and explores the role of the past in Perls' Gestalt therapy. The third part discusses Perls' therapeutic tools and 'techniques'. The fourth section describes the innovation of active experimentation, giving an example of one of Perls' experiments, together with explanatory commentary. The fifth and longest part describes various creative aspects of active experimentation, including Perls' use of fantasy, visualization, skilful frustration, attention to verbal language, enhancement of body language, movement, dance and 'intuition' and gives examples of the creative approaches discussed. The sixth part looks at how Perls worked with 'resistance' and the impasse in therapy and includes examples.[1] The last part of the chapter discusses Perls' approach to working with dreams and shows how he integrated all his individual practical contributions into a creative synthesis or whole in the dream seminars. Again transcripts of Perls' work are included.

Therapy and the Process of Change

Definitions of Therapy

Over forty years of practice Perls defined and described psychotherapy in many different, usually interrelated, sometimes conflicting, ways. In *Ego, Hunger and Aggression* (1947/1969a) he suggested that therapy needs to involve both synthesis and analysis of the patient's whole organism – psyche and body – and called his new approach organismic reorganization or concentration therapy. Perls, Hefferline and Goodman (1951/1973) were passionate and poetic in their discussion of the process of therapy. Trying to convey the essence of their personal definition of therapy, they use a series of different analogies and metaphors telling us that Gestalt therapy is an adventure in living which helps the patient re-establish her true nature by attending to the obvious; a chemical reaction which once started is self-maintaining; a training in phenomenology and a training in the emotions.[2] Therapy heightens the client's perceptions of her current functioning, while at the same time bringing sharply to her attention the unfinished business which continues to interfere with her present life. It consists of attention to and analysis of the internal structure of the present experience of the individual client in her immediate field. The *process* of interacting is as important as the content of the interaction; any aspect of the overall field is relevant:

> The therapy, then, consists in analysing the internal structure of the actual experience, with whatever degree of contact it has: not so much *what* is being experienced, remembered, done, said, etc., as *how* what is being remembered is remembered or how what is said is said, with what facial expression, what tone of voice, what syntax, what posture, what affect, what omission, what regard or disregard of the other person, etc. (Perls, Hefferline and Goodman, 1951/1973: 278)

Later Perls (1976) reiterates the theme of the client learning about herself and her interruptions but places more emphasis upon the client getting to know the disowned parts of the self, so that she can resume her growth and become more whole.

Aims of Therapy

Perls often made quite categorical statements about the aims of therapy. Again there is wide variation. He seemed to modify what he claimed to be the aim of therapy, according to the thesis he was currently expounding. Thus in his first book, he suggested that the aims of concentration therapy are to 'regain the feel of ourselves' (1947/1969a: 185) and to regain the ability to concentrate on or be fascinated in our ongoing process of living. In 'Theory and Technique of Personality Integration', Perls elegantly expressed the idea that the goal of therapy is to achieve just that amount of integration of the personality which facilitates its own development, and offered the following vivid image to illustrate his meaning: 'A small hole cut into an accumulation of snow sometimes suffices to drain off the water. Once the draining has begun, the trickle broadens its bed by itself; it facilitates its own development' (1948: 572). Perls, Hefferline and Goodman (1951/1973) emphasize that the aim of therapy is integration, increased awareness and contact, for these inevitably lead to change and growth. The aim is not to cure the client but to teach her how to learn about herself and to send her away with a tool box full of tools, so that she can solve not only her present but also her future problems. Later Perls repeats the image of giving the patient the 'tool of self support' (1976: 185) but also includes the more directed aims of teaching the client to balance her own needs with the demands of society.

The Role of the Therapist

In *Ego, Hunger and Aggression* (1947/1969a) Perls called the practitioner by the traditional term of analyst or psychoanalyst and included in the role of the analyst many functions which he later discarded (as for example the idea that the analyst's job is to 'recondition' the client and correct her 'wrong attitude'). However, there are already important glimmers of the radical changes which Perls was to introduce to the very notion of what a therapist is. For example Perls insisted that the analyst must stop being a distant, neutral figure and change into 'a human being on the same level as the patient' (p. 231) (see p. 87).

In 1951, Perls, Hefferline and Goodman dissociated themselves from the traditional model of the analyst-doctor, who is supposed to find out what is wrong with the patient and then cure her. They propose that the therapist's job is to invite the client into an active partnership, where she enables the client to learn about herself, and to develop an experimental attitude to life in which she tries out new behaviours and sees what happens. The therapist attends to and draws attention to all the obvious and often taken-for-granted features of the client's present functioning (the way she walks, breathes, moves or talks, for example) and thus helps the client develop self-awareness. The Gestalt therapist notices what is missing (i.e. what is presently in the background) as well as what is obvious.

Far from trying to remain neutral or objective, the therapist uses herself as a legitimate instrument in understanding the client. She empathizes with the client – 'Feels the patient's experience by means of [her] own experience' (p. 47). She shares her own awarenesses, feelings and reactions as they emerge – for '[S]he is not a therapist if [s]he refuses to be part of the ongoing processes of the psychiatric situation' (p. 19). She uses her skills, background training, careful observation and intuition to look for the urgency of the client's unfinished business in the present exchange. In partnership with the client, she designs experimental situations in which the client can explore her previously fixed attitudes, expand her options and become more fully herself: 'The task is to provide [her] with a problem in which [her] customary unfinished solutions are no longer the most adequate possible solutions . . . because they no longer achieve anything: their meaning has changed from technique to obstacle' (p. 509).

Later Perls (1976) defined 'empathy' very differently – seeing it as a kind of identification with the patient which excludes the personality and reactions of the therapist herself and so excludes half the field. At that time he believed that the empathic therapist often succumbs to her client's subtle manipulations and mis-guidedly provides all the environmental support that the client wants. The therapist must guard against this danger by consciously working both with sympathy/support and with frustration (see p. 107).

The Therapeutic Relationship: from Transference to Contact

In a radical redefinition of the therapeutic relationship, Perls moved the emphasis of psychotherapy from transference and inter-pretation to here-and-now contact.

In *Ego, Hunger and Aggression* (1947/1969a) he was already extremely critical of what he saw as the unreal and ritualistic aspects of the relationship in Freudian psychoanalysis: 'The psychoanalytic interview has changed from a consultation to a (nearly obsessional) ritual in which a number of unnatural – nearly religious – conditions have to be observed' (p. 82). In particular he believed that the traditional analytic relationship overemphasized the past ('Freud's "archaeological" complex, his one-sided interest in the past' (p. 88)) and the role of transference: 'We find the condensation of Freud's historical outlook in the concept of transference . . . whatever happens in psycho-analysis is not inter-preted as a spontaneous reaction of the patient in answer to the analytic situation, but is supposed to be dictated by the repressed past' (p. 88).

Instead, Perls (1947/1969a) emphasized the client's need for a much more real relationship in which client and therapist make human contact. In order to bring this about, he increasingly dispensed with the classical analytical arrangement in which the patient lies on the couch and the psychoanalyst sits behind her.[3] Instead, Perls was one of the first analysts to sit face to face with his clients for a part of each session. This was a fundamental and important practical innovation which had a huge impact on the future development of the therapeutic relationship: sitting face to face meant therapist and client met each other at an equal level and naturally made eye contact. The client 'has to see the human being and not a screen upon which [she] projects [her] "transferences" and the hidden parts of [her]self . . . [She] achieves genuine contact with reality in lieu of a pseudo contact with [her] projections' (p. 239). In this passage Perls moved the emphasis of the therapeutic relationship away from transference and towards contact.

Perls, Hefferline and Goodman (1951/1973) developed and refined the concept of human contact as the core of the therapeutic relationship. They saw the therapeutic relationship as a meeting and a dialogue, an existential encounter between therapist and client. Declining to hide behind the role or mask of the neutral doctor, the Gestalt clinician shares her own responses and reactions in an authentic dialogue with the client: '[S]he meets anger [for example] with explanation of the misunderstanding, or sometimes apology, or even with anger, according to the truth of the situation. . . This is different from . . . explaining it away as "negative transference"' (p. 297).

It may be hard for the reader of the 1990s who has assimilated thirty or more years of the human potential movement to fully conceive what a radical change this was from the ideal of the Freudian analyst who, at least in theory, made herself as neutral as possible in her interaction with clients. Perls did not deny the existence of transference as a phenomenon and many Gestalt therapists are trained to work with the transferential relationship as one aspect of the therapeutic process. However Perls' unique contribution was to affirm, in addition, the greater value for healing of the living encounter between two real human beings.

Although client and therapist are equal in their humanity and are together responsible for co-establishing a useful and creative working partnership, Perls (1976) explained that theirs is a special kind of equality in which the therapist at first has greater responsibility for developing the sort of atmosphere and relationship in which real human contact, person-to-person meeting and communication can take place.

Elaine Kepner (in Shepard, 1975) has described Perls' dialogic style in the 1950s:

> In his sessions in the early fifties he was never interpretive, nor had he yet developed his hot seat technique. . . He also stressed, much more than he did subsequently, the *encounter* between patient and therapist. If you were his patient he would quite explicitly work with your projections of what you thought was going on in him – all the things you were making out of him – and then he would tell you what he was *actually* experiencing . . . I remember working with him one time in Cleveland. I was depressed . . . I was claiming that he was never feeling anything but good. After I finished, he said, 'That's your fantasy.' Then he shared his own state, which was depressed, feeling pretty down and anxious'. (p. 66; present authors' italics)

Perls' habit of owning his own feelings without commonly accepted social euphemisms meant that he was sometimes refreshingly direct but he could also be experienced as abrasive and abrupt. He has certainly been criticized for his style (see Chapter 4). However his directness could also cut through social niceties and reach to the heart of the person.

The Place of Diagnosis

Perls, Hefferline and Goodman (1951/1973) were wary of the diagnostic methods popular in the medical and psychoanalytic fields at the time. They felt that diagnostic labels could encourage the therapist to objectify the client and treat her as a type of disease rather than a unique person. Mishandled, diagnosis can promote an objective or 'I–It' style of relating, and may be incompatible with a meeting or dialogue between people. What is more, Perls, Hefferline and Goodman tell us such categories of normal behaviour or adjustment to reality are unnecessary because of the observable qualities of the individual's process of gestalt formation. When the figure of the individual's present interaction is dull or lacking in energy, we may be sure that the person is not all there: something vital is being blocked out of his awareness.

Despite Perls' antipathy to diagnosis, Perls and his colleagues (1951/1973) do provide us with a typology allowing that the 'therapist needs his conception in order to keep his bearing, to know in what direction to look' (p. 507). They warn that the challenge of using any typology – including the one they offer – is to use it without losing the unique sense of the individual in the moment-to-moment exchange. They propose a diagnosis not of the person but of the *process* and go on to describe the *means* by which people interrupt their contact with present experience – confluence, introjection, projection, retroflection, egotism and desensitization (see pp. 72–7). They finish this section of the book by stressing that their typology should be used not to label a person but to describe the structure of a *single* behaviour.

Criteria for Therapeutic Progress and Success

Perls, Hefferline and Goodman's criteria for therapeutic progress do not depend upon increased 'social acceptability' or upon improved 'interpersonal relations'. Their approach is existential and puts more emphasis upon the client recognizing her own standards and values than on helping her conform to preset notions of appropriate behaviour. The client herself judges whether or not she makes progress through her own awareness of heightened vitality, more effective functioning or deeper sense of purpose and meaning. To be sure, her therapist and her friends are likely to notice the changes that the client feels, because the new ways she meets her needs and lives her life are noticeable and make a direct impact upon others. The formation and destruction of gestalts have specific observable properties. In a weak gestalt the figure is dull, confused, graceless and lacking in energy, whereas when an individual re-establishes a dynamic process of figure/background formation the dominant figure is interesting, bright and energetic, so that people around her are naturally responsive: 'The process of figure/background formation is a dynamic one in which the urgencies and resources of the field progressively lend their powers to the interest, brightness and force of the dominant figure' (Perls, Hefferline and Goodman, 1951/1973: 278). So the individual's friends will directly experience her increased vitality and commitment to life in their own responses to her.

If the therapy is successful, the client will have more sense of the meaning and direction of her unique life and will become more self-supportive, no longer at the mercy of interrupting forces which she cannot control (Perls, 1976). In particular the client learns to recognize when she goes out of contact with reality, to identify how and where she is out of touch and then to recontact what her actual present experience now is:

> If [she] learns a technique of awareness, to follow up, to keep in contact with the shifting situation, so the interest, excitement and growth continue, [she] is no longer neurotic, no matter whether [her] problems are 'inner' or 'outer'. . . *When in emergency the self can keep in contact and keep going, the therapy is terminated.* (Perls, Hefferline and Goodman, 1951/1973: 526, present authors' italics)

The Change Process
For Perls, change does not come about by effort, self-control or avoidance. Indeed he frequently points out that willed or deliberate change is short-lived or ineffective. The control of our behaviour in childhood, by parents and teachers, has certainly taught most of us 'self-control', but this self-control creates enormous and unnecessary internal conflict for us. The inner being is as though at war with itself. The controlling part restricts the natural impulse of the more spontaneous parts. We are constantly oscillating between what we 'should be' and what we actually are. We try to avoid life's challenges by hiding behind roles and comfortable habits. In a radical innovation, Perls insisted that the therapist must not join with the coercive side of the individual (which he often called the topdog) in cajoling the other parts into obedience, change or action. Equally the therapist must not collude with the avoidant side of the individual.

Perls, Hefferline and Goodman (1951/1973) believed that change and growth are the natural and *inevitable* outcomes of facing oneself and the nature of existence through full awareness, vibrant contact and assimilation (see p. 55). In a quintessentially existential paradox, change occurs when the person faces and becomes fully what she already *is*, not when she tries to become what she is not (see Beisser, 1970).[4] Gestalt therapy does not *aim* for change in itself. The therapist's job is to help the client to develop her own awareness and make full contact with how she currently *is*. Change can only occur when the client abandons, at least for the time being, her endeavours to become what she would like to be and instead experiences as fully as possible what she is. Perls highlights the fact that deliberate change does not work in a session with Ellie:

> Ellie: My name is Ellie. . . Well, I feel a fluttering in my chest, now, and I'd like to loosen up.
> F: That's a program.
> E: What?
> F: That is a program – when you say, 'I'd like to loosen up.'
> E: I'm trying, now.
> F: 'I'm trying.' This is also a program. You mix up what you *want to be* with what *is*.
> E: Now I'm – I'm moving my arms, to feel at ease. And I would like to talk about my . . .
> F: Let me tell you something, Ellie. The basis of this work is the *now*. All the time you are in the *future*. 'I want to work on this.' 'I want to try this,' and so on. If you can work, start every sentence with the word *now*.
> E: Now I'm saying to you, Dr Perls, that I am uncomfortable. Now, I feel my chest going up and down. I feel a deep breath. I feel a little better now.
> F: You see, instead of trying to escape into the future, you got in touch with yourself in the now. So of course you feel better. . .

Perls concludes his work with Ellie with the following remarks on change:

> We are all concerned with the idea of change, and most people go about it by making programs. They want to change. 'I should be like this' and so on and so on. What happens is that the idea of deliberate change never, never, never functions. As soon as you say, 'I want to change' – make a program – a counter-force is created that prevents you from change. Changes are taking place by themselves. If you go deeper into what you are, if you accept what is there, then a change automatically occurs by itself. This is the paradox of change. (Perls, 1969b: 175–6, 178)

Methods

A natural outcome of the paradoxical concept of change, discussed above, was a method of therapy which relies primarily upon present awareness and phenomenological investigation. Perls (1947/1969a; 1976) proposed that the only psychological reality is the present. We live our existence in the present, in this very moment now and here (see pp. 44–5).

Working with Present Awareness

Perls did something new in the field of psychotherapy: he offered people an experimental method to study present behaviour, devising a system of exercises whereby the individual (patient, therapist or lay person) can explore the data of subjective human behaviour in the present moment and thus develop fuller awareness of herself. 'The basic endeavour is to assist you to become aware of how you are now functioning as an organism and as a person. Since you are the only one who can make the necessary observations we shall, of course, be dealing with what we discussed previously as "private events"' (Perls, Hefferline and Goodman, 1951/1973: 42).

Perls proposed that a similar investigative approach is central to psychotherapy. In what he called a unitary approach, he suggested that the Gestalt therapist pay and draw attention to all aspects of the client's being – body, facial expression, gestures, muscular activity, voice tone, habitual stance or walk and so on. Becoming more fully aware of ordinary everyday behaviour, reveals in very specific and observable ways how the client approaches, contacts and manipulates her environment and meets her needs. It can also show both therapist and client how the client is interrupting her contacting and how and when she, at present, fails to meet her needs. The therapist also pays attention to her own process and reactions – as an equally important aspect of the client/therapist field – and shares them when they seem relevant.

For Perls everything was aware process and sometimes he maintained that the awareness technique alone could produce valuable therapeutic results (1976). The first part of Perls' work with Ellie (p. 91) shows how he encouraged the client to stay with awareness of the present and sometimes frustrated the client's attempts to break out of the present.

Phenomenological Methods of Investigation

Perls employed phenomenological methods to heighten present awareness. In the phenomenological approach the therapist describes what she perceives without inference or interpretation. She suspends previous assumptions about what is significant in the client's behaviour or description and gives equal significance to all aspects of what is seen, heard or felt. The seemingly simple method of phenomenological investigation of the field can help us be in touch with existence: me, as I, am in my me-ness; you, as you, are in your you-ness, the core and pulse of the universe. As we describe the thing or the person as such, there is a capacity to know the essence. Both patients and therapists often undervalue or take for granted the obvious and look instead for the arcane or the complicated.

Already in the 1940s, Perls (1947/1969a; 1948) was arguing that description is a powerful tool which distinguishes humans from animals, which puts us in touch with the present and allows the possibility of re-creating experiences. He urged the psychotherapist to keep to the surface and to the obvious, to remain with what is, really to notice what she sees and hears: 'Peculiarly enough, all great progress was made by examining the obvious. After taking over unsuccessful cases from other therapists, I have frequently discovered that the obvious had been taken for granted, not only by the patient, but by the therapist as well' (Perls, 1948: 577). Perls gave some graphic illustrations of instances where the obvious had been overlooked. An artist for example had remained stubbornly unable to work and had obsessional thoughts of killing his wife, despite psychoanalysis with a progressive analyst. After only one or two sessions with him, Perls suggested that the artist experiment with sculpturing the killing of his wife. The artist was able to return to work with passion and interest and ceased to be plagued with fantasies of murder. 'The obvious that was overlooked in his case was that modeling, not language, was his means of expression' (Perls, 1948: 578).

Perls, Hefferline and Goodman (1951/1973) repeatedly asked the reader to set aside her preconceptions, and past assumptions and interpretations: 'Without preconceptions, without models of any sort, without an official road map of whatever kind, *come to yourself*' (p. 116). Far from being trivial, the uppermost surface of our behaviour is, in fact, the expression of our present dominant need and of our unfinished business. The phenomenological approach offers us the chance to be again as a child, innocently seeing, tasting, touching, smelling or feeling the thing in itself.

Perls himself had a genius for phenomenological investigation. His ability to notice all the phenomena of the client/therapist field was astounding. He observed and drew to the attention of the client tiny, seemingly insignificant details of her way of being or commented upon obvious or habitual aspects of her process. These observations often brought to awareness important but previously ignored internal conflicts or surfaced all sorts of unfinished situations from the past which the client needed to deal with. On several occasions (see p. 24) he would describe the body posture and facial expression of people he did not know with such accuracy and insight that they were astonished by what he had been able to discover about them just by attending to their presenting phenomena. This chapter includes several examples of therapeutic exchanges, in which Perls draws the client's attention to some 'obvious' phenomenon of the field with effective therapeutic outcomes – as when he comments upon Maxine's voice quality (p. 111) and the young woman's reluctance to use her legs (p. 114). Often participants of Perls' workshops put his efficacy down to intuition or magic, because they themselves were unable to follow his acute observation and accurate phenomenological investigation.

Perls encouraged the therapist to ask the questions 'How?' and 'What?' rather than the question 'Why?', for the former encourage phenomenological exploration and description of the actual structure of the present situation.[5] The questions 'How?' and 'What?' thus develop the client's organismic awareness of her present field and way of functioning in it and her holistic discovery of what is. Perls (1976) on occasion maintained that the essence of the Gestalt awareness technique can be encapsulated in three key questions: 'What are you doing?', 'What are you feeling?' and 'What do you want?' 'We had to shift the concern of psychiatry from the fetish of the unknown, from the adoration of the "unconscious", to the problems and phenomenology of awareness' (Perls, Hefferline and Goodman, 1951/1973: 15).

In the following example, Perls has been working on a dream involving a spider with a client called Liz. He persistently uses the questions 'What?' and 'How?' to encourage her to investigate and describe phenomenologically her reaction to the spider:

L: Feels like a spider.

F: *What* do you feel? *What* do you experience personally?

L: Do you mean physically?

F: Physically, emotionally, so far we have mostly think-think, talk-talk, things. . .

L: I feel like I'm – there's a spider sitting on me and I want to go do something.

F: *What* do you experience when the spider sits on you?

L: It feels like black up here.

F: No reactions to the spider? If a spider really would crawl over you now *what* would you experience?

L: Adrenalin and jump and scream.

F: How? [Liz half-heartedly brushes away spider] Again. Spider's still there. . .

L: I'd scream and –
F: How? . . . *How* would you scream?
L: I c– I don't know if I could do it. I can hear it though when
I do it. It just comes out.
F: How? (Perls, 1969b: 86–7, present authors' italics)

Perls (1979) described how, inspired by Husserl's phenomenology, he encouraged the client to concentrate upon the very symptoms which brought her to therapy and upon the processes by which she maintained those symptoms. He gave an example of the detailed phenomenological description by which one of his clients really got in touch with the essence of himself and his process and evoked and worked through powerful unfinished business from the past:

> 'The front of my head is aching, my mouth is dry, my head wants to push back into the pillow. Now I am breathless. I see myself running down the street. A motor car is running over me, but does not touch me. I don't know whether this really happened. My knees are very heavy, my eyes want to close, I feel as if I want to cry, but I can't. I have not cried for six years.' Then he starts talking about his father who was run over by a motor car and killed. He relates this and the details of the accident and death in a matter of fact voice. The moment, however, he visualizes the coffin, he bursts into a loud, intense, and genuine crying. (Perls, 1979: 16–17)

The Role of the Past in Gestalt Therapy

Perls' tremendous emphasis on the phenomenological description of the here-and-now has led to a popular misunderstanding of Gestalt psychotherapy. Those who have not studied Perls and other Gestalt theorists sometimes believe that Gestalt psychotherapists do not deal with the individual's past. This is not generally true. If client and therapist pay careful attention to the internal structure of the client's present interaction, unfinished situations from the client's past will often come to her present awareness. In these cases, many Gestalt psychotherapists may work with the client to explore those experiences from the past. Perls certainly worked with some of the past scenes and elements of the client's life in the present. The point that Perls is making is that client and therapist cannot revisit the past; nor do they wish to. This would only lead to a repetition and possible retraumatization of the client. They explore elements of the past in the changed conditions of the present moment.[6] In doing so, the client has the opportunity to complete the unfinished situations from her past and to find and make herself anew, transforming her earlier decisions and image of herself.

The example given above shows how the phenomenological

description of present processes often can lead to the discovery of and working through of unfinished business (the father's death) from the past. The description of a therapy session on p. 114 illustrates how a powerful unfinished situation arose spontaneously from a phenomenological investigation of all aspects of the present field, which brought to awareness the previously ignored but 'obvious' fact that the client did not move her legs. This turned out to be an expression of the powerful unresolved feeling that the client still had towards her tragically handicapped sister. Jean's dream mentioned on p. 104 shows another example of Perls' extraordinary skill in helping the client bring the past alive and find emotional resolution of *past* situations *in the present moment*. These extracts are inevitably short and the reader is encouraged to read the complete transcripts in order to appreciate fully the impact of Perls' work with the past.

Therapeutic Tools

The tools and 'techniques' developed and used by Perls have been the subject of much controversy. Perls and his followers have claimed that he did not use techniques but invented unique responses, experiments and interventions in answer to each fresh therapeutic dilemma which he encountered with individual clients:

> At present, my technique is based on function and experiment. What I will do next year, I cannot tell. (Perls, 1948: 574)

> Fritz would say to trainees, 'A technique used without understanding is a gimmick' . . . Fritz developed tools to arrive at gestalt, which is a natural process; there are many different ways of arriving at it, but basically people who use 'techniques' haven't understood what Fritz was all about. (Barry Stevens in Gaines, 1979: 361)

> My experience of Fritz was that he was not *doing* Gestalt therapy; he was *creating* it every moment. He had a certain repertoire but the essential element was to be with what was happening from minute to minute, *every* minute. (Claudio Naranjo in Gaines, 1979: 298)

Because what Perls did was dramatic and effective, relatively untrained people imitated what they *thought* he did. They did things which *looked* like what Perls did without his years of clinical experience and without an understanding of the whole context in which he did them, that is without a knowledge of Gestalt therapy's theory and practice. Employed in this way, Perls' creative and individual exchanges are reduced to mere gimmicks which may be dangerous as they seem to promise instant cure or immediate thrills: 'Unfortunately, this workshop approach has become widely accepted as the essence of Gestalt therapy and applied by ever growing numbers of therapists to whomever they are working with. Thus, Gestalt therapy is reduced to a purely *technical* modality. . .' (Laura Perls, 1992). Towards the end of his life, Perls himself became concerned about the misuse of the sorts of methods which he and others had so widely publicized at Esalen. In Lake Cowichan he wrote a preface to *Gestalt Therapy Verbatim* (1969b), in which he warned his readers against the dangers of thinking that achieving breakthrough is the same as cure:

> These techniques, these tools, are quite useful in some seminar on sensory awareness or joy . . . But the sad fact is that this jazzing-up more often becomes a dangerous substitute activity, another phoney therapy that *prevents* growth. . . . In Gestalt therapy, we are working for something else. We are here to promote the growth process and develop the human potential. We do not talk of instant joy, instant sensory awareness, instant cure. The growth process is a process that takes time. . . In therapy, we have not only to get through the role-playing. We also have to fill in the holes in the personality to make the person whole and complete again. (Perls, 1969b: 1–3)

Nevertheless, as Naranjo and Stevens have indicated, Perls did use an extremely effective and innovative repertoire of therapeutic approaches and tools. Yontef (1992c) has pointed out that Perls himself sometimes used his own creative inventions repetitively so that, on occasion, they did become rather gimmicky techniques, despite his own claims to the contrary.

The next two parts of this chapter explore the creative tools which Perls integrated into his therapeutic work, especially his exploration of dreams. Having described Perls' theoretical ideas (Chapter 2) and his overall view of the therapeutic process (this chapter), we trust that the reader will not adapt the tools we now explore as gimmicks, but will understand them as an integral part of the whole that is Perls' practical and theoretical contribution to psychotherapy.

Active Experimentation

Perls often maintained that full awareness (involving sensation, feeling and understanding) does itself bring about growth, but at times he suggested that awareness alone is a slow method of achieving change (1976). In addition Perls introduced the idea of active experimentation. He gave the word 'experiment' a broader meaning than that of the scientific laboratory experiment. He used it to describe a therapeutic situation in which a client is encouraged to try out new behaviours and see what happens. The Gestalt therapy session is itself broadly experimental because if therapist and client are fully human and concentrating on moment-to-moment awareness, neither of them is controlling or able to predict the outcome of the interaction. The client is given the opportunity to experience herself more fully and to explore by trial and error through living out the events of the therapy session.

The creative challenge for the therapist is to imagine (or design in cooperation with the client) experiments which are at the same time relevant to the client's present interests, real enough to provoke the client's unaware or suppressed feelings and yet 'safe' enough for the client to be willing to try them. Perls, Hefferline and Goodman (1951/1973) described the creation of this subtle balance as the excitement of a 'safe emergency'. They emphasized the finesse of designing experiments and suggested that the task is to provide the client with a problem or experiment in which her customary unfinished solutions are no longer the most adequate possible solutions; so she can give up her fixed behaviour (or gestalts) because they no longer achieve anything.

Perls, Hefferline and Goodman (1951/1973) gave quite detailed guidelines for how to design a Gestalt experiment, which we have simplified as follows:

Precondition   A precondition for setting up any experiment is that the client is willing actively to attend to what she is feeling, thinking, doing, saying and to enhance her awareness through imagery, body sensation, non-verbal communication, description, possibly movement or enactment.

Stage 1   The theme of the experiment must be something of immediate interest to the client, so that she does not need to deliberately try to attend to it, but is naturally drawn to it. It must be something about which she is vaguely, but not fully aware.

Stage 2   The therapist suggests (or designs in cooperation with the client) an experiment *through the actual doing of which* the client can explore the current field and increase her awareness, irrespective of the outcome.

Stage 3   The client is invited to either (a) exaggerate and amplify her present behaviour or attitude, or (b) inhibit her present behaviour or attitude.

Stage 4   As contact with the denied behaviour or feelings gets stronger, the client's excitement/anxiety will inevitably be aroused or mobilized. She will experience the experiment as some sort of emergency or existential crisis and may therefore feel stuck between excitement and fear. This stuck point is also called the impasse.

(Both client and therapist know that the felt emergency is in fact also safe.)

Stage 5 In the safe emergency, the repressed or unaware feeling, attitude, behaviour or memory can come fully into awareness and thus change the client's experience of her self or of her I-boundary.

Stage 6 The client accepts the repressed part of herself as her own, now feeling that 'it is I who am feeling, thinking, doing this.'

Centrality of Anxiety to Active Experimentation   Perls emphasized that what is new about this particular approach to therapy is that the experiencing of anxiety is not an unfortunate by-product of the process, but an essential ingredient. For only if the client feels anxiety will she have the opportunity genuinely to undo the fixed gestalt and, maintaining her courage, stand her ground or speak out as she wished to (see p. 80 for a discussion of anxiety).

Example of a Gestalt Experiment

Perls (1976) gave a simplified example of an experiment, which we reproduce here, together with a commentary to show how each of the above guidelines for the design of Gestalt experiments were put into practice:

Perls' patient has been complaining that no one treats him with enough respect. Something happened in the company restaurant which disturbed him but he cannot understand why he was upset. [*Stage 1: the subject matter is of immediate interest to the client and is something of which he is vaguely but not fully aware.*]

Perls asked the patient to return in fantasy to the incident that bothered him and retell the experience in the present tense. [*Stages 2 and 3: the therapist suggests an experiment through the actual doing of which the client can increase his awareness; while the returning in fantasy and repeating his experience in the present tense is a way of inviting the patient to amplify his present attitude of vague upset.*]

Patient: I am sitting in our cafeteria. My boss is eating a few tables away.
Therapist: What do you feel?
[*Stage 3(a): the therapist concentrates on increasing the patient's present awareness through phenomenological investigation and thus at the same time amplifies the patient's contact with his present attitude of vague upset.*]

Patient: Nothing. He is talking to someone. Now he is getting up.

Therapist: What do you feel now?

[*Stage 3(a): the therapist continues to investigate phenomenologically and concentrates on increasing the patient's changing awareness from moment to moment and thus amplifies his present attitude.*]

Patient: My heart is pounding. He is moving towards me. Now I am getting excited. He is passing me.

[*Stage 4: as contact with the previously denied attitude or behaviour gets stronger, the client's anxiety/excitement is aroused.*]

Therapist: What do you feel now?

Patient: Nothing, absolutely nothing.

[*Stage 4: the patient reverts to feeling nothing. This may well be the point when he is holding some attitude or feeling out of full awareness and is stuck between excitement regarding the emerging feeling and fear of recognizing and owning it.*]

Therapist: Are you aware that you are making a fist?

[*Stage 5: the therapist draws the patient's attention to his non-verbal behaviour, thus bringing an ignored element of the field to his awareness.*]

Patient: No. Now that you mention it, though, I feel it. As a matter of fact, I was angry that the boss passed right by me but talked to someone else whom I dislike very much. I was angry at myself for being so touchy.

[*Stage 5: a previously ignored feeling of anger now comes into the patient's awareness. However, perhaps still afraid to identify fully with his anger towards someone else, he appears to retroflect his anger instead.*]

Therapist: Were you angry with anybody else, too?

[*Stage 6: the therapist invites the patient into a wider exploration of his anger and the possibility of undoing the retroflection.*]

Patient: Sure. With that guy the boss stopped to talk to. What right has he got to disturb the boss? See – my arm is shaking. I could hit him right now, the dirty apple-polisher.

[*Stage 6: the patient now feels the previously alienated anger as his own.*] (Perls, 1976: 89)

Perls' experiments were of course generally more complex than the one given above, and while he often worked through the stages described, he equally frequently back-tracked or side-stepped or even introduced a sub-experiment within the main experiment.

Bringing Therapeutic Interactions into Open Demonstrations

One of Perls' most important practical innovations (Yontef, 1992a) was the way in which he brought therapeutic interactions into open demonstrations. He had criticized psychoanalysis for its tendency to mystify and emphasize the arcane. By contrast, Perls explained what he meant by his theoretical writings and was willing to demonstrate how his theory could be embodied in practice (1969b). In particular his demonstrations really showed what is meant by active engagement and phenomenological experimentation. He did demonstration sessions in front of hundreds of people and arranged for many of his sessions in the 1960s to be tape-recorded and transcribed. He then allowed these transcripts to be reproduced and circulated in book form. He also had videos and films made of himself working and made these available to the interested public. He thus made his work widely available for observation and evaluation. This required courageous commitment to demystifying therapy and it is notable that many of those who criticize Perls have not allowed their own work to be so openly studied. These transcripts and films have been an invaluable resource for trainee therapists and have opened up therapeutic processes to public scrutiny and accountability in a way which has been to the benefit of many clients since.

Creative Approaches in Active Experimentation

Perls included in his experiments creative and active elements, such as fantasy, role-playing, movement, dance and voice modification. These were a crucial innovation and a radical departure from psychoanalysis, sometimes called a talking cure, in which, at least at the time when Perls first wrote, any form of active expression was seen as acting out and the analysand was required to lie rather passively upon a couch while free-associating. Perls' emphasis upon creative activity in therapy was based on his holistic belief that body and mind are two interconnected aspects of the whole person, so it does not make sense to work with one without the other; and on his knowledge of the learning process, by which people learn more effectively by *doing* something than by talking about it. If for some practical reason the individual cannot currently actually *do* whatever he wants to learn, he can still learn much better by *doing something in fantasy* than by talking about it (Perls, 1947/1969a).

Developing and Grading Experiments

The previous section in this chapter, entitled 'Active Experimentation', described in some detail what Perls and his colleagues meant by an experiment and gave an illustrative example of a simple experiment with commentary. Perls improvised on the theme of experiment in many varied ways. He suggested grading experiments, using a range of creative approaches, to meet the level of risk which the client is currently prepared to take. For example a client might start by imagining a scene with another person, then develop a verbalized fantasy of an exchange with that other person, then graduate to a written-down dialogue and finally enact a scene as a psychodrama.

This section describes how Perls used various creative approaches (e.g. visualization, enactment, frustration support, attention to verbal and body language, movement/dance etc.) to work with the present awareness of the individual; the pressing unfinished business of the individual and the exploration of the individual's polarities within the general context of active experimentation. The section also illustrates a number of different experiments, each designed or graded specifically for that client at that moment in time. Subsequent sections explore how Perls worked with 'resistance',[7] with the impasse and with dreams, using a full range of creative approaches to active experimentation.

Fantasy and Visualization

Although Perls often pointed out the negative and draining effect of living in unaware fantasy as a way of avoiding contact with reality, he also enthused about the potential for deliberate creative exploitation of fantasy in therapy, devoting a large part of a paper (1978a) to the exploration of fantasy. He suggested (1947/1969a; 1978a) that the client use fantasy as a way of increasing contact with herself, and with people that she cannot presently contact in reality, giving an example of a man who was quite unmoved by talking about his father but burst into tears when asked to visualize him because of the greatly increased sense of contact with the old man that he experienced as soon as he did so. Later (1969b), Perls developed the use of fantasized retreat as a means of self-support, suggesting that when people feel overwhelmed, they can learn to withdraw in imagination to a place where they feel good and then return to reality with renewed freshness: 'Get in touch with your fantasy of being on an island or in a warm bathtub. . .This will give you a lot of support when you return to reality' (1969b: 61).

Perls described how he worked with fantasy when the client feels blank:

If we ask a patient to visualize something, he may tell us that his fantasy images are hazy. When we ask him to go on, he might continue and report that it is as if they are in a cloud or a fog. . . If the patient can stay with his fog long enough, it will clear up.

Take the case where the fog cleared into a whitish grey, which the patient reported was like a stone wall. The therapist asked the patient if he could fantasize climbing over that wall. And when the patient did, it developed that there were green pastures there. (Perls, 1976: 99)

Psychodrama, Enactment and the Resolution of Unfinished Business

Already in *Ego, Hunger and Aggression* (1947/1969a), Perls suggested the idea that the client could express *aloud* to a fantasized other person whatever feelings of love or hatred she experienced in response to that person. This was a first glimmer of the acting methods which he later popularized. Perls' demonstrations in the 1960s and all his later books (1969b; 1969c; 1976) are very obviously influenced by Moreno and psychodrama (see p. 20). He (1976) fully acknowledged his great debt to Moreno, while also highlighting how much he himself transformed psychodrama into a new method (1969b); for Perls modified psychodrama considerably to suit his own style as a therapist and to fit in with his theoretical stance.

Instead of inviting other people in the therapy group to play the different roles of the client's past unfinished situation or dream (as Moreno, 1964 had proposed), he asked the client to play all the roles. He made this change in order to help the client explore all aspects of the situation and increase her sense of identification with, and responsibility for, the parts of herself that she unawarely projected on to other people: 'If I let the patient do *all* the roles, we get a clearer picture than when we use Moreno's technique of psychodrama, pulling people in who know very little about you' (Perls, 1969b: 121).

Two-Chair Work

In order to make this quite substantial modification to psychodrama, Perls had to invent some means of representing the other role(s). He chose a simple prop – an empty chair – and thus created 'two-chair' work. Perls invited the client first to imagine that the other person was sitting in that empty chair and to address 'him/her' and then, switching roles, to become the other person and to respond. Perls thus enabled the client to enact a dialogue in which she could explore all aspects of her unfinished business with the other person. This active approach often allowed the client to express herself more fully and directly than merely talking about the unfinished situation.

The following example of Jean talking with her 'dead mother' gives some idea of the tremendous potential that this type of enacted dialogue has for the emotional resolution of unfinished business:

F: Can you say to your mother, 'Goodbye Mother, rest in peace'?

J: I think I did tell her . . . Goodbye, Mother. (like a cry) Goodbye!. . .

F: (gently) Talk to her. Go to her grave and talk to her about it.

J: (crying) Goodbye, Mom. You couldn't help what you did. It wasn't your fault that you had three boys first, and then you thought it would be another boy, and you didn't want me and you felt so bad after you found out I was a girl. (still crying) You just tried to make it up to me that's all. You didn't have to smother me . . . I forgive you, Mom . . . You worked awful hard. I can go, now . . . Sure, I can go.

F: You are still holding your breath, Jean. . .

J: (to herself) Are you really sure, Jean?. . . (softly) Momma, let me go.

F: What would she say?

J: I can't let you go.

F: Now *you* say this to your mother.

J: I can't let you go?

F: Yah. You keep her. You're holding on to her.

J: Mom, I *can't* let you go. I need you. Mom, I don't need you.

F: But you still miss her. . . don't you?

J: (very softly) A little. Just somebody there. . . what if nobody was there?. . . what if it was all empty, and dark? It's not all empty and dark – it's beautiful. . . I'll let you go. . . (sighs, almost inaudible) I'll let you, go, Mom. . . (Perls, 1969b: 153)

An analysis of the principles involved in two-chair work is given on p. 107.

Enactment and Exploration of Polarities

Perls took the existential position that people are intrinsically neither good nor bad. He believed that we all have a capacity to embody any human characteristic, but that often we disown potential characteristics because they are unacceptable to us, perhaps because family, teachers or friends have forbidden or ridiculed them. Ignoring or disowning parts of the self results in a hidden inner conflict or stalemate in which the aware or dominant part struggles with the denied or background part. Energy is tied up in keeping the denied polarity out of awareness but it is wasted energy, for the disowned characteristic will pop up in unexpected ways and sabotage the apparently victorious part of the personality.

Perls (1947/1969a; Perls, Hefferline and Goodman, 1951/1973; Perls 1969b; 1976) believed that 'polarities' are dialectical: they form two ends or poles of one continuum. You can't have stoicism without complaint, or vice versa; the one defines the other. Opposite characteristics are not contradictory: they form two sides of the same coin and are complementary. If one characteristic is foreground (stoicism for example), then another polar quality (say, whining complaint) must be in the background of the field. Perls' complex and paradoxical view of dialectical polarities is similar to that of existential counselling as described by van Deurzen-Smith (1988: 61–2):

> All too often people have opted for one side of a polarity, believing the truth to be simple and partial rather than complex and paradoxical. They short-circuit themselves this way and burn up all their energy in the hopeless attempt to maintain a lopsided position. Others recognize the polarities but are frightened of their implications. They try to manage contradictions by effacing them; synthesizing and compromising until all potency is drained from life.

Topdog/Underdog

The most famous of the polarities discussed by Perls are the topdog/underdog polarities. Perls called the dominant aspect of the individual her 'topdog' and named the less aware or background part her 'underdog'. The topdog commands, gives instructions or nags. The underdog by contrast appears helpless and put upon; she sabotages the resolutions of the topdog through her passivity and helplessness. Perls (1969b) has pointed out that although she appears so self-effacing, the underdog is in fact covertly powerful and often wins in any conflict between herself and the topdog, by preventing the topdog from taking effective action.

Perls believed that essential vitality is tied up in the denial of any human characteristic and in the struggle between the dominant (or figural) and denied (or background) aspects of the personality. His aim in working with the polarities is to bring the two characteristics into awareness; to show that polarities coexist; and to make overt any hidden conflict between them, exploring its meaning for that particular client. He often invited his clients to become first one polarity (e.g. the topdog) and then the other polarity (e.g. the underdog) and address each other in imaginary dialogue, again using an empty chair to represent the part not talking. Through the contact and dialogue enacted between the two parts or chairs, some greater knowledge of the previously split-off polarity is sought. The following example shows Perls working with Liz's topdog and underdog and includes Perls' thoughts on the theme:

F: Are you by any chance suffering from the curse of perfectionism?
L: Oh! *Yes.* (chuckles)
F: So whatever you do is never good enough.
L: Right.
F: Say this to her.
L: You do things adequately but never right, never perfectly.
F: Tell her what she *should* do, what she should be like.
L: She should. . .
F: '*You* should –'. Never gossip about anybody who is present, especially when it's about yourself. (laughter) Always make it into an encounter. Talk *to* her.
L: You should be able to do anything and everything and do it perfectly. You're a very capable person, you've got the native intelligence to do it and you're too lazy.
F: Ah! You got the first appreciation – you are capable. At least she admits that much.
L: Well she was born with that. She didn't – (laughter)
. . .
F: Yah. Now we have got here the typical topdog, underdog situation. The topdog is always righteous – sometimes right, but not too often – and *always* righteous. And the underdog is willing to believe the topdog. Now the topdog is a judge, is a bully. The underdog usually is very canny and controls the topdog with other means like *mañana* or 'You're right,' or 'I try my best,' or 'I tried so hard,' or 'I forgot,' things like that. . . (Perls, 1969b: 85)

As a person gets to know her polarized characteristics and to feel that apparently opposite qualities are in fact complementary and can coexist, she increases her range and ability to move subtly between the poles of her existence. She develops her potential for acting as a flexibly integrated whole organism, rather than as a group of separate factions at war with themselves.

Although topdog and underdog are the polarities that Perls made famous, the range of polarities within an individual is pretty much infinite. Each individual is a never-ending sequence of polarities:

tyrant/victim, saint/sinner, witch/spellbound, 'headmistress'/'hurt baby', 'jumping beans'/'heartbroken child'. Each person has her own distinctive polarities, often with names of their own.

One of the most popular and well known practical innovations of Fritz Perls is the two-chair dialogue, described and illustrated in the previous sections. Many therapists who say 'I use Gestalt techniques' mean that they occasionally use a form of enacted or symbolic dialogue or encounter between different aspects or embodiments of the self. Unless trained in the Gestalt approach, such therapists inevitably use it without an awareness of either the full implications of Gestalt psychotherapy, or the integrative context and phenomenological idiom of genuinely assimilated Gestalt.

Authors such as Greenberg (1975; 1979; Greenberg and Clarke, 1986) have moved two-chair work to great levels of sophistication, and have even succeeded in making it friendly to outcome research. Greenberg and Rice (1984) give a description of the use of two-chair work, particularly in terms of intrapersonal conflict resolution. They itemize the principles behind two-chair work and indicate three different ways in which such work can be highly effective:

> The therapist uses two-chair work in order to separate the two parts of the [intrapersonal] split and then create contact between them. Even though much of the Gestalt approach relies on the creative intuition of the therapist, there exist some basic principles around the two-chair technique that can be abstracted and used as guides toward the resolution or integration of the opposing aspects of clients' splits (Greenberg, 1975). The five basic principles of two-chair work are (1) separation and the creation of contact, (2) the responsibility of the client, (3) the attending function, (4) the heightening function, and (5) the expressive function . . . The possible ways of resolving conflict in Gestalt two-chair work appeared to be (1) a resolution by some form of integration; (2) a resolution by a release of previously unexpressed feelings, in Gestalt terms, an explosion (Perls, 1969b); or (3) a resolution by a change of perspective which made the conflict no longer appear relevant. (pp. 71–4)

Use of Skilful Frustration and Support

Perls believed that the process of maturation is a 'continuous process of transcending environmental support and developing self-support, which means an increasing reduction of dependencies' (Perls' 1969 note in Perls, Hefferline and Goodman, 1951/1973: 9). The healthy adult prefers to generate self-support rather than depend unnecessarily upon the support of others. Many people are unwilling to take this sort of responsibility for themselves and seek to manipulate the environment to provide support. Perls contended that it is mainly through meeting and overcoming frustration that the individual child or adult develops inner strength and the ability to support herself. He therefore believed that the therapist must learn to work with a fine blend of frustration and support. He indicated that some of the ways that the Gestalt therapist can legitimately offer support are her 'exclusive attention' and lack of blame (Perls, 1976: 51).

Perls skilfully frustrated the client's attempts to gain support manipulatively and offered her opportunities to meet her needs without manipulation, sometimes reminding clients that he would not get sucked into their games (1976). If Perls perceived that a client was manoeuvring him into providing the support she lacked, he often used humorous exaggeration of the client's manipulative efforts, in order to bring them fully to the client's awareness. This is illustrated in the following exchange, where Perls has been working with Claire, who keeps asking him questions which he perceives as efforts to cajole him into providing her with answers and self-support which, in the final analysis, only she can provide:

> C: And so now I say, well, how can I deal with this? I'm still stuck with this.
> F: 'Give me answers. How can I deal with this? Come on, come on, give me, give me, give me.'
> C: I – you know – really, I don't even *want* the answers any more, because nobody is really, you know – everybody's got an answer and it isn't doing me any good.
> F: 'Come on, give me the right answer, the one that's really nourishing, get me out of my impasse.'
> C: So I'm back to the same thing. I'm the one that has to give me the answer how to get out of the impasse.
> F: No. Answers don't help.
> C: Well what the fuck does?. . . What does help?
> F: Another question. 'Come on, come on.' (Perls, 1969b: 250)

[*Perls highlights how the client keeps asking questions and thus tries to get the therapist to provide support instead of generating her own self-support. He humorously exaggerates what Claire is doing by echoing her words in heightened form. Thus 'Come on, come on' and 'give me, give me' indicate what Perls believes is the real message behind Claire's words.*]

Perls also frustrated the client's attempts to get him to give help or guidance. He sometimes asked a client to be her own 'Fritz' and thus to offer herself all the wisdom or support she sought. This had the advantage of simultaneously frustrating the client's manipulations and teaching her one way of becoming self-supporting:

> I, this Fritz, can't go home with you. You can't have me as a permanent therapist. But you can get your own personalized Fritz and take this along with you. And he knows much more than I do because he's your own creation. I can only guess or theorize or interpret what you're experiencing. I can see the scratch, but I cannot feel the itch. (Perls, 1969b: 109–12)

Attention to Verbal Language

Perls (1947/1969a; 1948; 1969b) emphasized that the way we use language reflects our overall attitude to life. He therefore suggested that both therapist and client pay attention to the manner in which they structure their sentences and use words, thus noticing the unaware messages that they are giving themselves and other people.

As discussed in Chapter 2, Perls based Gestalt on a core philosophical assumption that people are responsible for their own feelings and behaviour. He demonstrated how many people avoid this awesome sense of responsibility by using static linguistic forms and impersonal phrases, such as 'it feels bad' instead of 'I feel bad'; 'people think', rather than 'I think'. Such language embodies a form of projection. The experience or process is externalized or put outside of the organism. The individual has partially disowned the feeling, thought or behaviour.

Inspired by Harry Stack Sullivan and Kurt Goldstein amongst others, Perls encouraged clients first to notice how they depersonalize and deaden their language, then to explore what this means to them and then to experiment with changing their turn of phrase, in order to re-identify with the disowned and projected feelings, thoughts and behaviours, and thus understand that living and contacting are processes not static structures. These themes are illustrated in the following exchange with Max:

> M: I feel the chair, I feel heat, I feel the tenseness in my stomach and in my hands –
> F: *The* tenseness. Here we've got a noun. Now *the* tenseness is a noun. Now change the noun, the thing, into a verb.
> M: I am tense. My hands are tense.
> F: Your hands are tense. They have nothing to do with you.
> M: I am tense.
> F: You are tense. How are you tense? What are you doing? You see the consistent tendency towards reification – always trying to make a thing out of a process. Life is *process*, death is *thing*.

M: I am tensing myself.

F: That's it. Look at the difference between the words 'I am tensing myself' and 'There's a tenseness here.' When you say 'I feel tenseness,' you're irresponsible, you are not responsible for this, you are impotent and you can't do anything about it. The world should do something – give you aspirin or whatever it is. But when you say 'I am tensing' you take responsibility, and we can see the first bit of excitement of life coming out. So stay with this sentence. (Perls, 1969b: 107)

Another way in which Perls (1970) felt that people disown responsibility for themselves and for what they are really saying is by asking questions. They may ask a question as a way of trying to get the other person to solve their problems or as a way of avoiding voicing their own opinion. He therefore encouraged clients to take the risk of turning questions into statements, as for example when he was working with Beverley:

B: How did I manipulate you?

F: You see, again. This question, for instance. This is very important for maturation – change your questions to statements. Every question is a hook, and I would say that the majority of your questions are inventions to torture yourself and torture others. But if you change the question to a statement, you open up a lot of your background. This is one of the best means to develop a good intelligence. So change your question to a statement. (Perls, 1969b: 130)

Creative Enhancement of Body Language

Perls saw a commonly assumed split between body and mind as central to the discomfort of the modern neurosis or disturbance. He believed that the psychoanalysts of the 1940s worked primarily with the individual's thought processes and verbal expression and he criticized them vociferously for thus reinforcing this damaging split. As has been discussed in Chapters 1 and 2, Perls was deeply influenced by Wilhelm Reich. Although Perls (1947/1969a) did at times criticize Reich for his overemphasis upon the body at the expense of attention to understanding the individual in her surroundings, he learnt a great deal from Reich and himself developed an exceptional flair for observing and working with body language and other means of non-verbal expression.

Perls often claimed that the non-verbal language of the individual is more important than the verbal language: 'A good therapist doesn't listen to the content of the bullshit the patient produces, but to the sound, to the music, to the hesitations. Verbal communication is usually a lie. The real communication is beyond words. . . So don't listen to the words, just listen to what the voice tells you, what the movements tell you, what the posture tells you, what the image tells you' (Perls, 1969b: 53). In this passage, as so often, Perls exaggerated his case to the extreme in order to really shake his trainees out of their complacence and make them see how important and fundamental is the often ignored expression of the body. He did not really mean that therapists should *never* listen to words, for at other times (1976) he tells therapists to shuttle their attention backwards and forwards between words, gestures and facial expression.

Perls' own genius consisted in his fine attunement to both verbal and non-verbal language and his ability to work, in a truly holistic fashion, first with one, then with the other and sometimes with both almost simultaneously. He was very aware that there is a somatic and emotional as well as an intellectual component to all experiences and looked for ways of getting his clients to feel this for themselves and to integrate all three dimensions into their living. Examples of Perls' attention to the varied non-verbal expressions of his clients abound (1969b; 1976). In fact there are few exchanges between Perls and a client where Perls does *not* draw attention to some aspect of body language.

Believing that the first gestures or words a person makes or speaks are especially significant, Perls paid attention to the individual's opening statements, frequently observing aloud his phenomenological impressions of a person's initial body postures or movements. These descriptions often accurately represented that person's life situation or her unexpressed, possibly unowned, feelings and thus enabled the client to move rapidly to the core of what she wanted to deal with. The following exchange between Perls and Maxine illustrates both Perls' uncanny ability to notice significant non-verbal expression in the first few seconds of a therapy session, and one of his methods of working with incongruence between the verbal message and the non-verbal expression:

Maxine: My dream is that I'm at home at my parents' house and. . .
Fritz: Well, will you first play your voice. 'I am Maxine's voice. I am loud, soft, droning, musical, I'm alive. . .'
M: I am Maxine's voice and I am very lifeless . . . little feeling in it, and I feel very different than my voice represents.
F: Okeh, then have an encounter with your voice. Put your voice here, and you sit there. You say, 'Voice, I have no relationship with you. You're different from me.'

M: Voice, you're different from me. I feel altogether different
from – from – from the way you sound. I'm nervous, I'm
trembling, and I'm scared to death. . .
F: That's what you feel.
M: My stomach is – my stomach is – is jumpy.
F: Okeh, now be your voice.
M: I – I know that you don't – you don't want me to – to,
uh – to express how you really feel, so I'm helping you to
cover it up. . .
M: But I don't want you to cover up what I feel. I want to –
I want you to let my feelings out, I want you to –
F: Say this again. 'I want you to let my feelings out.'
M: (more lively) I want you to let my feelings out, I want you
to let me be a person. (Perls, 1969b: 131–2)

[*As the dialogue continues Maxine becomes more insistent that
she no longer wants to cover up her true self and as she insists
she becomes more and more authentic and vital.*]

Movement and Dance

Perls had studied with the innovative theatre director Reinhardt
and the expressionistic dancer Palucca in Europe and with the
Living Theater in New York (see Chapter 1), and was keenly
interested in integrating movement and dance into his active
therapy as a means of self-expression. In the 1960s Perls was able
to develop and fulfil his passion for expressive movement by working with professionals in the field such as Anna Halprin, the
creative choreographer and dancer, and Janet Lederman, an
innovator in expressive movement. Perls did a series of Gestalt
workshops for Anna Halprin's dance company. 'He loved it
because everyone was so responsive. We actually did the whole
Gestalt workshop as dancers and as theater people. We'd dance
and act out and everything. He would do Gestalt therapy by
getting us up on our stage and saying, "Now be this. . . now be
that. . ." and everybody would be it by dancing it' (Anna Halprin
in Gaines, 1979: 200).

The influence was two way. Not only did Perls train the dancers
in Gestalt therapy; he integrated the dance into Gestalt therapy. He
quite frequently suggested that a client move, mime or dance a feeling or an aspect of herself, thus mobilizing her energy, invoking
her creativity and enhancing her vitality. For example when he was
working with Meg who has dreamed about a dog and a couple of
rattlesnakes, which have frightened her, Perls asked Meg to be the
dog and then to dance the rattlesnake. The transcript illustrates

Perls' unique style of working with a blend of enactment, body sensation and expressive dance, while staying closely in touch with the client's non-verbal process:

[*Meg is currently enacting the dog*]

F: Close your eyes. Enter your body. What do you experience physically?

M: I'm trembling. Tensing.

F: Let this develop. Allow yourself to tremble and get your feelings. . . [her whole body begins to move a little] Yah. Let it happen. Can you dance it? Get up and dance it. Let your eyes open, just so that you stay in touch with your body, with what you want to express physically. . . Yah. . . (she walks, trembling and jerkily, almost staggering) Now dance rattlesnake. . . (she moves slowly and sinuously graceful). . . How does it feel to be a rattlesnake now?

M: It's – sort of – slowly – quite – quite aware, of anything getting too close.

F: Hm?

M: Quite aware of not letting anything get too close, ready to strike.

F: Say this to us. 'If you come too close, I . . .'

M: If you come too close, I'll strike back. (Perls, 1969b: 164)

[*Meg has spontaneously found a means of expressing herself through dance and thus gets fully in touch with a very different side of herself – one that is able to strike back when threatened. With a little more exploration of her body sensations, she ends the work feeling warm and real, with more confidence.*]

Dance, mime and play are often considered to be activities associated with the right hand side of our brain (Ornstein, 1972). By integrating these forms of creative expression along with verbal expression (which is more associated with the left hand side of the brain), Perls was working holistically to enhance all aspects of the person and to enable the individual to be herself in the fullest possible sense (see p. 36).

Intuition and Fine Phenomenological Observation

Perls was highly intuitive and demonstrated and legitimized the use of intuition and of hunches in therapy. He would often openly own that he was working on a hunch especially when he made a therapeutic intervention that appeared to be going off at a tangent or to be a *non sequitur*. Many of his intuitive leaps were not in fact as magical as they seemed but were based on his phenomenological exploration of all aspects of the field, particularly his observation of non-verbal expression: 'He didn't miss a thing. He saw where people were in their body. That's why he saw people so clearly' (Gabrielle Roth in Gaines, 1979: 263).

The following example of supposedly intuitive work (described by Schwarz in Gaines, 1979) demonstrates the importance of fine phenomenological observation to intuition – in this case the observation of body language *and* of what was *missing* from the whole field (i.e. the *absence* of movement in the client's legs).

[Fritz] said, 'You are not using your legs.'

She ignored that and went on.

He said again, 'Now get your legs into the act.'

She said, 'How? I don't know how.' But she got up, walked two steps, stopped. . . She seemed unaware that her legs would not participate. . .

[*Fritz asked her to contact people with her feet. To her amazement, she discovered that her feet felt paralysed. After staying with the feeling of paralysis for a while, she regained sensation in her feet and felt the texture of the carpet as though for the first time. She was excited and grateful to Fritz and wanted to sit down, but Fritz encouraged her to return to the hot seat and work a little longer.*]

. . .he said, 'Now go into yourself again. What do you see?'

She said, 'I'm in the back of a car,' and all of a sudden it was apparent that the joy was gone.

'Are you there alone?'

'No, my sister is with me.'

'What do you see?'

'You know, my sister once. . .'

'I'm not interested in your memories, just tell me what you see.'

'NO!'

'*Look* at her.'

'NO, NO!' She began to cry bitterly.

He laid one hand on her arm and talked to her, but she said, 'I can't, I can't. . .'

'Tell her you can't talk to her.'

She hesitated, then she started with the statement, 'You're so pretty and so gifted. It's a terrible tragedy you were born with only one leg.'

We all gasped, amazed that he had sensed there was

something to do with the legs. As he [continued to] work with her, it turned out that since childhood she had not allowed herself to use her legs freely. Fritz finally had her say to her sister that she would not change places with her for all her beauty and talents. (Gideon Schwarz in Gaines, 1979: 253–5)

[*It was the observation of the inhibition of the use of her legs which Perls had noticed near the beginning of the session which led to the dramatic discovery of the client's unfinished business with her sister and allowed for its expression (in the tears) and resolution in the re-owning of the sensation in her feet and the final statement at the end of the work when the client reclaimed her own selfhood and right to exist as herself.*]

'Resistance' and the Impasse

Working with 'Resistance'
At the beginning of therapy or at the beginning of any single therapeutic session, the client is likely to embrace the attention to her present functioning and the participation in active experimentation which are the hallmarks of her chosen therapeutic approach. But fairly soon a client in Gestalt therapy, as in other forms of therapy, will express or demonstrate some form of ambivalence or inner conflict regarding the therapeutic exploration.

Perls' contribution to the theory of 'resistance' is the high value he placed on it, which led to a questioning attitude about the very concept of 'resistance'. Perls (1947/1969a; Perls, Hefferline and Goodman, 1951/1973) pointed out that 'resistance' is the dialectical opposite of assistance – assistance and 'resistance' being two poles of one continuum – and reminded his readers that what is now termed 'resistance' was once a life-enhancing decision, an assistance to the life of the individual. Although he several times suggested that 'resistance' could be renamed assistance, he did in fact use the term 'resistance', but often placed it in quotations marks, as we shall do, to indicate that he was not using the term in the current psychoanalytic sense.[8] He stressed (1947/1969a) the importance of not dissolving the 'resisting' forces of an individual, explaining that people need flexible and permeable defences, which they can adapt to the environmental conditions. People who demonstrate a total absence of defence or 'resistance' become confluent with the environment and may get overwhelmed by environmental forces or act very impulsively and dangerously; while other people are so identified with their 'resistance' that without it they would have no energy or interest in living. Perls pointed out that all 'resistances' are *somatic* (that is present in the tightening of the muscles, restriction of breathing), *intellectual* (justification, rationalization) and *emotional*.

Perls, Hefferline and Goodman (1951/1973) explained that the Gestalt experiment is designed with the intention of arousing unaware 'resistance': 'If these experiments simply sent you about your ordinary business, you would experience little conflict, for in those situations, you know very well how to avoid conflict. Instead this work is designed with the express purpose of making trouble for you. It is intended to make you aware of conflicts in your own personality' (p. 73). The 'resisting' forces in the individual are as much a part of the individual as the part which comes to therapy and wants to solve her problems. So instead of trying to ignore or attack 'resistance', Perls, Hefferline and Goodman suggested that the therapist and client heighten and concentrate upon it, exploring its somatic, intellectual and emotional aspects, in order to find out the purpose and meaning of the muscular contracting, intellectual rationalization, scare or anxiety. Concentrating in this way ensures that the individual actually experiences that her so-called 'resistances' *belong to her* and are as much part of her as whatever they 'resist'.

> they, the resistances – belong to us, are ours, just as much as whatever they resist. This is difficult, for it involves discovering that we ourselves interfere with our own activity – in short, that, without being aware of it, we launch counter-attacks against our own effort, interest, or excitement. (p. 70)

Perls was particularly skilled at picking up a body gesture or voice tone which was incongruent with the overtly declared verbal message of the individual and might indicate some ambivalence. He would then invite the client to heighten her awareness of it by amplifying or exaggerating it, in order to explore the significance of the incongruence.

The following transcript shows Perls working with May, who has complained that she feels as though she has a wall between herself and other people. Perls does not ignore or attack this obstacle between May and her surroundings, but encourages her to become the wall, thus embodying, exploring and re-identifying with the energy and power she invests in this wall or 'resistance' to contact:

F: Now, May here, wanted to come up and work. She told me that she has a wall between herself and the world. Of course here we have an *it* to work with. She says she has got a *thing*: something outside, something May is not responsible for. It

just happens that she's a victim of circumstances. . .
F: . . . Will you play the wall now?. . .
M: I will not let you come in contact with anyone.
F: Say this to me. You're the wall and I'm May.
M: May, I will not let you contact anyone completely. You can know them and you can see them but you can never fully come in contact with them as a human being, as a person, and I refuse to let you do this. . .
F: Why not? (plays despondent) What have I done to deserve that?
M: Just being there you deserve it. I'm a very mean wall and I will not let you out.
F: Okeh, change roles now. Now be May. The wall has just spoken to her. . .
M: Like, you keep me from ever enjoying anything completely. I'd like to. . . I've got to find a way through you, wall. . . And the wall says, All right, I'll retreat just a little bit; just enough to make you feel a little bit more comfortable, but I'm always there. . . And when you don't expect it, then I'll really get big again and crush you down.
F: Say this again to me.
M: (strongly) Oh, when you don't expect it I'll get *big* again and I will *crush* you.

[*May has now really begun to get in touch with and to re-own the strength and energy tied up in the wall and Perls makes a new suggestion, designed to help her amplify and re-own still further the power of the wall which 'resists' contact:*]

F: Can you play a witch. . .? (Perls, 1969b: 100, 102–3)

Working with the Impasse

The impasse is the point in therapy when the individual feels stuck. It is the third layer of Perls' five-level model of neurosis (see p. 78). Perls proposed that every neurosis has at its core this stuck point or impasse. The impasse is the stage in the therapeutic exploration when the apparently contradictory polarities in the personality reach a stand-off. The growthful and the 'resisting' forces are caught in a struggle. Here we endlessly repeat our fixed gestalts or rigid patterns of behaviour. We cannot assimilate novel information and grow. We are truly stuck. According to Perls most of us avoid experiencing this layer of ourselves because of fear of the confusion or existential anxiety which would be generated by taking responsibility for our stuckness and for our ability to choose to experience things differently. The impasse can be a point of existential despair:

When approaching the existential impasse (and this does not mean minor hang-ups), the patient gets into a whirl. [She] becomes panic-stricken, deaf and dumb – unwilling to leave the merry-go-round of compulsive repetition. [She] truly feels the despair which Kierkegaard recognized as 'sickness unto death'. The existential impasse is a situation in which no environmental support is forthcoming, and the patient is, or believes [herself] to be incapable of coping with life on [her] own. (Baumgardner and Perls, 1975: 13)

All the individual's available energy is tied up in this contrary struggle, turned inwards, hooked into the deadlock. Perls described the holding on and inward-turned energy which is typical of this stage as the implosive layer of the personality (see p. 79). In the implosive layer the individual has no energy available for the outward impulse which could loosen the impasse and lead to explosion and authenticity. The individual is paralysed by the fear of the unknown. She is either physically tense or excessively limp. Her images and dreams are metaphors which reflect the paralysis.

Perls sought and found the impasse as fast as possible, because since this is the place where most energy has accumulated, it is also the point at which there is greatest potential for change. Perls invited the client to really go into the impasse and feel just how stuck, confused, empty or despairing she is. He often suggested that the client describe in detail or enact the sensation of stuckness and exaggerate whatever physical sensations of tension she has. As the client amplifies how she locks her energy, turning it in on herself, the implosion gets so great that eventually it cannot turn any further inwards, but all the energy must go somewhere, so it explodes outwards into the authentic layer. The client shakes in fear, laughs, sings, jumps for joy or just does something different. The impasse is resolved and the individual moves in a fresh and authentic direction. The 'explosion' is often followed by important insights and a time of great creative energy and excitement. Perls' genius for working with impasse phenomena is illustrated by the amplification of the 'implosion', the resolution of the 'impasse' and the 'explosion' seen towards the end of the work with May:[9]

[*This extract begins after a long piece of work in which Perls has stayed with May's persistent sense of stuckness and image of a wall between herself and others.*]
F: . . . Go on; how would you crush yourself?
[*Here Perls is inviting May to amplify the implosive layer: see p. 79.*]
M: I don't know. I ah, I don't know what I'm doing. . .
F: That's a lie. You know quite well what you're doing. How are you crushing yourself?. . .

M: I'm not – I'm keeping a wall there, and I'm not letting myself get through it.

[*May is still at an impasse and once more becomes aware of just how stuck she feels with this sense of a wall between herself and others.*]

F: How do you crush yourself?. . . How do you crush yourself?. . .

[*Perls investigates phenomenologically.*]

M: I'm closing myself up and not talking.

[*May becomes more aware of her imploding energy at the impasse.*]

F: How do you crush yourself?. . . Yah? What happened right now?

[*Perls notices a change in non-verbal expression – he does not interpret it but investigates its significance phenomenologically.*]

M: I don't crush myself at all.

[*The impasse appears to be resolved: May is no longer stuck or caught in the physical implosion and tenseness of crushing herself. She voices a sudden insight, moving in a fresh and authentic direction.*]

F: You don't crush yourself at all. You played a game.

M: Yeah.

F: What do you feel now?. . . I noticed you stopped torturing me with your game. . .

M: (lively) Well, right now? I don't know, I just kind of feel sort of silly.

F: Look at the audience. (May laughs) . . . Look at them.

[*Perls senses that May is through the impasse and available for contact in the present and makes a suggestion to heighten contact.*]

M: They're all there.

F: Say this to them.

[*Perls again suggests that May make direct contact with others.*]

M: (excitedly, almost crying) You are all there, and I can see your eyes, and your faces looking at me. And you all have beautiful faces. . .

[*May is showing the energy and excitement which Perls associates with the explosion into the authentic layer of the personality.*]

F: Could you go down and touch somebody you see.

M: I could touch all of you. (May goes and touches and hugs people and begins to cry)

[*May appears to be her 'authentic self' in full and vibrant contact with her own feelings and with other people.*] (Perls, 1969b: 105–6)

In the transcripts of Perls' demonstration work there are many examples of heightening and then resolving an impasse within one short session. However, resolving a lifetime dilemma is not generally so quick; in long-term therapy a client may well remain at the impasse or stuck point over a number of sessions. This is uncomfortable for both the client and the therapist; here again the therapist's job is to stay with the client's stuckness, confusion and despair and encourage her to explore the impasse – often no easy task. Even in Perls' demonstrations there are plenty of impasses which do not get resolved immediately and then he usually contents himself with really underlining the impasse – which is the best therapeutic work that he can do *at that moment*, because he is emphasizing the reality of what *is*, and hopes thus to heighten the client's awareness (see p. 90):

> F: . . .Well, I want to finish here. All I can say is, you are a beautiful example of being stuck. You are stuck in your marriage, you are stuck with your fantasies, you are stuck with your self-torture. . . (Perls, 1969b: 157)

Dreams, the Royal Road to Integration

Perls particularly enjoyed working with dreams. A high proportion of the transcripts of his demonstration work in the 1960s are of dream workshops, where most of the individual sessions take the client's dreams as the starting point. He was exceptionally gifted in the use of dreamwork as a tool towards increased self-under-standing and self-actualization. His exploration of dreams shows him at his most perceptive, creative and intuitive, integrating all the other innovations already discussed in this chapter.

Perls believed that dreams are very important. He said that they were the most spontaneous expression of the existence of the human being and claimed that the problems of existence of any individual are most clearly indicated in her dreams. He described dreams as the 'royal road to integration' (Perls, 1969b: 66) and as 'existential messages' (Perls, 1976).

Dreams as Projections

Although Perls described dreams in a variety of ways, his most well known view of the dream is of a spontaneous expression of the dreamer in which each part of the dream represents different projected and disowned aspects of the personality. His radical contribution to dreamwork was to replace the analytic method of interpretation with active exploration of the meaning of the dream through enactment or psychodrama. He stressed that the therapist must never, ever interpret because that prevents the client from discovering for herself the meaning of her dream and it is only through active discovery that human beings learn and make meaning of their experience: 'Let me warn you, there's only one great mistake you can make. That is to interpret. If you start interpreting, you're lost. You make an intellectual, Freudian game out of it, and at best, you will be filing away some very interesting insights into some intellectual filing cabinet, and make sure nothing real happens. Don't interpret, just be that thing, be that plate, be that pot, be that friend of yours' (Perls, 1976: 184).[10]

Perls' aim in working with a client's dream was to get the client to identify with and explore all the parts of herself and her field represented in the dream. His primary method of working with dreams was to ask the client to retell the dream in the present and then to become each of the dream components in turn. Perls asked the client to enact objects, animals or supernatural forces as well as human beings, because he considered all aspects of the dream to be projected parts of the dreamer and, working phenomenologically, he tried to suspend his prior judgements about which aspects were most important. The role-playing often led the client to unexpected discoveries about some aspect of the dream (or of herself).

Here is a dream which illustrates Perls' method of inviting the client to role-play the different parts of her dream and shows how Perls integrated enactment, dance, movement, attention to verbal and non-verbal language and the heightening of awareness in a fresh and creative unfolding dialogue with the client. In the spirit of Perls' last intervention in the piece, we do not add a commentary to the transcript but allow the work to speak for itself:

Fritz: Wait, stop here. Close your eyes. Go on dreaming. Now the waking up is a beautiful gimmick to interrupt the solution to the dream.
Madeline: The . . .
F: You came back to us. Did you go on dreaming?
M: The same dream? It took a long time before I came to the dream. I saw the lights in my eyes and feeling of, of very busy.
F: Gesticulate this. Go on.
M: Very busy. (Moves arms about and laughs)
F: Dance it. (She does a dance mostly with arm movements.)

All right. Now let's have the story of the figure of the statue.
You're now the statue.

M: I'm a statue in the middle of a lake.

F: To whom are you talking?

M: I was trying to talk to Helen. (Laughs) I'm grey and sort
of, uh, I'm pretty classical looking. I'm looking like most little
statues of little boys you would see. And I hold a vessel. It is
a vase that has a small neck and big in the bottom. And I hold
it, and though I'm in the water, I pour it – I pour this water
in the lake. I don't know where it comes from, but this water
is extremely pure, and you would really benefit from drinking
this water. You would feel all good all over because you had
water on the outside of your body from the lake I am sitting
in the middle of. And the water is really good outside of your
body. But then, I really want you to drink the water I'm giving
from my vessel because it will really make you feel good inside,
also. I don't know why, but sometimes, you cannot drink it,
you just come to drink it – you're all happy and then you're
swimming and you want to drink it and then you can't drink
it. I cannot bend to you. I can just keep on pouring my water
and then hoping you can come and drink it.

F: Say that last sentence again to us.

M: I cannot come down and give the water to you. I just can
keep on pouring it and hoping that you will come and drink
it. I just can keep on pouring it.

F: Okay. Now, play the water. Tell us. You're now the water.

M: In the vessel?

F: Yes, the water in the vessel. What's your script? What's your
story, Water?

M: (Pause) I don't know much about myself.

F: And again.

M: I don't know much about myself. (Pause, begins to cry) I
come. I don't know how I come but I know I'm good, that's
all I know. I would like you to drink me because I know I'm
good. I don't know where I come from . . . I'm in that big
vase. It's a black vase.

F: Now, get up. Say this to each one of us. Stand up. Go to
each one of us and tell us this. You're the water.

M: (Crying and sniffing) I'm water in a vase and I don't know
where I come from. But I know I'm good to drink. I'm water
in a vase.

F: Use your own words now.

M: I look like water and they call me water and I'm just there
in the vase. And there's no hole in the vase. I don't know

where, nobody, I'm just there all the time, I'm just pouring
out, and I'd like you to drink me.
F: Go on to the next.
M: I'm there and I'm white and pure, and if you ask me where
I come from I can't tell you. But it's a miracle, I always come
out, just for you to drink me. You have to get out of the other
water and come. (Goes to the next person, crying) I'm a vase,
and I don't know where I come from but I'm coming out all
the time, and you have to drink me, every little bit of it.
F: Now what are you doing with yourself?
M: I'm holding myself.
F: Do this to me. (M goes over to him and rubs his arms)
Okay, sit down. So what do you experience now?
M: I feel I've discovered something.
F: Yeah? What?
M: I used to think, I thought of the dreams, I used to think
the water in the vase was spirituality.
F: Mmhhmm,
M: Beauty of, of birth and . . . it's such a mystery for me, the
beauty of life, and I thought that the vase was a secret, and I
wasn't high enough to drink the water. That's why I woke up.
When I was very small, it didn't bother me – I was just happy
with swimming. I didn't care not drinking the water, waking
up. But as I grew older I got more and more resentful not to
be able to drink the water . . .
F: All right. This is as far as I want to go. Again, you see the
same thing that we did before with dreams. No interpretation.
You know everything; you know much more than I do and all
my interpretations would only mislead you. It's again, simply
the question of learning, of uncovering your true self. (Perls,
1976: 192–4)

Nightmares

Perls especially encouraged us to enact those aspects of the dream
which we most abhor or fear, because those often represent the
parts of ourselves from which we are most alienated. There is
usually tremendous vitality and power in these feared parts; they
appear in our nightmares as magicians, witches, torturers, bullies,
ogres, terrible animals, as all-powerful creatures, whereas we often
see ourselves as the victim of the nightmare apparition. To become
whole and stand up for our needs in the world we need to reclaim
the disowned power of the ogre or monster. So with nightmares,
Perls would suggest that the client play the part of the 'baddie'. He
frequently promised that if the individual would enact the fearsome

aspect of her nightmares often and thoroughly enough, she would eventually reintegrate the alienated and disowned power so completely that the nightmares would cease: 'If you are pursued by an ogre in a dream, and you become the ogre, the nightmare disappears. You re-own the energy that is invested in the demon. Then the power of the ogre is no longer outside, alienated but inside where you can use it' (Perls, 1969b: 164). One example of this idea in action is the instance quoted earlier when Meg dances the rattlesnake that has frightened her in her dream.

Dreams as Existential Messages
Perls (1970; 1976) also viewed dreams as existential messages or expressions of the way the dreamer relates to the world or life:

> This, for me, is the meaning of the dream – an existential message. It's not just an unfinished situation, it's not just a current problem, it's not just a symptom or a character formation. It's an existential meaning, a message. It concerns your total existence, concerns your lifescript. . . And you can be sure if there is a repetitive dream, it's a very important existential issue at stake. (Perls, 1976: 186)

He frequently encouraged the client to work with the dream in the manner already described, until she got the existential message regarding herself and her relational stance to the world, as is shown at the end of an exploration of Ann's dream of trains and a station:

> Ann: [*playing the station in her dream*] . . .Why do you. . . it doesn't make any sense that you keep moving on, getting on another train and going off somewhere and you don't even know where you've been and where you're going or. . . you have friends here and you leave them behind.
> Fritz: Well, this sounds already like a little bit of an existential message. Okay, this is as far as I want to go. (Perls, 1976: 188)

Absent or Forgotten Dreams
Perls developed ways of working with fragments of dreams, forgotten dreams and the dreams of people who feel that they never dream. Perls demonstrated how it is possible to work with the merest fragment of the dream or even with only the residual mood left by a completely forgotten dream. He would invite the client to enact a dialogue between herself and the fragment or the mood of the dream.

When the client really couldn't remember anything at all about her dream(s), he suggested that the individual place the fugitive dream(s) upon the empty chair and address it/them in fantasy, saying to her dream(s) how she feels about it/them. Perls then invited the client to sit on the empty chair and respond as her dreams and thus to hold a dialogue between the person and her dreams. This is a powerful method which often offered insight regarding the individual meaning of forgetting dreams for that client.

Conclusion

This chapter has considered Perls' important additions to the discussion of the definition of what therapy is and to the exploration of the nature of change. It has outlined his innovative contributions regarding the role of the therapist and the therapeutic relationship. It has described and given examples of Perls' therapeutic methods, including the heightening of present awareness through phenomenological investigation and active experimentation. Lastly it has explained and illustrated his individual synthesis of creative approaches such as fantasy, visualization, enactment, movement and intuition in his experimental practice and demonstrations.

Perls' theoretical and practical contributions, as well as his personal values and ethics, have stimulated both warm appreciation and fierce criticism. Chapter 4 now addresses itself to some of the controversies surrounding Perls' work, person and style.

Notes

1. Perls (1947/1969a; Perls, Hefferline and Goodman, 1951/1973) questioned the validity of both the concept and the term 'resistance', as used in the orthodox psychoanalysis of the period. He pointed out that 'resistance' is the dialectical opposite of 'assistance', that is 'assistance' and 'resistance' are the two poles of one continuum, and suggested that 'resistance' could be renamed 'assistance'. The concept of 'resistance' is hotly debated amongst Gestalt theorists (see for example Breshgold, 1989; Laura Perls in Rosenblatt, 1991; Davidove, 1991; Polster, 1991).
2. See pp. 46, 92 and 113 for descriptions of phenomenology.
3. Perls (1947/1969a) first wrote about making this important change in the 1940s, but Isadore From (in Wysong and Rosenfeld, 1982) and James Simkin (in Gaines, 1979) have explained that he still used the couch some of the time in the 1940s and 1950s.
4. Drawing from Perls' comments upon, and examples of, the paradoxical nature of change, Beisser (1970) has evolved the paradoxical theory of change which has since become central to the development of Gestalt thinking regarding change.
5. Perls persistently criticized the use of the question 'Why?' as an intervention, believing that it encourages the client to be cognitively introspective, to intellectualize and to look for rationalizations, rather than to explore her own

phenomenology. It gives the client the illusion that her behaviour or problems can be explained by a single cause and encourages her to believe that explanation will help her resolve her present problems.

6. For an exploration of the relevance of the past in Gestalt therapy, see pp. 45, 95 and 130 and Polster (1987) and Clarkson (1988).

7. See note 1 to this chapter.

8. The concept of 'resistance' continues to be debated amongst Gestalt theorists: see note 1 to this chapter.

9. An earlier excerpt from the work with May is quoted on pp. 116–17.

10. Despite Perls' insistence that the therapist should not interpret, he did in practice occasionally interpret both dreams and other processes of the client.

4

Criticisms and Rebuttals

Introduction

The purpose of this chapter is to review some of the assessments and criticisms of Fritz Perls' theory and practice. We have chosen to examine the opinions of authors whose work has reached a wide audience and has therefore had the most effect in influencing how Perls is seen. The four main sources of assessment and criticism discussed are Kovel (1976, reprinted 1991), Masson (1989), Dublin (1977) and Yalom (1980; 1985). Kovel and Yalom are the authors of widely read reference books and Masson is the author of a much publicized attack on the whole field of psychotherapy, including Fritz Perls and Gestalt therapy; so it is therefore from these sources that many students of psychotherapy and members of the interested public get their impressions of Perls' work.

We shall attempt to show that the later, much publicized work of Perls is *not* synonymous with Gestalt and has in fact been identified as 'Perls-ism' by Dublin in order to distinguish it from Gestalt as a whole. We hope thus to correct the popular misconception that what Perls did at Esalen in the 1960s is the only or even the main form and style of Gestalt. Although we have on the whole restricted ourselves to the discussion of specific criticisms of Perls, and not attempted to examine all criticisms of Gestalt therapy, we have therefore made one important exception to this limitation. Some commentators, such as Kovel, have described and criticized something which they *call* Gestalt therapy but which is in fact a description not of Gestalt therapy as a whole, but of the work that Perls did or published in the 1960s. In such cases we have examined criticisms of 'Gestalt therapy' as though they were criticisms of Perls, while making it clear that we are doing so.

Perls was deliberately provocative in what he said, did and wrote. He was by nature a man of many facets, a strong personality, with varied and sometimes extreme characteristics. In addition he chose to confront accepted theory and practice in the medical and psychoanalytic fields, to question the established authority of society and to overturn social and professional conventions. Not surprisingly, then, Perls has not left people indifferent. There are no objective witnesses to Fritz Perls and his work – only a range of subjective impressions. He and his practice have provoked – and still provoke – strong reactions. He has been as vociferously challenged as he was challenging and as pointedly ignored as he sometimes ignored or dismissed others. Our task in this chapter is to present the criticisms as honestly as possible, and then to discuss which aspects of the criticisms are justified and which are not, or with which qualifications.

Gestaltists' criticisms of Perls are more fully explored in Chapter 5, as part of a discussion of Perls' influence upon the development of Gestalt therapy. Gestalt theorists and practitioners have vociferously debated both Perls' person and his practical and theoretical contributions. In many cases criticisms of Perls have led to new theoretical perspectives and fresh methods of practising Gestalt therapy, which later Gestalt therapists have adopted in place of, or in addition to, some of Perls' original ideas and techniques. This process of critique and evolution within Gestalt has gone on since its inception and has grown richer and more varied in the last twenty years.

We review first Kovel's description of Gestalt therapy and Perls' work, and then Masson's attack on Perls. Next we discuss the common but mistaken assumption that Perls' work and Gestalt therapy are synonymous and we outline Dublin's distinction between Gestalt therapy and Perls-ism. Finally we explore Yalom's generally sympathetic view of Perls' work and examine the specific criticisms which he makes.

Kovel's Description of Gestalt Therapy

Kovel (1976) has written a consumer's guide to the field of psychotherapy from a psychoanalytic point of view. It gives a brief description of different forms of psychotherapy and attempts to offer guidance about the strengths and weaknesses of each approach. Kovel describes as Gestalt therapy the limited version of Gestalt therapy which is most commonly associated with the practice of Fritz Perls, without acknowledging that this is what he is doing.[1] We therefore take Kovel's remarks regarding Gestalt therapy as remarks relating to Fritz Perls.

First we will summarize the aspects of Kovel's assessments of Perls and of Gestalt therapy which seem to us to be a reasonable if inevitably condensed synopsis of the spirit of his work. Then we will discuss Kovel's criticisms.

Summary of Kovel's Description

Kovel (1976) begins his description positively and is unusual in that he fully acknowledges the innovatory nature of Perls' contributions. In particular he comments favourably upon Perls' challenging of the use of verbal language as the prime means of communication and upon Perls' rejection of the psychoanalytic concentration upon the psyche as opposed to the whole organism of the person: 'Gestalt therapy . . . while not eschewing language completely . . . makes the decisive break into non-verbal experience. By denying the special status of mind. . . Gestalt therapy also undercuts language, the tool of thought, and clears the way for an approach that is explicitly *organismic*' (p. 165). Again positively and unusually, Kovel appreciates and points out to his readers that the popularization of Gestalt on the West Coast of America has led many to forget that Gestalt therapy has an elaborate theoretical base that is firmly grounded in the traditions of modern psychology and psychotherapy, including Freudian psychoanalysis. Later Kovel makes a fair-minded attempt to summarize Perls' key idea that awareness is an active process that moves towards the construction of meaningful organized wholes between an organism and its environment and has curative value as a therapeutic method that was overlooked by Freud. Kovel commends the positive existential approach of Gestalt therapy and apparently quotes Perls favourably regarding the simplicity of paying attention to the obvious.

Kovel's Criticisms

After a positive description, Kovel concludes his chapter on Perls and Gestalt with a number of criticisms, which are summarized here:

1 Perls minimizes the past and insists that everything is dealt with in the here-and-now.
2 Gestalt therapy takes place almost exclusively in groups and favours a short workshop format.
3 Gestalt/Perls has no theory of group process.
4 Gestalt/Perls offers no theory of transference to speak of.
5 Gestalt/Perls plays down verbal explanation.
6 Perls pays almost exclusive attention to projection as the major form of disturbed communication between the self and other people.
7 Gestalt (or Perls') therapy is so emotionally demanding that it can induce a state of near hysteria, and because of its emphasis upon emotional as against intellectual experience it creates an opening for mystification and hysterical possession.

If Kovel is justified in these allegations, particularly the last one, then his critique is a serious one for Gestalt. What evidence is there to justify or refute Kovel's statements? We will take the above statements and examine each in turn.

Does Perls Minimize the Past and Insist that Everything is Dealt With in the Present?

Kovel suggests that the Gestalt therapist's task is to forestall any excursion into the past or outside the immediate therapeutic situation, by refusing to tolerate any talking about or reference to other matters. Certain words of Perls may seem to indicate such an attitude. For example, he enthusiastically reiterated the discoveries of field theory that the only psychological reality is the present and that a person's behaviour can only be explained in terms of the phenomena of the present field. However, to suggest that Perls minimizes the past is an oversimplification of Perls' emphasis upon present awareness.

Far from denying the importance of the past to Gestalt therapy, Perls, Hefferline and Goodman (1951/1973) said that one aim of the Gestalt therapist is to look for, and to work with, the urgency of the past unfinished situation which is seeking attention in the present. One of Perls' most important contributions was that he, together with his colleagues, developed therapeutic methods which allowed for the *completion* of past unfinished business in the *present* therapeutic experiment (see pp. 45 and 95 for a discussion of the place of the past in Gestalt therapy). Although, Perls was certainly a past master at present centredness, he was equally skilled at facilitating the re-enactment of early life experiences. He did explore past experiences with his clients in a vital fashion in the present field, which allowed for their emotional resolution. Chapter 3 gives a number of examples of Perls' work with spontaneously arising unfinished business from the client's past (see especially pp. 104 and 114).

Kovel's statement that Gestalt minimizes the past and tolerates no comment *about*, or reference *to*, is not, then, in our view an accurate description of either Perls' theoretical or practical work. However, Perls did reiterate certain phrases, which have contributed to Kovel's and other commentators' misunderstanding of the role of the past in Perls' work and Gestalt in general.

Kovel's view is especially misrepresentative of current Gestalt therapy which fully values and acknowledges the past as background to the present and has developed a still more flexible approach to the individual's life story (Polster, 1987) and an ability to synthesize here-and-now figure with historical background

(Clarkson, 1988; Yontef, 1987; 1991). 'Gestaltists may at times encourage a reliving of the past, occasionally be neutral, or occasionally prevent it (e.g. particularly if repeated regressions to past experiences appear to be serving as an avoidance of good contact in the here-and-now)' (Clarkson, 1988: 75).

Does Gestalt Therapy Take Place in Groups and Favour a Short Workshop Format?

Kovel tells us that Gestalt therapy is usually conducted in groups, which do not meet over a period of time but happen in a concentrated workshop setting. Even at the time Kovel wrote, it was not accurate to state that Gestalt therapy in general was conducted in groups or short-term workshops. This was only true of Perls in the second half of the 1960s and even he distinguished between his workshop demonstrations and Gestalt therapy (1969b). Previously Perls himself had seen clients in individual long-term therapy.

Then, and now, many other Gestalt therapists were, and are, doing different modes of Gestalt therapy, including short-term work, long-term work, individual, family and group therapy with people in a variety of different settings, ranging from private practice to mental hospitals. By the time that Kovel's book was reprinted (1991), the modes of Gestalt therapy were diverse and well documented (Fagan and Shepherd, 1970; Polster and Polster, 1974; Kempler, 1973; Zinker, 1978; Feder and Ronall, 1980; Frew, 1983; Hill et al., 1983; Harman, 1984; Nevis, 1987; and others).

Is There a Theory of Group Process in Perls' Work or in Gestalt?

Perls himself did not write or talk about group process; nor did he actively work with group process to our knowledge. Indeed in the public demonstration workshops that he gave at Esalen and elsewhere in the 1960s he sometimes discouraged the spontaneous participation of group members. His preferred way of working was with volunteers from the audience who came up one by one to occupy the 'hot seat' and do individual work in front of the others. Perls certainly used the group to heighten the impact of the work and as witness to whatever took place. Sometimes he invited a client to engage with other members of the group or get feedback from group participants (Perls, 1969b). In his workshops, there was no group process as it is understood in psychoanalytic groups or as is now common in Gestalt groups.

As we have already said, Kovel seems to be assuming that Gestalt therapy is the therapy that Perls described and did in the late 1960s. So if his assumption were correct, he would be right that *at that time* (1976) Gestalt therapy had no theory of group process. But as we have pointed out, his assumption was wrong. *Gestalt Therapy Now* (Fagan and Shepherd, 1970) was a collection of articles by leading Gestalt practitioners, psychologists and psychiatrists of the time, including Elaine Kepner, Erving Polster, Laura Perls and James Simkin. Some of these writers describe the integration of Perls' hot seat method with group interaction, others describe Gestalt in interactive therapy groups. Polster and Polster (1974) had already published a thorough exploration of Gestalt theory and practice, in which they devoted a chapter to groups and group process. They specifically pointed out that the hot seat method of working in a group was Perls' style, not the theory which supports his style. They did provide some supporting theory for the hot seat approach but they also described, both practically and theoretically, other ways in which they were doing Gestalt group therapy.

Between 1976 when Kovel first wrote his critique, and 1991 when his book was most recently reprinted, the picture has changed dramatically. *Beyond the Hot Seat* (Feder and Ronall, 1980) is a collection of theoretical discussions of group process in Gestalt, some of which are described on p. 165 of the present book. Therefore, although Kovel's proposition, with the notable exceptions of Fagan and Shepherd's (1970) collection and the Polsters' book (1974), was partially justified in 1976, it was wholly inaccurate when reprinted in the 1990s.

The false ideas that Gestalt therapy is usually practised in groups and makes no use of group process are unfortunately still being repeated (as for example in Brown and Pedder, 1991).

Is There a Theory of Transference in Perls' Work or in Gestalt?
Kovel says there is no theory of transference in Gestalt. What is the evidence in Perls' work to refute or support this statement? We will consider first his practice and then his theory.

Perls, together with many of the other Gestalt therapists of the 1950s, had been fully trained in psychoanalysis and was therefore perfectly competent in recognizing and dealing with transference phenomena in practice. However, in the 1960s Perls dismissed transference with scant explanation. Unfortunately at that time some people who had attended a few Gestalt workshops began to call themselves Gestalt therapists, without sufficient clinical background, and without a knowledge of Gestalt theory or of the importance of the ongoing therapeutic relationship or the phenomena of transference and countertransference. So at the time when Kovel first wrote (1976), there was almost certainly considerable justification for his belief that some so-called Gestaltists did not *in practice* acknowledge or know how to deal with transference. (Even in the 1960s there were, of course, Gestalt therapists, such as Laura Perls, Erving Polster, Gary Yontef and others who fully acknowledged both the psychoanalytic and the Gestalt theories of transference.)

However, Kovel's supposition that there is no *theory* of transference in Gestalt is less easy to understand. It is true that in his later publications (1969b; 1976), Perls does not discuss transference at any length. It is also true that even in his earlier works, Perls does not explain the psychoanalytic theory of transference. He takes it for granted that his readers will have that knowledge. In his earlier publications (Perls, 1947/1969a; Perls, Hefferline and Goodman, 1951/1973), Perls pays considerable attention to the *concept* of transference. He does not deny its existence but he criticizes the orthodox psychoanalysts of the time for reducing all the reactions of the client to mere transference, rather than acknowledging them as valid in the present exchange.

Kovel's criticism completely ignores the fact that Perls made a major *contribution* to the theory of transference and of relationship in therapy. He introduced the concept – novel at the time – that the real relationship or contact between therapist and client is *as* valid and important as the transferential relationship. Perls proposed that dismissing the client's reactions as mere transference is devaluing of his authenticity and personhood: 'Whatever happens in psychoanalysis is not interpreted as a spontaneous reaction of the patient in answer to the analytical situation, but is supposed to be dictated by the repressed past' (Perls, 1947/1969a: 88). He suggests instead that the psychotherapist (while not denying to himself the possibility of a transferential element) can accept the client's feelings as valid in themselves and respond to them authentically person to person: 'He meets anger with explanation of the misunderstanding, or sometimes an apology, or even with anger according to the truth of the situation' (Perls, Hefferline and Goodman, 1951/1973: 297).

As Yontef has pointed out (1991), now that psychoanalysis has integrated many of the contributions of humanistic psychology, including a positive evaluation of the real or present relationship, it is hard to imagine how rigid psychoanalysis in the 1940s and 1950s had become, particularly regarding transference. It is therefore not easy for us to understand why Perls was so insistent in his criticism of the psychoanalytic overemphasis upon transference. And it is difficult to grasp what a major innovation his notion of real contact was to the theory of therapeutic relationship.

Since the 1960s, Gestalt therapy has largely recovered from the sometimes casual practices of that time, drawing on the better informed theory of the 1950s, as well as developing and refining new theory. There are ample references in the Gestalt literature to refute Kovel's claim that there is no theory of transference in Gestalt (Polster and Polster, 1974; From, 1984; Yontef, 1988; 1991; Clarkson, 1989), including a recent exploration of transference in Gestalt theory and practice (Mackewn, 1991). Yontef acknowledges that, 'one cannot do good therapy without dealing competently with the transference phenomena. One cannot do good therapy and ignore developmental issues either. However, in Gestalt therapy we do deal with both of these, using the dialogic and phenomenological perspectives we have been discussing' (1991: 18). Current Gestalt training programmes include training in transference and countertransference and/or require their trainees to have already gained that as a prerequisite of entry.

Does Perls Play Down Verbal Explanation and Verbal Knowledge?

Kovel tells us that in Gestalt verbal explanation and verbal knowledge are played down. This is certainly true of Perls' later publications (especially Perls, 1976), where he goes so far as to tell us that words are often lies and that non-verbal language is much more authentic. However it is not true of the more considered theoretical explorations of Perls, Hefferline and Goodman (1951/1973), who emphasize a holistic method of therapy which concentrates on *all* aspects of the person and the field. They advocate that the therapist pay attention to the client's verbal communication, to his voice tone, his gestures, to the therapist's own reactions and so on, as different parts of the whole therapist/client field become figural (see p. 42).

Does Perls Concentrate on Projection as the Major Form of Disturbed Communication?

Kovel accuses Perls of almost exclusively concentrating on *projection* as the major form of disturbed communication between the self and other people. Perls certainly refers to projection a good deal but he does not do so exclusively or even predominantly. He and his co-authors describe six major means of interruption to contact or communication: introjection, confluence, retroflection, projection, egotism and desensitization. In his overall work, he pays as much attention to introjection as to projection (Perls, 1947/1969a; Perls, Hefferline and Goodman, 1951/1973; Perls, 1969b; 1976). Although he may not refer to confluence, egotism, desensitization and retroflection as much as he does to projection, he explains them fully and he and his colleagues devote a whole chapter to each of retroflection and introjection as well as one to projection. They also point out that the various interruptions to contact cannot be understood in isolation but are interlinked. Kovel's misapprehension may arise from Perls' much publicized method of working with dreams as projections of the dreamer (Perls, 1969b).

Did Perls Induce a State of Near Hysteria?

In the last page of his ten-page assessment of Gestalt, Kovel tells us that 'because Gestalt therapy is so emotionally demanding, it can induce a state of near hysteria' and because it has a 'pronounced emphasis on emotional as against intellectual experience . . . [it] creates the opening for mystification and hysterical possession' (Kovel, 1976: 174). This comes as a surprise, for nothing in the foregoing text has led the reader to expect such a serious indictment of the therapeutic approach described. To be sure Kovel has explained that Gestalt attends to the emotional life of the whole person, but he has not proposed that Perls suggested that the therapist should attend to the emotions *instead* of the intellect, only *as well* as the intellect. He has talked of the dramatization and enactment of the topdog/underdog split as though they *were* Gestalt therapy *instead* of one of the many ways it has been demonstrated (Laura Perls, 1992). And he has informed us, however inaccurately, that Gestalt mainly heals through fostering intense emotional experiences in a group setting. However none of this amounts to near hysteria or hysterical possession.

   Is there anything in the work of Fritz Perls which could justify such a statement? We think there is. In the 1960s Fritz Perls, the Esalen Institute and the political and social attitude of 'anything goes' were instrumental in popularizing a new model of Gestalt therapy. Yontef has dubbed this style of Gestalt 'boom-boom-boom therapy' and has characterized it as 'a theatrical and highly catharsis oriented approach, arrogant, dramatic, simplistic, and promising quick change' (1991: 8). Some examples of Perls' *own* work (as portrayed in the transcripts) do seem to be primarily aimed at dramatic catharsis rather than awareness, understanding and dialogue (Baumgardner and Perls, 1975: 147, 156; Perls, 1969b: 80, 139, for example). This kind of therapy attracted therapists who had a need to be charismatic and to feature 'peak' or dramatic experiences over careful phenomenological exploration and respect for the safety of the client and his natural tendency to grow.

Many trainees either imitated Perls' more dramatic work or did what Perls *appeared* to do, without Perls' background knowledge or his genius for fine observation. Lieberman, Yalom and Miles' research (1973) into different group therapies featured one Gestalt therapist who fitted into this category (see pp. 158–9). Perls did belatedly realize that his theatrical and sometimes simplified presentation of Gestalt had done the approach harm and he spoke out against the style that he himself had promoted (1969b). Unfortunately he spoke too late. The damage was done. Many, such as Kovel, equated (and still equate) Gestalt therapy with the dramatic, active, sometimes abrasive and confrontational style that Fritz Perls *sometimes* demonstrated on the West Coast. Yontef (1991) has argued that even in the 1960s at least two contrasting styles of Gestalt were already developing – the one theatrical and cathartic and the other hardworking, person to person, dialogic and equally pioneering. He proposes that the latter style and an emphasis upon the paradoxical theory of change have now largely replaced the cathartic model of Gestalt therapy.

Thus, we fully acknowledge the basis of catharsis-oriented work from which Kovel *may* have drawn his impression of 'near hysteria', but we ourselves differentiate between catharsis and hysteria and find no support in the work of Perls for this particular word.

Masson's Accusations

Jeffrey Masson was professor of Sanskrit at the University of Toronto from 1970 to 1980, during which time he underwent a clinical training in psychoanalysis at the Toronto Psychoanalytical Institute, graduating as a psychoanalyst and member of the International Psychoanalytical Association in 1978. In the preface to his book *Against Therapy* (1989) he tells us that because of his doubts concerning the validity of psychoanalysis, he did not practise as a psychoanalyst.

Masson alleges that Perls behaved unethically by having sexual contact with his clients; that he was extremely self-important and made grandiose claims for himself and for Gestalt therapy; and that he arrogated to himself the powers of a traditional guru, including the power to cause great pain and destruction to others. These are extremely serious accusations which have reached a wide readership and must be carefully considered. We will examine each in turn.

Did Perls Behave Unethically by Having Sexual Contact with his Clients?

As Masson has said, Perls made no secret of the fact that he had sexual contact with clients. He wrote about it openly in his autobiography. A number of visitors to Esalen have spoken or written about his sexual approaches to them (Gaines, 1979) and Marty Fromm has spoken and written at length about her fairly prolonged relationship with Perls (Gaines, 1979; Shepard, 1975).

In Chapter 1, we have already made clear our personal attitudes to this aspect of Perls' behaviour. We completely agree with Masson that Perls acted unethically and irresponsibly in this respect. Sexual contact between therapist and client is against current codes of ethics for the practice of Gestalt therapy, and qualified Gestalt therapists and Gestalt trainees in the UK now work to a code of ethics. So Perls' unethical behaviour would not be tolerated within most Gestalt communities of the 1990s. It was also abhorred by many therapists at the time (Alexander Lowen as quoted in Gaines, 1979, for example).

We do not defend Perls in any way, but we contextualize his behaviour by drawing attention to the fact that he and Paul Goodman were anarchistic, intent on challenging convention in principle, and this unfortunately included the flagrant flouting of the necessary boundaries and taboos on sexual contact between therapist and client. Masson criticizes Perls for his brazen avowal of his sexual relationships with patients. We do not agree with Masson that the avowal makes the offence worse. The open acknowledgement of a sexual relationship between therapist and client does not excuse the offence but also does not render it any more serious than that of the many psychotherapists of all orientations who have transgressed this boundary secretly (Rutter, 1990). Indeed some would argue that on grounds of honesty and the degree of harm done, openness makes the offence less, not more, serious.

Did Perls Make Grandiose Claims for Gestalt and for Himself?

Perls believed passionately in the importance of the therapeutic approach which he had been instrumental in developing and, like most other proponents of new approaches or newly synthesized approaches, sometimes made sweeping statements about the pre-eminence of Gestalt: 'But how do we open the ears and eyes of the world? I consider my work to be a small contribution to that problem which might contain the possibility of the survival of mankind' (Perls in Masson, 1989: 254). How far, if at all, does research corroborate his claims for Gestalt?

There are continuing controversies about the relative merits or 'depths' of different psychotherapies. On the other hand, the Fiedler studies (1950) showed growing recognition that there is less difference between competent and experienced therapists from different psychotherapeutic approaches than between inexperienced and experienced psychotherapists within any one approach. Recent research by clinicians throughout the world supports the view that the crucial components in effective therapy are client characteristics and the helping relationship, and not necessarily the choice of psychotherapy system. Neither empirical studies nor comprehensive reviews indicate that any one therapeutic approach can be shown to be superior to another (Bergin, 1971; Frank, 1979; Landman and Dawes, 1982; Luborsky, Singer and Luborsky, 1975; Smith, Glass and Miller, 1980). Considering the weight of such objective evidence, due caution must be exercised when comparing one system of counselling or psychotherapy with another (Clarkson, 1988).

Research, then, does not support Perls' claim for the pre-eminence of Gestalt as a therapeutic approach: so Masson's criticism that Perls made grandiose claims for Gestalt is justified.

Perls' Personal Grandiosity and Self-Importance
Masson quotes extensively from Perls' autobiography to support his claim that Perls was self-important and we accept that this criticism was valid at least some, maybe a good deal, of the time. We also agree with Masson when he suggests that perhaps some of Perls' particularly grandiose claims had a humorous as well as a narcissistic ring to them: 'I believe that I am the best therapist for any type of neurosis in the States, maybe in the world' (Perls in Masson, 1989: 254).

Many others have corroborated Masson's criticism of Perls' personal self-importance (Enright, Naranjo and Hall, for example, in Gaines, 1979). Even affectionate descriptions of Perls during the Esalen period confirm the image of a man who adored being the centre of attention: he has been described as a showman (Yalom, 1985), a ringmaster and a director (Gaines, 1979). Recently Yontef (1991), who also did some training with Perls in the 1960s, affirmed 'Fritz was theatrical, outrageous, narcissistic. . . [F]reed from the influence of the New York City Gestalt therapy group, his tendencies to show off, look for excitement . . . his theatrical background all rose to the fore' (p. 7).

However, as Yontef has succinctly said, Perls engaged people as well as enraging them and there are almost as many people who talk of his love, tenderness and even of his humility as of his narcissism. George Brown for example has said, when describing a tender moment between Perls and Brown's wife, Judith, 'It's sad that you don't hear that kind of thing very often about Fritz, because he was at times a very loving man, tender and caring' (Gaines, 1979: 230). Gabrielle Roth also enthused about his loving softness. Barry Stevens, authoress of *Don't Push the River* (1970), has spoken of his humility and flexibility:

> I knew him during the last three years of his life, and I saw him changing during that time. He was *always* learning and changing. There was a true humility in Fritz, too, which showed up in different ways. It was present when he said he'd discovered he was wrong about something. (Gaines, 1979: 362)

The papers which Perls (1948; 1979) published or delivered in the late 1940s also show instances of his ability to be open and humble about his own work at that time. In the paper he gave at the William Alanson White Institute in 1946–7, he uses a case story in which he feels he has made a mistake as an illustration of his theme, and at the end of the paper he delivered at the Association for the Advancement for Psychotherapy he concludes by modestly inviting the benevolent scepticism of his audience:

> I shall be very happy indeed, if my paper has encouraged you to be benevolently sceptical towards both your own and my present convictions and to make the transition from any compulsive dogmatism to the experimental, insecure, but creative, pioneering attitude for which I can find no better example than the courage of Sigmund Freud. (Perls, 1948: 586).

Was Perls a Guru who Caused Great Pain and Destruction to Others?

However, Masson goes much further in his criticisms of Perls: he feels that Perls was more than narcissistic. He proposes that Perls arrogated to himself the traditional powers of a guru, including the power to cause great pain and destruction to others. We will first discuss the implication that Perls caused pain to others and then consider the question of whether or to what extent he was a guru.

There is no doubt that Perls caused great pain to members of his own family: Masson quotes his daughter's bitter memories of her father. Many have vouched for the fact that his treatment of Laura was often dismissive, rude and very inconsistent. However, in judging their relationship, it is important to bear in mind what Virginia Satir has said: 'The way in which he managed Laura at times . . . awful! But I know enough to know that these things are transactional and not just unilateral' (in Gaines, 1979: 235) – that is that Laura, as well as Fritz, had some responsibility for the field that they co-created. We have briefly touched on his relationship with his children in Chapter 1, and this and his relationship with Laura are amply documented in Shepard (1975) and Gaines (1979).

Masson (1989) implies that Perls also caused pain and destruction in his workshops, 'either directly or by causing the group to turn on, attack, and brutalize one of its members' (p. 257). In the transcripts of Perls' demonstration workshops (Perls, 1969b; 1976; Baumgardner and Perls, 1975), we have not found evidence of the latter. Perls did not to our knowledge incite group members to turn on, attack or brutalize other participants. Indeed he discouraged the participation of other group members. However his own style of doing therapy in these workshops could be *extremely* challenging and confrontative. If a client did not listen to him or seemed phoney and uncooperative, Perls would sometimes dismiss him or her abruptly from the hot seat, for example, with scathing words. Many participants have spoken of the fear or trepidation that this sort of behaviour inspired in them, even though they also often insist that Perls' sharpness led to insight, which they appreciated. Schutz,[3] while acknowledging how much he learnt from Fritz Perls, has criticized some of his more extremely confrontative behaviour as unnecessarily hurtful:

> The Fritzian model is a bit show-offy. On the other hand I've picked up something important from him – the idea that you're responsible for yourself. . . But I don't like the way he handled it. I think he carried it to extremes. When somebody wouldn't do anything, when they were in the hot seat, Fritz would fall asleep or kick them out or something, which was very dramatic and usually effective, but I think, debilitating. (Gaines, 1979: 179)

Again there are many who defend Perls and say he has been misunderstood. Barry Stevens drew attention to the other person's role in the transaction: 'People who think of him as cruel are perceiving him that way' (Gaines, 1979: 307); while John Stevens, author of *Awareness* (1989), and Rollo May, existential psychotherapist and author, have emphasized how discriminating Perls was in his use of confrontation. Virginia Satir, widely published family therapist, who was a colleague and friend of Perls in the 1960s, encapsulates the controversy: 'The man had many sides to him. I've often said that when Fritz was gestalting he was magnificent; when he was Fritzing, he could be a bastard' (Gaines, 1979: 267).

Masson, then, seems justified in suggesting that Perls could cause great pain. Masson does not, however, give a full picture of Perls who had tremendous range as a therapist and could be exquisitely attentive, respectful, present, tender, playful, supportive, gently humorous and extraordinarily perceptive – as is illustrated in the transcripts of his demonstrations and as we hope we have shown in our discussion of his contributions to practice in Chapter 3. Many, many clients spoke of his unique ability to reach and help them:

> I felt he was absolutely trustworthy and had an absolute genius as a therapist. (Sam Keen in Gaines, 1979: 288)

> Fritz had extraordinary attention, immediacy, simplicity, concentration. (Erving Polster, 1992)

> He was one of the first people in my life that I could just play with, totally, without any thought patterns. We would go into mime movement or theater spaces and be absurd together. . . Fritz was right there when I first began to do movement with groups of people. I was very insecure because I had no theories about it; I had no education in it. . . And Fritz really encouraged me to do that. He certainly supported it. (Gabrielle Roth in Gaines, 1979: 262–3)

The confrontative style sometimes associated with Perls and his followers in the 1960s is now considered by many Gestalt therapists to be one rather limited style of Gestalt therapy and was certainly not even the only style that Perls used in his lifetime. Gestalt practice today embodies dialogue, presence and support as well as creative confrontation based on the Gestalt principles of phenomenological awareness and field theory. It is richly flexible as the background to Gestalt therapy and the environment of psychotherapy itself changes (Yontef, 1991; Clarkson, 1991b).

Masson (1989) maintains that Perls clearly thought of himself as a guru, because he dressed and looked the part, with long white beard and hair, beads, sandals, and flowing robes. It is indisputable that Perls did dress as described during his years at Esalen and his short stay at Cowichan, but at the time this was not necessarily the style of a guru, but of a whole generation of hippies and flower children. Also, Perls certainly did not present himself like this for the vast majority of his professional life; photos of him in Germany and in South Africa show a much more traditional-looking analyst. However, Masson is not alone in seeing Perls as guru-like in the late 1960s; Simkin has also suggested that Perls had a tendency to act as a guru.[4]

Others join in criticizing Perls' self-importance. Yontef (1991) says that Perls and the therapists who adopted his theatrical style often led by charisma rather than dialogic contact and phenomenological focusing. Philip Reif, the Benjamin Franklin Professor at the University of Pennsylvania, and Sol Kurt have said that Perls was an egomaniac and a megalomaniac (in Gaines, 1979). Erving Polster (1992) has said that 'I think that Fritz's views have been upstaging Gestalt therapy forever and it has been difficult, over the years, to go beyond his persona and into emphasizing the new ideas he has influenced.'

However none of these witnesses even approach the leap with which Masson (1989) ends his assessment of Perls: 'Perls made no bones about arrogating to himself all the privileges and power of a traditional guru. . . All gurus. . . are only a few steps away from Jonestown' (p. 257). The cult of Jim Jones was exclusive and secretive. He earned between 5 and 10 million dollars in 1978. He had an American Congressman shot and he and his bodyguards arranged the mass suicide of approximately 900 people, including Jones himself. Equating Perls with Jones is nonsense. Whatever his faults – and they were many – and whatever his personal style, Perls was one of the first psychotherapists to allow filming of the process of therapy. His work, more than that of almost any other psychotherapist (excluding Rogers), has been available for public scrutiny. By his sudden association of the violent massacre of Jonestown with the person and practice of Fritz Perls, Masson devalues rather than supports his own arguments.

As we will show in the subsequent development of this chapter, Kovel and Masson were unfortunately not alone in making allegations about Gestalt which render Gestalt virtually unrecognizable to present-day Gestalt theorists and practitioners. Why has Gestalt been reduced and trivialized and attracted such criticisms? We have already indicated that Perls himself contributed to the misrepresentation not only of Gestalt but also sometimes of his own theoretical work. We will now examine in more depth how, and in what ways, Perls invited reductionism and misunderstanding.

Dublin and the False Equation of Gestalt Therapy and Perls-ism

Dublin (1977: 141) has clearly differentiated Gestalt therapy from what he calls 'Perls-ism'. He referred to Perls-ism as that kind of Gestalt which is *neither* Gestalt therapy *nor* existential Gestalt therapy, but a particular articulation of Fritz Perls' 'biological-hedonistic existentialism' (Clarkson, 1991c). Dublin indicated that there are a good many features associated with Perls' ideas and practice in the 1960s which are not *intrinsic* to Gestalt therapy. His paper is important because many people (including Masson and to a lesser extent Kovel) have erroneously assumed that Perls-ism is synonymous with Gestalt therapy. They have described and assessed the practice of Perls as they experienced it in his work-shops or through his published transcripts, and they have assumed that in doing so they are describing and assessing Gestalt therapy. This is not the case. We hope that Chapters 4 and 5 of this book amply illustrate that from the beginning there were other important exponents of Gestalt therapy and that since Perls' death, over twenty years ago, Gestalt therapy has developed and changed and is radically different from the therapy associated with Perls' demonstration workshops. Unfortunately this means that many of the popular summaries of 'Gestalt therapy' (Kovel, 1976; Brown and Pedder, 1991, for example) are misleading, and may in some respects amount to caricatures of Perls-ism rather than any true assessment of Gestalt therapy.

The aspects of Perls-ism which Dublin says are not intrinsically part of Gestalt therapy are mainly direct criticisms of Perls' work and include:

1 his anti-intellectual attitude
2 his view of maturity as extreme hedonistic isolation as represented in the Gestalt prayer
3 his unsupportive stance as a therapist.

We will consider the merits of each of these criticisms in turn.

Perls' Anti-Intellectual Stance
Dublin claims that Perls did not merely minimize or de-emphasize intellectual processes, but outlawed them from his kind of Gestalt therapy, calling them 'mind-fucking'. It is true that Perls described intellectualization, rationalization and most theoretical discussion in this way. Indeed he goes further and dismisses talking about, small talk, and the exchange of social clichés as 'chickenshit'; rationalization and explanatoriness as 'bullshit'; and high-powered intellectual discussion or theorization (such as his own talks on therapy) as 'elephantshit' (Perls, 1969b; 1970). Many have joined Dublin in criticizing Fritz Perls (and hence 'Gestalt') for his/its anti-intellectual stance (Corey, 1991; Rooth, 1987). This criticism was fuelled by Fritz's lack of scholarship (Wysong and Rosenfeld, 1982: 12, 15; Dublin, 1977: 133, 141; Yontef, 1982: 23), his distaste for establishment academia and, in the latter part of his life, his scathing disapproval of intellectual effort.[5]

Although we therefore believe the criticism of anti-intellectualism to be well justified by Perls' own words as well as by witnesses, the charge is not true in *all* respects and deserves to be contextualized.

Perls did not develop his stridently anti-intellectual stance until the 1960s – and indeed he put considerable effort and energy into making intellectual contributions in the earlier part of his career. For example, Fritz, with his wife Laura, co-wrote an academic paper and presented it at the International Psychoanalytic Conference in 1936, travelling all the way from South Africa to Europe to participate in this intellectual debate *par excellence*. In cooperation with Laura he wrote *Ego, Hunger and Aggression* (1947/1969a) at the beginning of the 1940s, which in retrospect can be seen as the embryonic outline of the Gestalt approach, and which Yontef (1992b) has called 'a clear, albeit disorganized, exposition of field theory' (p. 102). In the late 1940s, Perls prepared and presented academic papers (1979, delivered 1946–7; 1948) to the most respected academic associations in New York – the William Alanson White Institute and the Association for the Advancement of Psychotherapy. 'Theory and Technique of Personality Integration' (1948) in particular is a clear, well thought out and coherent presentation of his ideas and includes apt illustrations from his clinical practice. Both the papers mentioned make an eloquent case for the idea that the psychotherapist's philosophy or theoretical position will inform his practice. Perls continued to write papers and give addresses throughout his life (1978a; 1978b; 1970) and many manuscripts currently remain unpublished (Joe Wysong, 1992).

Perls also co-authored *Gestalt Therapy* (Perls, Hefferline and Goodman, 1951/1973), of which the second volume provides a substantial theoretical treatise on Gestalt therapy. Although the literary style of this volume suggests that Goodman was largely responsible for its development and refinement and much of its final writing, From (in Wysong and Rosenfeld, 1982) has said that Perls provided an initial manuscript. A comparison of *Gestalt Therapy* (1951) with *Ego, Hunger and Aggression* (1947/1969a) and 'Theory and Technique of Personality Integration' (1948) suggests that Perls contributed many of the ideas as well as some of the examples and images for the later book – even if they were in a more rudimentary form.

Even in the 1960s, when he derided intellectualization and theoretical discussion, Perls continued to give short theoretical talks to illustrate and explain his practical demonstrations – while sometimes poking fun at himself for doing so. When he realized how others were copying his techniques without understanding the theory of Gestalt, he spoke out against instant therapies, which made rash and oversimplified claims for themselves (Perls, 1969b).

In considering Perls' attitude, it is also important to understand his aims and the context in which he attacked intellectualization. Psychoanalysis had in many instances become rigid (Yontef, 1991) and Perls felt that it had become stuffy and dryly theoretical. He wanted to shock people into sharing his viewpoint and realizing that healing is achieved by real, immediate human contact and not by talking or by erudite theoretical discourse. According to Erving Polster (1989), Perls was gifted at creating slogans which challenged people's ordinary perceptions; he often did this kind of thing. When Fritz Perls said, 'Lose your mind and come to your senses', he was probably sloganeering to undermine intellectualization. But Perls was not seeking to undermine intelligence. Clearly he was an intelligent man, who valued intelligence in others.

However, Perls' challenge to the academicism of his time created an overreaction or an imbalance in the opposite direction so that, for a decade after his death, Gestalt therapists – with notable exceptions – were generally unenthusiastic writers and made relatively few theoretical contributions (Yontef, 1991) (see pp. 161–2). Perls meant to redress the overly intellectualized development of the psychoanalysis of his time. But his emphasis in the 1960s upon the body and feelings, apparently in preference to the mind, was actually contradictory to his own earlier theoretical innovations, that is to Gestalt psychotherapy's holism, which emphasizes wholeness and organismic unity of the organism/ environment field. In any field perspective, the passions of the heart and body cannot be divorced from the mind and still lay any claim to holism (Clarkson, 1988; 1991b). Modern Gestalt therapy has witnessed a return to a valuation of thinking, theory and intellectual creativity, as well as an emphasis on sensory aliveness and emotional expressivity.

Perls' View of Maturity as Autonomy

Perls (1969b; 1976; 1969 preface to Perls, Hefferline and Goodman, 1951/1973) defined maturity as a continuous process of transcending environmental support and developing self-support, with an increasing reduction of dependencies. Dublin (1977) says that there is a terrible aloneness to that definition of maturity which he thinks is most clearly shown in the 'Gestalt prayer':

> I do my thing and you do your thing.
> I am not in this world to live up to your expectations
> And you are not in this world to live up to mine,
> You are you and I am I,
> If by chance we find each other, *it's* beautiful.
> If not, *it can't be helped*. (Perls, 1969b: 4 in Dublin, 1977, Dublin's italics)

Dublin elegantly points out that if Perls had substituted the word 'I' for 'it' as he frequently exhorted others to do, the implication for

Perls would have been grave because the final lines of the 'prayer' would read: 'If by chance we find each other, I'm beautiful / If not, I can't be helped.' Dublin quotes Tubbs' radical revision of Perls' 'prayer' as a reminder of the social interdependence which is actually intrinsic to all but the most extreme 'late-Perlsian' styles of Gestalt:

> If I just do my thing and you do yours,
> We stand in danger of losing each other
> And ourselves.
> I am not in this world to live up to your expectations;
> But I am in this world to confirm you
> As a unique human being,
> And to be confirmed by you.
> We are fully ourselves only in relation to each other;
> The I detached from a Thou
> Disintegrates.
> I do not find you by chance;
> I find you by an active life
> Of reaching out,
> Rather than passively letting things happen to me,
> I can intentionally make them happen.
> I must begin with myself, true;
> But I must not end with myself:
> The truth begins with two. (Tubbs, 1972 in Dublin, 1977: 142)

Perls' intention in his 'prayer' was succinctly to challenge inauthenticity. He originally said it at a time when many members of the helping professions were coming to train with him at Esalen. He believed that some of them were deluding themselves into thinking that they were doing everything they did in order to be 'helpful' to their patients. He wanted to shake their complacency and get them to look deeper at their motivations and concentrate on their own growth, rather than on 'phoney' altruism (Miller, 1989). Again he shocked with a catchy, easily popularized slogan, which caught the attention but oversimplified and was only one extreme of a continuum. His 'prayer' has come to represent the uncaring polarity of Perlsian theory that sometimes makes individualism and responsibility for the self a higher priority than responsibility for the self-and-others-in-community (Clarkson, 1991c).

Many Gestaltist theoreticians and practitioners have been horrified by the almost compulsive autonomy and isolationism expressed by Perls in his prayer and often in other aspects of his later work. Wheeler (1991) for example has criticized Perls for consistently devaluing anything interpersonal by comparison with anything autonomous in his posthumously published books.

Laura Perls obviously felt 'the prayer' was the antithesis of

Gestalt therapy as she, one of its co-founders, conceptualized it:

> He had this ideal of being independent and self-sufficient. But it's adolescent to say, as he did in the Gestalt prayer, 'I am doing my own thing' or 'I am my own person,' because the adolescent comes home, drops his dirty clothes, changes into clean ones and goes out, and takes for granted that Mother takes care of everything. Talking about taking total responsibility for one's life is arrogance: one's life is always interdependent with the lives of other people and to ignore that means to ignore contact. I think Fritz ignored that to a great extent. (in Gaines, 1979: 12)

> While Fritz emphasized the 'confrontation' side of contact at a boundary, Laura emphasized the support side. For example, she would encourage me not to reach out unless I had adequate support. (Serlin, 1992)

Perls' later emphasis upon autonomy rather than upon interdependence as a sign of maturity was not only in direct opposition to the views of the co-founders and other major Gestalt theoreticians of the 1950s and 1960s, it was also in contradiction to his own views. Perls, Hefferline and Goodman (1951/1973), for example, acknowledge the intrinsic social interconnectedness of mature and healthy human nature in several places:

> The underlying social nature of the organism and the forming personality – fostering and dependency, communication, imitation and learning, love-choices and companionship, passions of sympathy and antipathy, mutual aid and certain rivalries – all this is extremely conservative, repressible but ineradicable. And it is meaningless to think of an organism possessing drives which are 'anti-social' in this sense, opposed to his social nature, for this would be a conserved inner contradiction; it would not be conserved. But there are, rather, difficulties of individual development, of growing-up, of realizing all of one's nature. (Perls, Hefferline and Goodman, 1951/1973: 386)

At different times over the twenty-five years that he was speaking and writing, Perls emphasized both extreme individualism and the need for interdependence. Over these twenty-five years he often contradicts himself on this, as on other matters. Sometimes he states one polarity and sometimes the other. The essence of the Gestalt view of polarities is that they coexist, define and determine each other, both representing aspects of the whole:

> The whole is thus represented in any fragment of itself. It is in the nature of holons or wholes that we experience different facets differently at different times. This does not negate the intrinsic wholeness of the phenomenon. But neither does it exclude its containment of opposites.

Whatever is said fully and completely, the opposite also begins to be true. . . This is in the nature of the notion of polarities, turning into each other at their apotheosis. Both Jung [1968] and Perls refer to this by the name of 'enantiodromia'. In chaos theory this phenomenon is known as the 'flipover' effect and in Gestalt we are familiar with it in terms of the paradoxical theory of change. (Clarkson, 1991c: 28)

Was Perls an 'Unsupportive' Therapist?

The implications of Perls' definition of maturity (as the transcendence of environmental support and the acquisition of autonomy or self-support) for his therapeutic practice during the 1960s were great. Dublin (1977) says that the 'Perlsian' style of therapist who adopts this definition of maturity is 'almost utterly and consistently non-supportive' (p. 143). In Chapter 3 (p. 107) we have explained and contextualized Perls' belief that *one* of the important roles of the therapist is to frustrate the client's attempts to get the therapist to provide the environmental support which the client craves. Dublin does not deny that the role of therapist may sometimes be to frustrate, but he says that Perls was not merely a frustrator but a radical frustrator who took the art of frustration to extremes, refusing to answer questions or 'help' the client in any way.

This is really overstating the case, for Perls always stressed that the therapist must work with support *as well as* frustration (see pp. 86–7 and 107). Transcripts of Perls' work do show many instances of his behaving in a deliberately challenging fashion. Sometimes his deliberate lack of support did appear to help the client find his own creative vitality. Other times Perls' unsupportive style became so extreme that he seemed to be mocking the client in a way that now seems offensive. However the transcripts also show many examples of Perls working with great patience (as for example the work with May and the wall, featured in Chapter 3: Perls, 1969b) and with gentle and tender support (as for example in the work with Jean, also featured in Chapter 3: Perls, 1969b). Participants in his workshops have described how attentive and tender he could be on occasion (see p. 141) and how his frustration and confrontation could at times be profoundly supportive in their existential quest for understanding of themselves and search for meaning. Polster (1992) has said that a lot of the work chosen for the films and books featured colourful, dramatic confrontations and he suggests that there were also many interactions between Perls and clients, even in the 1960s, where the client felt supported and in tune with Fritz.

Yalom's View of Perls

Yalom (Professor of Psychiatry at Stanford University of Medicine) is author of three authoritative works: *Existential Psychotherapy* (1980), *Theory and Practice of Group Psychotherapy* (1985) and *Love's Executioner and Other Tales of Psychotherapy* (1989); as well as co-author of a thorough and extensive research investigation of different approaches to group psychotherapy (Lieberman, Yalom and Miles, 1973).

Yalom's descriptions of Perls' contribution to existential therapy (1980) and to group therapy (1985) were generally favourable and showed a real understanding of the essence of Gestalt therapy and the depth and complexity of its theory. He identified the fact that Gestalt theory and practice are often seriously misrepresented and asked the key question, 'How has it come about that so many have mistaken the substance for the essence of the Gestalt approach?' His answer to his own question is that 'The cornerstone for the error was, unwittingly, laid by the founder of Gestalt therapy, Fritz Perls, who had a creative, technical virtuosity which acted in such consort with his flair for showmanship so as to lead many to mistake the medium for the message' (Yalom, 1985: 447).

Yalom's and Perls' Attitude Towards Support and
Responsibility
Yalom (1980) discusses Perls' attitude regarding confronting the client with his own essential responsibility for himself and acknowledges Perls' contributions to this debate in a generally positive fashion, showing much greater understanding of Perls' existential view than most commentators:

> Of the proponents of an active therapist style in the approach to responsibility, none have been more vigorous or inventive than Fritz Perls. Perls's approach rests on the basic concept that responsibility avoidance must be recognized and discouraged. (p. 246)

> This approach to symptoms – asking the patient to produce or augment a symptom – is often an effective mode of facilitating responsibility awareness. . .Though they have not conceptualized it in terms of responsibility assumption, several other therapists have simultaneously arrived at the same technique. Victor Frankl, for example . . . Don Jackson, Jay Haley, Milton Erickson, and Paul Watzlawick have all written on the same approach, which they label 'symptom prescription'. (pp. 247–8)

However, after continuing to commend Perls for his insights regarding responsibility, Yalom criticizes Perls for the way he said he typically started his workshops in the 1960s:

> So if you want to go crazy, commit suicide, improve, get 'turned on,'

or get an experience that will change your life, that's up to you. I do my thing and you do your thing. Anybody who does not want to take responsibility for this, please do not attend this seminar. You came here out of your own free will. I don't know how grown up you are, but the essence of a grown-up person is to be able to take responsibility for himself – his thoughts, feelings, and so on. (Perls in Yalom, 1980: 250)

Regarding this passage Yalom takes a position similar to Dublin's, saying that this is an extraordinarily severe position regarding the personal responsibility of clients and suggests that it requires modification.

We think that Yalom and Dublin are fully justified in criticizing Perls for declining to take almost any special responsibility for his clients in the instances quoted and we believe that the therapist does have specialist forms of professional responsibility. Without detracting from the individual's potential for taking personal responsibility for his life, it is necessary to recognize that realistically many clients enter therapy disturbed or distressed and are not *at that time* able or willing to take as much responsibility as the therapist. For example many Gestalt clinicians, from the very beginning of the history of Gestalt until the present day, have described the particular responsibilities of the therapist in the therapeutic relationship (Laura Perls, 1992; Yontef, 1980; Hycner, 1985; Jacobs, 1989; Clarkson, 1989; 1991b; etc.). Another example of specialist professional responsibility is that some therapists of all orientations, including Gestalt, ask highly stressed or suicidal clients to make a 'no harm' contract (Shearman, 1993), in which they agree not to harm themselves or others or go mad for a specified period of time. Such an approach can significantly diminish risk to the client. In addition reputable Gestalt training courses no longer take anything resembling Perls' irresponsible attitude regarding their trainees. It is invariably a prerequisite of substantial Gestalt training that trainees are in personal therapy themselves at least for the duration of their training course, so that they have a safe place to explore issues that are raised as a result of their experiences in their training group and so as to ensure that they have done the personal exploration that is essential if they are to become safe and responsible psychotherapists.

Perls and the Reduction of Gestalt to Gestalt Techniques
Gestalt is frequently mistakenly thought to be a set of techniques or structured exercises, such as role-play, two-chair work or awareness exercises. This reductionistic attitude towards Gestalt is exemplified by comments such as 'I used Gestalt on my dream' or 'I use a bit of Gestalt in my practice.' Even Yalom (who, as we

have said, showed a real understanding of the essence of Gestalt) occasionally reduces the Gestalt approach to a set of techniques, as when he talks of sending patients to try a weekend of 'powerful. . . Gestalt affect-arousing techniques' (1980: 307) as though that could be a way of researching the efficacy of Gestalt therapy.

Gestalt therapy is not, however, about techniques or quick catchy gimmicks: it's a process of working with phenomenological awareness, experimenting, creating and dialoguing. According to Resnick, a true Gestaltist would be barely affected if every technique that any Gestalt therapist had ever used before were never used again. 'Gestalt therapy has as its core holistic, phenomenological, existential, humanistic and dialogic elements whose matrix is ignited and grows, limited only by the therapist's background and creative richness' (Resnick, 1984: 19).

How, if at all, did Perls contribute to this misunderstanding? He himself claimed that he did not use techniques as such (see pp. 96–7 for a further discussion of this controversy). In his best work he invented new experiments, to explore the difficulties or interruptions to awareness which arose in the dialogue between each individual client and himself. 'Although he sometimes appeared to use similar or slightly repetitive experiments, they always had a unique quality which is not fully conveyed by the transcripts. He always looked for freshness' (Polster, 1992). He discovered new challenges and found opportunities to stretch and develop people in ever newly minted ways. Some of the spontaneous elegance and originality with which Perls often creatively transformed moment-to-moment encounters is illustrated in Chapter 3.[6] Perls' best work may be contrasted with the forced application of so-called 'Gestalt techniques', for example the routine or unimaginative use of two-chair work, where there is no incomplete Gestalt calling for this kind of completion.

However, the experiments which Perls created in the moment were effective and often dramatic. Many people either copied Perls' more crude and repetitive work or did what Perls appeared to do without understanding the Gestalt theories of phenomenological awareness, dialogue, or experiment. Perls' *repetitive* work and the *imitations* of his style *were* often techniques and gimmicks and that is how Gestalt has often come to be seen as merely structured exercises (see above).

In a later publication Yalom (1985) demonstrates that he has well understood the common error which reduces Perls' contributions to a series of virtuoso exercises. He states that Gestalt therapy as a major source of structured exercises has been 'considered by some as a speedy, pre-packaged, gimmick-oriented therapy, whereas in fact it offers a therapeutic approach based on the deepest and most unpalatable of truths' (p. 447). Yalom emphasizes that, on the basis of Perls' client sessions (Perls, 1969b; 1976), as well as his theoretical essays, Perls was essentially 'concerned with problems of existence, of self-awareness, of responsibility, of contingency, of wholeness both within one individual and within the individual's social and physical universe' (p. 447). A true Gestalt therapist does not base himself or herself on the techniques of Perls or of any other therapist but abhors technique or gimmicks devoid of understanding (Clarkson, 1989).

Contradictions between Perls' Ideas and his Practice
It is frequently suggested that in certain specific respects, Perls preached one message but practised another, often without any recognition that he did so. Yalom (1980) has drawn attention to one important illustration of this discrepancy: Perls told his clients to assume responsibility for themselves and yet his personal style contradicted his words. Yalom suggests that the client's lived experience was in fact of an enormously powerful, charismatic, actively directive, wise old man who gave the verbal advice 'Assume responsibility' while at the same time conveying the non-verbal communication of 'And I'll tell you precisely how, when and why to do it.' The client was therefore receiving two contradictory messages simultaneously – one explicit and one implicit. Transcripts of Perls' work abound with instances where his active and authoritarian or directive style offer the client little choice and leave him little space to take personal responsibility in the here-and-now interaction, as is illustrated by the following example, where Perls has been working with Elaine on a dream in which she is afraid a priest because she has no control of the situation:

> F: Okeh, put the turmoil in this chair. Talk to your turmoil. . .
> E: You have no- My tur-. . . You have no, no means of – I have no means of *dealing* with you.
> F: Yah. Now be the turmoil that controls you. 'Elaine, I am your turmoil. I control you.'
> E: I will keep you moving. / F: Say this again. /
>   I will keep you moving. / F: Again. /
>   Uhuh, moving. / F: Again. /
>   I will keep you moving. / F: Say this to the audience. /
>   I will keep you moving. / F: Say this to a few people here.
>   /
>   I will keep you moving. I will keep you moving. I will keep you moving.

F: So how do you do this? How do you keep people moving?. . .

E: By letting them become involved – in what I'm saying. / F: Umhum. / But I'm in control.

F: Umhum. Now talk again to the group and give us a speech of about a minute. 'I am control mad. I have to control the world, I have to control myself –.'

E: I'm control mad. I have to control people. I have to control myself. I have to control the world. When I control the world, then I can deal with it, but when I'm in control, I have no means of dealing with it. So then I become lost, so I'm. . . (Perls, 1969b: 145)

[*With one important exception, all Perls' frequent interventions in this passage are directions. Not only does he repeatedly tell Elaine what to do, e.g. 'talk to your turmoil' or 'talk to the group', but he even makes up her speeches for her!*]

On the basis of this and much other evidence, we agree with Yalom that Perls did not resolve (and probably did not recognize) the paradox between his own active, directive style and his belief that the therapist must not accept the burden of the patient's responsibility. In this transcript Perls is working with Elaine to get her to re-own the power and control she has projected on to the priest in the dream. But with the undoubted advantages of distance and time, we wonder whether Perls may not also have been projecting *his own* unrecognized need to control upon Elaine?

In Perls' defence, this work can be reframed as an example of exaggerating one polarity, in order to be more fully in contact with what *is* and thus, by the paradoxical theory of change (see p. 90), facilitate change. Indeed the interaction actually finishes with Elaine exploring the opposite polarity – her lostness – in a way that is unique to her and which Perls makes no attempt to control. He seems in fact most respectful of her own personal space at this point:

F: What happens when you get lost?

E: (relaxed) Oh, I'm slowly moving, at peace with myself.

F: Yah. / Swirling . . . soft . . . absence of tension.

F: Does it feel good?. . .

E: In contrast. Yes.

F: Yah. . . So what happened when you got lost? When you are not in control?. . .

E: It's . . . I can – I can describe it – it's a movement of the sea when the tide and the surf is slowly rolling, and – only – I am a part of the movement and the swirl, it's not violent.

And I slowly move, in a circle. I am turning, my body is slowly turning, as the sea turns – that's how I feel. (Perls, 1969b: 145)

Conclusion

In this chapter we have considered the main criticisms which have been levelled at Perls and his work. Some of these criticisms we have found to be fully justified, as for example the accusation that Perls behaved unethically by having sexual contact with clients and the charge that Perls made grandiose claims for Gestalt and for himself. Some of the criticisms – such as that Perls caused pain, that he sometimes played down verbal explanations and that he used techniques and gimmicks – we have found to be partially justified. Other criticisms of Perls we have shown to be one-sided and misrepresentative of Perls as a whole, if taken out of context. We have attempted to contextualize the criticisms which fall into this category – as for instance Perls' anti-intellectual stance, his view of maturity and his attitude towards support and responsibility. Finally some of the criticisms seem to us to be entirely unjustified and based on gossip, prejudice or a very partial understanding of Perls. Unjustified criticisms of Perls include the suggestions that Perls minimized the past and that Perls had no theory of transference.

In addition, Chapter 4 shows that Perls is not Gestalt therapy. Chapter 5, which follows, develops the theme of how far Perls is, or is not, synonymous with Gestalt therapy by discussing Perls' overall influence upon the subsequent development of Gestalt psychotherapy and upon the whole field of counselling and psychotherapy.

Notes

1. This common error is fully explored in the third section of this chapter (see p. 142).

2. The style of Gestalt therapy which Kovel describes is that represented in these transcripts, and three out of four of his references are to this book.

3. Schutz, author of *Joy* (1967) and one of the founders of the encounter movement, was a trainer in residence at Esalen at the same time as Perls; many have witnessed to the rivalry between Schutz and Perls at the time.

4. Masson and Simkin both seem to be using the word 'guru' in a rather negative, limited Westernized sense. Originally it was not meant as an insult but signified an honoured spiritual leader (Albery, 1992).

5. Yontef (1982) has written that: 'Perls' style was often unscholarly and brash. His knowledge of Gestalt psychology was limited. His popular, cliché-level statements have attracted attention and have been treated by many as representing

Gestalt therapy. This style is antithetical to any good scholarship, including the careful scientific approach of the classical Gestaltists. Moreover, taken without careful definition and without an adequate, overall Gestalt therapy perspective, some of these statements not only appear discrepant from Gestalt psychology, but are internally contradictory as well.'

6. Yontef (1992c) has pointed out that Perls himself sometimes used his own creative inventions repetitively so that, on occasion, they did become rather gimmicky techniques, despite his own claims to the contrary and his passionate conviction that a Gestalt therapist can respond freshly to each unfolding moment.

The Overall Influence of Fritz Perls

Introduction

This chapter discusses the influence of Fritz Perls upon the subsequent theory and practice of Gestalt therapy and upon the overall field of psychotherapy and counselling. The first part of the chapter appraises the influence of Perls upon theory and practice in Gestalt. It describes his general role as co-founder and disseminator of Gestalt therapy; it then examines his practical impact upon the reputation and practice of Gestalt, as well as upon the theory of Gestalt, arguing that in both cases his personal impact both helped and hindered the evolution of Gestalt. The second part of the chapter is a section on developments in Gestalt since Perls' death in 1970. It describes some of the many new theoretical and practical contributions which have developed in Gestalt and discusses whether or not Perls has had any influence upon these later developments. The third part of the chapter looks at how some of Perls' ideas have now been absorbed into the broad field of psychotherapeutic and counselling theory or have been 'reinvented' since his death by theoreticians of many schools. Finally the conclusion explores some of the questions raised by the attempt that we have made in this book to summarize or encapsulate the essence of Perls' work.

Co-founder and Disseminator of Gestalt Therapy

Fritz Perls is still widely described as the founder or primary founder of Gestalt therapy (Nelson-Jones, 1982; Corey, 1991, for example). In Chapter 1 we have demonstrated that he was not the sole founder of Gestalt therapy but one of the three main co-founders – Fritz Perls, Laura Perls, Paul Goodman – who in turn developed their early ideas in discussion with other important contributors. The exact proportion of Fritz's role – as opposed to that of Laura or of Paul Goodman – continues to be debated. However, rightly or wrongly, of the three co-founders he was and still is the best known in the wider world, beyond the confines of the discipline of Gestalt therapy.

Perls was extremely energetic in his efforts both to establish Gestalt as an independent school of psychotherapy and especially to ensure its spread through the United States and Canada. Within a few years of his arrival in New York, he established an itinerant lifestyle in which he travelled all over the USA in order to promote his ideas. For example in 1950 he spent part of the year in Los Angeles, where he and Isadore From tried to spread his 'here-and-now' approach to therapy and where he saw a number of clients for individual therapy. In the early 1950s he, Isadore From and Laura Perls made regular visits to Cleveland, where he contributed to the training of the young Erving Polster and others who soon became the founder members of the Cleveland Gestalt Institute.

This highly mobile lifestyle continued. From New York, he went to Florida; from Florida, he went to Ohio and back to Florida. He left Florida again when he was invited to become a consultant to the Mendocino State Hospital – a golden opportunity to introduce Gestalt therapy to professionals in the state system of psychiatry and psychology. Then it was San Francisco and Los Angeles, from where he made weekly trips along the freeways, holding train-ing/therapy groups at various hospitals and centres *en route*. Finally established at Esalen, he remained resident for five years, but continued to give talks and demonstrations throughout the United States and Canada, as well as attracting visitors to Esalen from all over the world.

The Gestalt approach which Perls co-founded and was so energetic in disseminating is now established and flourishing. Train-ing centres exist in many places including Israel, South America, Canada, France, Germany, Yugoslavia, Czechoslovakia, Scan-dinavia, Russia and Japan, in addition to those in the United States. In many of these countries the Gestalt approach has been integrated into the provision of a wide range of psychotherapy and counselling services, including for example in medical and psychiatric settings, in educational settings, in social work settings and in private prac-tice. The Gestalt approach is also used in organizational and consultancy work in both the USA and the UK (see Nevis, 1987; Clark and Fraser, 1987; Clarkson and Shaw, 1992, for instance).

Perls' Personal Impact on the Practice of Gestalt

Thus Perls co-founded a school of psychotherapy which has become widely established in the Western industrialized world. However his impact upon the establishment of Gestalt therapy and other therapies is more complex than that statement suggests. Perls both helped and hindered the establishment of Gestalt as a discrete and respected school of psychotherapy.

Perls brought Gestalt therapy to the attention of a wide public by doing innumerable workshop demonstrations, by making recordings, videos and films of his work and by seeking publicity through interviews, television and journalistic cover – so that Gestalt therapy, as Perls practised it at Esalen, became well known to many lay, as well as professional people. Perls also sought to make the theory which informed his therapy understandable to an average intelligent reader by continually trying to simplify his message (Perls, 1969b; 1976; Baumgardner and Perls, 1975). In addition Perls had a talent for inventing clever and witty phrases (see p. 26 for examples) which caught on and also furthered the spread of a popular form of Gestalt therapy.

However all these contributions towards the dissemination of 1960s Perlsian Gestalt therapy had drawbacks, because they tended to popularize and reduce a serious and richly complex approach. Many people who did not know the earlier substantial theoretical works of Perls and his colleagues, and who did not understand or experience Perls' intuitive genius and range, saw Gestalt as a clever, abrasive and sensationalist approach which over-emphasized catharsis and confrontation. In Chapter 4 we have argued that this form of Gestalt was not Gestalt therapy but one style of Gestalt which imitates Perls' 'techniques' without his flexibility or creativity. Borrowing from Dublin (1977) we have called this style of Gestalt 'Perls-ism' or Perlsian Gestalt. The way we teach and use Gestalt in the nineties is as an integrative, theoretical and methodological system, encompassing physiology, emotionality, behaviour, intellectual nourishment, societal connection and spirituality. However the excesses of some of the practitioners of the 1960s resulted in a widespread and pervasive distrust of Gestalt therapy in public as well as professional domains, which has only gradually and recently begun to shift. There are still Gestaltists who cling to the outdated ethos of a belligerent and hostile style as the hallmark of Gestalt. But as Perls himself said, 'How can you have sameness in this rapid-changing world?' (1969b: 30).

The widespread and at the same time ambiguous nature of Perls' personal impact upon the practice of Gestalt in the 1970s is well illustrated by Lieberman, Yalom and Miles (1973), who reviewed and assessed the style and efficacy of seventeen groups representing nine different types of groups or 'group technologies' popular around the time of Perls' death.[1] Two out of sixteen of the leaders described themselves as Gestaltists, while another two claimed to be substantially influenced by Gestalt.

One of the Gestalt therapists (leader of group number three) was described as being anti-intellectual, active and using a high number of 'structured exercises'. He was more interested in here-and-now interaction (both intra- and interpersonal) than in historical material or abstract issues. He was open and self-revealing regarding his own here-and-now feelings and personal values. He was considered highly challenging, and engendered a group which affirmed confrontation and emotional expression. He was also seen as very supportive, competent and warm. Overall this Gestalt group leader was rated second by participants and almost equally highly by the observers. There were no psychological casualties in this group.[2] The influence of Perls' style and practice upon this leader seems fairly evident and the outcome was excellent. Such research findings certainly support the claim for the efficacy and benefits of the Gestalt approach, including a well integrated (not introjected) Perlsian style of Gestalt.

However a second Gestalt therapist (leader of group number four) was found to be attention-seeking, dominant, melodramatic, anti-intellectual, irresponsible. He seems to have copied and exaggerated the worst aspects of Perls' charismatic style without Perls' experience, originality or genius. For example he ridiculed and insulted people in the group, regularly fell asleep (or feigned sleep) as Perls had done on individual occasions, and even used almost identical phrases to those Perls is recorded as saying. He also took Perls' demanding position on personal responsibility (see Chapter 4, p. 149) to a further extreme. His blaming attitude may be contrasted with Perls' sometimes painstaking work with clients who felt stuck at an impasse (see pp. 116–20). Finally this Gestaltist fondled both male and female members of the group in an overtly sexual way (as Perls had done).

This group had the largest number of psychological casualties in the study and members generally reported a lowered sense of self-esteem, became less lenient towards themselves and saw the environment as less lenient. Members of the group would not have wanted to be in a group with this leader again. They felt he was too obtrusive and one member of the group felt he was destructive. The leader showed sarcastic disinterest when an investigator later alerted him to the psychological injuries suffered by members of the group.

Although Perls cannot be held responsible for therapeutic work, either good or bad, done by other Gestaltists, both the beneficial and the damaging *influence* of his personal style upon the practice of Gestalt therapy in the 1970s is evident from these two examples.

As Yontef (1991) has concluded: 'Clearly, how the therapist prac-
tises results in a wide range of results, from very therapeutic to
precipitating psychotic breakdown. And the label used by the
therapist, e.g. Gestalt therapist, does not in itself indicate the
quality of the therapy' (p. 12).

Widespread though Perls' influence was upon the practice of
Gestalt in the 1960s and 1970s, Yontef (1991) has pointed out that
his was not the only influence even at this period. For example,
Simkin had a very different style – concerned, contactful, actively
present and emphasizing the existential theme of responsibility
without pressurizing the client. Simkin ran training workshops at
Esalen and in Los Angeles, both with Perls and alone, and thus had
a considerable influence upon a whole wave of Gestalt therapists,
including Yontef who has, in turn, made a widespread impact upon
the development of Gestalt, especially through his prolific and
scholarly writing. From the 1950s, Paul Goodman, Isadore From,
Laura Perls and others were also training Gestalt therapists in a
different style of Gestalt in New York, Cleveland and elsewhere:

> The style that Fritz Perls developed in demonstration workshops for
> professionals during the last few years of his life has become widely
> known . . . The dramatization of dreams and fantasies is a beautiful
> demonstration method. . . But it is only *one* aspect of the infinite
> possibilities in the Gestalt approach. It is not useful in working with
> very disturbed people and not usable at all with the real schizophrenic
> or paranoid patient. Fritz Perls knew this very well and simply by-
> passed workshop participants where he sensed the schizoid or paranoid
> disturbance. (Laura Perls, 1992: 51)

However the influence of the other co-founders and trainers of
Gestalt in the early years was not so dramatic or far-reaching, and
Fritz Perls' impact remained dominant until other voices began to
publish their ideas and examples of clinical practice in the later
1970s and 1980s and thus eventually reached as wide an audience
as Perls had done in his lifetime: 'They spoke out later, after the
theatrical demonstrations of Fritz and his imitators had made an
indelible impression on the professional and lay public' (Yontef,
1991: 10).

Perls' Impact upon the Theory of Gestalt

Together with Laura Perls and Paul Goodman, Perls started a
radically new psychotherapeutic approach. With contributions
from Laura Perls, Perls wrote *Ego, Hunger and Aggression*
(1947/1969a); he wrote 'Theory and Technique of Personality
Integration' (1948) and other papers; and he co-authored *Gestalt*

Therapy (Perls, Hefferline and Goodman, 1951/1973). Perls (1947/1969a) and his colleagues (1951/1973) emphasized what people can learn through developing their awareness. Perls (1947/1969a) introduced the idea that therapist and client grew by being actively present and engaged in the contact of the therapeutic exchange, and validated the client's moment-to-moment experience rather than insisting on sometimes arcane interpretations of that experience in terms of transference and a complex theory of childhood development.[3] He and Goodman developed the powerful and innovative ideas of experimentation and active therapy. Clients were encouraged to try out something new and allow increased awareness and insight to emerge from the experimental behaviour. Efforts to learn by trial and error (Perls, 1947/1969a) were validated, instead of being labelled 'acting out'. Perls helped to popularize the field ideas of Wertheimer's Gestalt psychology and Kurt Lewin with their emphasis upon the psychological reality of the present and the interconnectedness of all aspects of the perceived field. He also helped to nurture an interest in process rather than content and causality. (See Chapter 2 of this book for a summary of Perls' theoretical contributions.)

Perls' contributions to theory have remained the foundations and cornerstones of Gestalt therapy. Fifty years have not invalidated them or brushed them aside. Knowledge and understanding of the theoretical contributions of Perls and his colleagues are still essential to the student of Gestalt therapy or anyone else who wishes to understand the Gestalt approach. Workshops based on Perls, Hefferline and Goodman are still offered in training centres around the world, to help the student destructure, chew over and assimilate a book which is not easy to understand on first reading, rather as Isadore From taught Gestalt theory from Perls, Hefferline and Goodman's text in the early days of the Cleveland Institute. Thus Perls' influence in past, present and probably future Gestalt theory remains crucial.

However, Perls' impact upon the theoretical development of Gestalt was not all beneficial. Although he and his colleagues contributed the first theoretical foundations of Gestalt as discussed above, Perls' later anti-intellectual stance had an inhibiting effect upon the development of Gestalt theory in the 1960s and 1970s. It is a puzzling and regrettable phenomenon that so many of the best of the original founders and theoreticians of Gestalt didn't write. Laura Perls, for example, was kind, considerate, intellectual – psychologically the opposite pole from the extroverted performer she married. Although she was one of the finest repositories of responsible, careful, well informed Gestalt psychotherapy, she published only a few articles and no book on Gestalt in her lifetime.

Was there anything about Perls and his ambience that discouraged colleagues, trainees and graduates from writing? Did the Gestaltists of the period simply prefer the oral tradition? Or were they reluctant to do the hard work of formulating and organizing material which is involved in writing? Perhaps their small written output was partly due to Perls' frequent scathing condemnation of intellectualization, or 'chickenshit, bullshit and elephantshit', to use his terms (From, 1984: 9–10). Knowing that the man they looked up to was likely to demolish intellectual effort, with such patent disregard, would probably have been a major disincentive for those amongst Perls' trainees who might otherwise have been inclined to write. Perls' theoretical skill lay in his ability to assemble and synthesize much knowledge through a kind of osmosis from others who knew more and read more than he ever would; his acknowledgement and referencing of his sources was notoriously negligent or inconsistent; his practical artistry lay in the moment of discovery or engagement with a person. In short, his talents were not primarily scholarly and he found it difficult to accept that other ways of embodying or writing Gestalt could be of equal and different value to his own.

'As Fritz Perls himself would insist, any unipolar articulation of experience cannot truly be Gestalt since Gestalt always implies figure-in-background, organism in environment, content in context' (Clarkson, 1991c: 29). A Gestalt therapy which denies the intellect is as unholistic as therapies which underemphasize the body, emotions or spirit. Times have changed. To quote Perls (1947/1969a): 'Everything is in a state of flux – even the density of the same substances with differences of pressure, gravitation and temperature' (p. 22). Gestalt theory too is in flux. It continues in a process of change, frequently swinging from one polarity to another. Perls was reacting extremely to what he experienced as the over-intellectualized and rigidified approach of psychoanalysis. In the 1970s, the pendulum began slowly swinging back from Perls' extreme anti-intellectual later position and, in the last fifteen or more years, Gestalt thinkers have been developing and writing an abundance of new theory without losing the fresh, direct contactfulness of the Gestalt approach in practice.

Beyond Perls: Developments in Gestalt Theory since 1970

Gestalt therapy literature began slowly to augment in the 1970s. Fagan and Shepherd (1970) edited and contributed to an important book of papers on Gestalt. Perls' two posthumous books (1976; Baumgardner and Perls, 1975) were published. The Polsters (1974) wrote one of the most readable books on Gestalt today. Simkin (1974) and Latner (1974) wrote books on Gestalt therapy, while Zinker (1978) contributed a fresh, lyrical exploration of the creative process in Gestalt therapy, also still very popular. Two more composite books appeared, *Gestalt Is* (Stevens, 1975) and *The Growing Edge of Gestalt Therapy* (Smith, 1977); while the *Gestalt Journal* was begun in New York in 1978 and has stimulated, as well as disseminated, a growing wealth of theoretical debate and development in the 1980s and 1990s. The Cleveland Institute has published, among others, books such as *Organizational Consulting: A Gestalt Approach* (Nevis, 1987), *Body Process: A Gestalt Approach to Working with the Body in Psychotherapy* (Kepner, 1987) and *Gestalt Reconsidered* (Wheeler, 1991). In 1989 *Gestalt Counselling in Action* by Petrüska Clarkson was published by Sage, which has now been translated into both Russian and Italian. In the last few years and at the time of writing there has been an escalation of Gestalt publication, including *Living at the Boundary* (Laura Perls, 1991), *Personality Disorders* (Delisle, 1993), *Awareness, Process and Dialogue* (Yontef, 1992c) and *Presence of Mind – Literary and Philosophical Roots of a Wise Psychotherapy* (Schoen, 1993).

Important theoretical developments in Gestalt theory in the last decade abound and space precludes the discussion of all of them. We are choosing to briefly consider the following:

1 developments and diagrammatic representations of the Gestalt cycle
2 the development of theories of group process
3 the expansion of the concepts of relationship and phenomenological dialogue
4 the integration of knowledge and ideas from other disciplines, including psychoanalysis
5 the re-examination of the place of field theory
6 the retrieval of the creative life force – Physis – in Gestalt psychotherapy.

In this section, we will describe each of the above examples in turn, exploring how current ideas on these areas of theory have developed and differed from Perls' position, and reviewing how, if at all, Perls influenced them.

Developments and Diagrammatic Representations of the Gestalt Cycle
Many Gestalt theorists have developed and refined Perls' (1947/

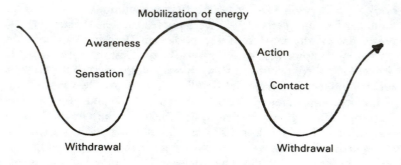

Figure 5.1 *Awareness-excitement-contact cycle (from* Creative Process in Gestalt Therapy *by Joseph Zinker, 1978)*

1969a) cycle of interdependency of organism and environment, and Perls, Hefferline and Goodman's (1951/1973) process of contact. Each has understood the cycle in his or her own unique way and configured it slightly differently, often giving it a new name (the cycle of experience, the cycle of contact and withdrawal, the cycle of Gestalt formation and destruction, for example). One of the most important developments of the cycle is the fact that many

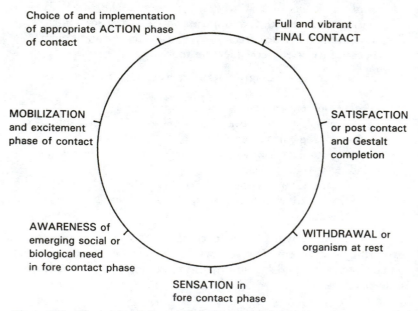

Figure 5.2 *The cycle of Gestalt formation and destruction (from* Gestalt Counselling in Action *by Petrūska Clarkson, 1989)*

theorists have chosen to represent it diagrammatically (Hall, 1977; Kepner, 1987; Zinker, 1978; Parlett and Page, 1990; Clarkson, 1989), either as a wave or as a circle. We give two examples of the many representations in Figures 5.1 and 5.2. We believe that this frequent and graphic representation has contributed to the fact that the Gestalt cycle is one of the best known and understood aspects of Gestalt theory.

How far did Perls contribute to the diagrammatic representation of the cycle? Although he himself never published an illustration of his cycle, a comparison of Zinker's stages with Perls' (1947/1969a) version and Perls, Hefferline and Goodman's (1951/1973) version (see p. 50) illustrates that he took Perls as his starting point. Zinker's stages are clearly based on Perls', and Clarkson states specifically that the cycle she uses is based on Zinker, Perls, Hefferline and Goodman, for which she demonstrates an antecedent in Smuts (Clarkson, 1989). Her particular contribution consists in using the cycle to frame and explicate the process of psychotherapy, its progressions as well as its interruptions.

Development of Theories of Group Process in Gestalt

Gestalt Therapy Now (Fagan and Shepherd, 1970) was an extensive collection of articles by leading Gestalt practitioners, psychologists and psychiatrists of the time, including Elaine Kepner, Claudio Naranjo, Erving Polster, Laura Perls, Ruth Cohn, Joen Fagan, Irma Lee Shepherd and James Simkin. Some of these writers describe the integration of Perls' hot seat method with group interaction; others describe Gestalt in family therapy and in interactive therapy groups where the participants are encouraged to make contact with each other and deal directly one with the other. Polster and Polster (1974) devoted a chapter to groups and group process and pointed out that the hot seat method of working was only one way of working with a group. They described, both practically and theoretically, other ways in which they were doing Gestalt group therapy.

Zinker (1978) outlined the principles of Gestalt group process as developed at the Gestalt Institute of Cleveland: '1) the primacy of ongoing group experience; 2) the process of developing group awareness; 3) the importance of active contact between participants; and 4) the use of interactional experiments stimulated by an actively involved leader' (p. 162). Zinker sees the group as a microcosm of society which has the capability of not only re-creating the social system but also modifying it.

This is obviously a major departure from the way that Perls practised in his demonstrations. However Zinker (1978) acknowledged the influence as well as the value of Perls' way of working in practice, telling us that the group members 'surrounded [him], observed and were often delighted with the skill and artistry of Fritz's work with the individual member' (p. 159).

Beyond the Hot Seat (Feder and Ronall, 1980) is a collection of theoretical discussions of group process in Gestalt. One of the most influential has been 'Gestalt Group Process' by Elaine Kepner. Kepner, also from the Gestalt Institute of Cleveland, described Gestalt group process as it has evolved at that Institute, with different emphases and in greater detail than Zinker (1978). She presented an integration of a systems perspective with Gestalt group practice, acknowledging her debt to other theoreticians such as Bion, Berne and Yalom. She considered therapy to be a process that takes place within the boundaries of a social system, and believed that within the boundaries of that social system, phenomenological processes are occurring simultaneously on three levels: the intra-personal level, the interpersonal level and the systems level, giving examples from her own practice to illustrate what she means by these three levels. Kepner outlined several stages of group development – identity and dependence, influence and counterdependence, intimacy and interdependence, reaching a closure – and argued that the group leader's tasks are different at each stage. Zinker's contribution to *Beyond the Hot Seat* (1980) also discussed several similar, although differently named, stages of group development.

Kepner's practice, like Zinker's, is obviously very different from that of Fritz Perls. As she said, 'it differs substantially from the popular notion of Gestalt groups, namely, that of individual therapy done in a group setting, as practised by Fritz Perls and others in their workshops' (Kepner, 1980: 7). However she went to great trouble to describe the historical background that gave rise to the Cleveland integrated group process model,[4] and pointed out that the Gestalt workshop was an ideal model for the trainees of the time and the purposes of Perls:

> The workshop method, developed by the Perls and later used by, among others, Isadore From, Paul Goodman, and Paul Weisz, proved to be a dramatic and effective teaching model and a powerful way of recruiting mental health professionals for training. It was an appropriate model for the needs and learning goals of the trainees. At that time, the participants in these workshops were either practicing therapists or advanced graduate students in one of the mental health disciplines. Many of them had some previous experience as a client in therapy. Most of them knew a good deal about psychotherapeutic theories and clinical practice, but little about what to do with a living client. Gestalt therapy, with its emphasis on what to do and how to do it, provided some sorely needed tools, and the workshop setting made it possible to see and experience the effects of the methods. (pp. 9–10)

Kepner also generously acknowledged that Perls 'through his many years of experience had discovered the power of a group in the process of individual change', but suggested the Gestalt group process model *'builds on what Fritz articulated in the theory of Gestalt but did not practice'* (p. 7, present authors' italics).

Perls' theory, although not his practice, has then contributed to the developments in the theory of group process which have occurred since his death. It has been synthesized with a re-evaluation of Lewin's emphasis, an integration of group process theory from other schools and the evolving experience of Gestalt practitioners from Brazil to Bristol (Ribiero, 1985; Clarkson and Clayton, 1992). Clarkson, Mackewn and Shaw (1992) have developed a new approach to Gestalt group process and chaos theory, called quantum group dynamics.

The Expansion of the Concept of the Relationship in Gestalt Therapy

Modern Gestalt theoreticians have developed Perls' radical innovation regarding the importance of the person-to-person contact in therapy and have explored the concept of this person-to-person relationship in Gestalt therapy, in much greater depth than Perls himself ever attempted. Most of the Gestalt theorists who have written about the therapeutic relationship have turned to Martin Buber's (1987) discussion of the I–Thou encounter as a source of inspiration. In this they may have emulated Laura Perls who met Buber once and was directly influenced by Buber's ideas in Frankfurt. Fritz Perls was also influenced by Buber (Perls, 1978b) in a more general way and indirectly through Laura (see p. 8).

Yontef (1980), Hycner (1985; 1991) and Jacobs (1978; 1989) have discussed Gestalt therapy as a dialogic approach. They have emphasized that the relationship is the medium through which awareness is increased and through which the client restores her growth. The meeting or relationship (not the therapist) is healing since the meeting is the sharing of inner selves. In particular an I–Thou relationship has the maximum power to heal. Yontef has defined an I–Thou relationship as person-to-person contact – or the contact of the core of one person to the core of another person: 'Such a healing relationship develops when two people, each with his separate existence and personal needs, contact each other recognizing and allowing the differences between them. This is more than a combination of two monologues but two people in meaningful exchange' (1980: 15).

Although the outcome or quality of exchange in the therapeutic relationship is determined by what happens between the two people and cannot be controlled or willed by either individual, Yontef has been quite specific about what the therapist needs to embody in order to create a climate where dialogic relationship can flourish. She must practise inclusion, show her presence, be committed to the dialogue, be non-exploitative, live the relationship and be an experimental phenomenological experiential guide: see Yontef (1980) for an explanation of these terms.

Hycner (1985) described clearly and simply the basic premises of Buber's philosophy of dialogue, explaining that dialogic gestalt therapy is a therapeutic application of this philosophy of dialogue (p. 26). He suggested that I–Thou relating and I–It relating are both valid aspects of dialogic relationship – which encompasses the rhythmic alternation of the I–Thou and I–It moments: 'To try to force an I–Thou relationship is to be guilty of modern "hubris". To attempt to do so paradoxically creates an I–It relationship!' (Hycner, 1991: 50). For Hycner awareness is a means of helping the client establish a better relational stance to the world, a healthier person/environment interaction. This better relational stance may occur through the relationship which can take place between therapist and client, when by a mixture of hard work and 'grace' (Buber, 1987) the individuals meet and touch each other as human beings.

Jacobs (1989) further explored the role of the relationship in the overall therapy process – both the importance of the relationship as a factor in healing and the extent to which the relationship *per se* is a focus of therapy. She explained how Buber's philosophy of dialogue meshes with the concepts of contact, awareness and the paradoxical theory of change, giving clinical examples. She paid much greater attention than Yontef or Hycner to the crucial issue of just how much the therapist needs to show of herself in order to be 'present'.

Clarkson (1990; 1991b) has distinguished, theoretically and by means of examples, five variations on the I–Thou relationship: the working alliance, the unfinished (transferential) relationship, the reparative/developmentally-needed relationship, the 'real' or person-to-person relationship, and the transpersonal relationship. She has also emphasized (1988; 1991b) that Gestalt does not work *either* with the existential and phenomenological present *or* with regressive states and transferential material, but encompasses both existential encounter and regressive exploration.

How far has Perls influenced these important developments regarding the relationship in Gestalt therapy? Although the most important source of inspiration is undoubtedly Buber, Perls has, we believe, had a seminal influence upon them in two almost contradictory ways. Perls himself was influenced by Buber (Perls, 1978b) both directly and indirectly through his wife Laura. One of his most important early innovations was his insistence (1947/1969a) that the therapist stop being a neutral, mirror-like figure and instead allow herself to be a human being on the same level as the patient: 'Not only has the psychoanalyst to understand the patient but the patient has to understand the psychoanalyst. [S]he has to see the human being' (p. 239). Perls, Hefferline and Goodman (1951/1973) developed the concept of real human contact as the essential core of the therapeutic relationship, using words which are not dissimilar to Yontef's and Hycner's: the therapy is a 'meeting' between two human beings. The Gestalt clinician shares her own responses and reactions in an authentic dialogue with the client.

Yontef (1980) confirms the view that Perls has had an influence upon the subsequent exploration of the relationship. He emphasizes the fact that Gestalt therapy has, since its inception, stressed treatment using the active presence of the therapist as a chief tool, and explains that although the language used was different, the early Gestalt literature was describing a form of therapy by dialogue, even when it did not specifically use the word 'dialogue'. Citing Perls' books (Perls, 1947/1969a; Perls, Hefferline and Goodman, 1951/1973) as examples, he concludes: 'In practice, Gestalt Therapy did show the presence of the therapist, which is the beginning of treatment by dialogue' (p. 2). Hycner (1985) also acknowledges the influence of Perls upon his discussion, by reminding his readers of some of the statements of Perls and his colleagues which grounded Gestalt therapy in the person–environment matrix and emphasized the 'between' that exists at the contact boundary. (See Chapter 3, p. 87, for a fuller discussion of Perls' concept of the therapeutic relationship.)

The second way in which Perls has influenced the rich subsequent discussion of the relationship in Gestalt therapy is much more indirect. In contrast to his earlier theoretical writings, Perls' later works and practice often emphasized individuality and self-reliance to the point that relationship and interdependence seemed sometimes to be forgotten, as in the much debated 'Gestalt prayer' (pp. 62–3 and 145). Perls' later emphasis upon insular self-sufficiency may well have contributed to the passion and poetry with which the Gestaltists discussed in this section have – in response – argued for inclusion, mutuality and dialogue. Like many modern gestaltists Perls, Hefferline and Goodman also emphasized the essential social nature of human beings (see p. 147).

This is the principle of 'enantiodromia' (Jung, 1968; Perls, 1969a; Clarkson, 1992b).

Assimilation of Knowledge from Other Disciplines into Gestalt

Yontef (1988) has argued that Gestalt therapy needs to integrate knowledge and ideas from other disciplines including psycho-analytic and diagnostic perspectives. Yontef has insisted (1991) that Gestalt therapists must have an understanding of transferential processes and know how to work with transferential and counter-transferential phenomena, for example. He proposed that Gestalt therapists need to extend their concept of here-and-now to include a richer tapestry of 'space–time zones', including the 'there-and-now', the 'here-and-then' and the 'there-and-then'. Erving Polster (1987) especially has encouraged Gestalt therapists to work with the concept of full engagement in the here-and-now in a much more flexible way. In contrast to Perls' frequent criticism of talking about, Polster demonstrates the simple and yet immense value of telling our life stories, of describing our past. He has wonderfully illustrated how the Gestalt psychotherapist – like the novelist – can help the client to notice the everyday drama and interest in herself and her story which she may have previously taken for granted or dismissed. By her skilful listening and genuine absorption, the therapist can draw the client's attention to the coherence, the directedness, the sequencing of the story and enable the client to regain authorship of her life:

> the here and now . . . the emphasis upon technique dramatically upstaged what was always methodologically crucial in Gestalt therapy, the common human engagement. This includes much that is ordinary: support, curiosity, kindness, bold language, laughter, cynicism, assimilation of tragedy, rage, gentleness, and toughness. . . These broader interests, especially as they are expressed by the novelist, may help therapists to encompass all they can about how people live, not only *here* but also *there*, not only *now* but also *then*. (Polster, 1987: 183)

Yontef (1988) has also suggested that Gestalt therapists need to be able to identify clients who are suffering from personality disorders, especially the narcissistic and borderline disorders, and know how to treat these clients appropriately, integrating concepts and approaches from object relations to do so. Tobin (1982) criticized the limitations of Perls' view of the self as process (as described on p. 59), particularly in respect to working with clients who show narcissistic disturbance. He writes that Perls, Hefferline and Goodman's (1951/1973) description of the self as an organizing process seems to imply that each person has an equally effective, well functioning self and fails to include in the concept of self the important self-functions of stability, groundedness, confidence and flexibility. Borrowing extensively from Kohut's (1971; 1977; Kohut and Wolf, 1978) definition of the self and from theories of the development of the self and stage-related pathology (Klein, 1964; 1975; Winnicott, 1958; 1965; Mahler, Pine and Bergman, 1975), Tobin offered some methods of treating the client with a self-disorder which involve an integration of Gestalt and self psychology approaches to self-disorders.

Greenberg (1989) described working with clients with borderline personality disorders, using a special adaptation of Gestalt therapy, borrowing from Mahler, Pine and Bergman (1975), Kernberg (1976), Masterson (1976; 1981; 1983) and Blanck and Blanck (1974). She pointed out that Gestalt therapy was originally designed for working not with such disorders but with 'over-intellectualizing neurotics' and makes a great many quite specific, practical and helpful suggestions for ways of working with clients who show borderline traits and of adapting Gestalt to meet their needs. McLeod (1991) has argued that Tobin's assimilation of psychoanalytic views of the self have diluted Goodman and Perls' conception of self as contact and thus in some sense also weakened Gestalt's holistic and relational stance. Delisle (1988) has developed a creative and useful model which integrates Gestalt approaches to diagnosis of the individual's *process* of contacting or supporting herself with DSM III R (American Psychiatric Association, 1987), the system of observed criteria for diagnosis.

What influence has Perls had on these important developments, in which Gestalt therapy has integrated knowledge and ideas from other disciplines, particularly from psychoanalytic practice and literature? Greenberg (1989) neither mentions Perls nor includes him in her list of references, so Perls has had little or no direct or specific influence upon her contribution, except in the broadest sense, in that she is a Gestalt therapist. Tobin (1982), on the other hand, quotes from Perls and seems, as he writes, to be in active dialogue with Perls and his colleagues, taking their definition of self as his starting point, building upon it and reacting against it. McLeod (1991) is extensively influenced by Perls and Goodman.

Clarkson's recent contribution is to show the continuity of Gestalt ideas from pre-Socratic Heraclitus through Perls, Hefferline and Goodman to the quantum physics and chaos theory of today. In '2500 Years of Gestalt' (1992b) she shows how these ideas constitute an unbroken thread of holistic, organismic, cyclic and relationship-oriented awareness since the beginning of Western philosophical tradition to the frontiers of science as we begin to perceive them reaching into the twenty-first century.

Perls himself, of course, borrowed from and reacted to psycho-analysis, thus providing a model for the current exchange of ideas between the Gestalt and psychoanalytic fields: 'We have always been an integrating framework. That's one of the things I love about Gestalt therapy' (Yontef, 1988: 6).

Re-examination of Field Theory and Gestalt

Wheeler (1991) has suggested that Perls did not have a thorough knowledge either of Gestalt psychology or of Kurt Lewin's field theory. In particular Wheeler maintains that the 'model of contact handed down to us by Goodman and Perls, and elaborated by many subsequent authors, is figure-bound, in a theoretical sense; that the analysis of this contact process (or awareness, or experience) is incomplete without direct consideration of organized features or structures of ground' (p. 3). Wheeler reassesses the work of Lewin and of Goldstein which he believes has been under-valued in Gestalt therapy. He claims that, because of Perls' over-emphasis upon the *figure* of contact, Gestalt therapy has tended to be preoccupied with episodic, dramatic contactful work and has paid too little attention to the assimilation into ground over time of these episodes of therapeutic work. Wheeler argues that Gestalt therapists need to work with the structure of ground as well as with the figure. His book explores field theory in great depth and includes case examples which illustrate the concepts.[5]

In 'Individuality and Commonality in Gestalt' (1991) Clarkson re-emphasised the validity of Lewin's field theory as one of the core Gestalt concepts which mediate the shift from object relations to subject dialogue, particularly as exemplified in the work of the phenomenologist Merleau-Ponty (1962). Parlett (1992) has recently given present-day examples to illustrate and explicate the field theory of Lewin. He recalls that field theory is basic to Gestalt therapy but argues that this fact has been too little recognized, because of a later emphasis upon individualism (Saner, 1989) and an under-appreciation of the importance of community in people's lives. Parlett strongly recommends the field theory approach, which pays as much attention to the ground of the individual's background as to immediate issues. He suggests a wonderful image of the individual's life space as layered or laminated and proposes that Gestalt therapy is brilliantly adapted to move between the layers and levels, switching frames or positions; so that on occasion therapist and client can reach deeply into the past in a regressive re-enactment, while at another time, they may look purely at the present relationship.

What influence has Perls had upon this renewed emphasis on field theory in Gestalt therapy? A crucial one in several respects. To begin with he, together with Laura Perls and Paul Goodman, first formulated the theory of Gestalt therapy, drawing upon ideas, methods, metaphors and outlooks taken from many different disciplines, *including the field orientation of Lewin and Wertheimer*, to conceive a magnificent new synthesis. Parlett (1992) reminds us that the original Gestalt agenda was to 'locate human distress and confusion not in the confines of a person's individual psychopathology, but instead in the interactions between people and their situations' (p. 5) and that Goodman and Perls, like Lewin, were social critics. Furthermore, Perls in later life was also at least partly responsible for the emphasis upon the polarity of extreme individualism (Saner, 1989), which has now led Naranjo (1982), Clarkson (1989; 1991b), Wheeler (1991) and Parlett (1992) to make such eloquent pleas for a re-examination of the other polarity of community, background and interdependence in the form of a better and more comprehensive understanding of field theory in Gestalt therapy. Clarkson has made a particular development in Gestalt therapy by a re-evaluation of the notion of the life force. Creative growth or holistic evolution between the important polarities of individuality and commonality can be mediated by a third life force which Heraclitus called 'Physis', a generalised creative force of nature. Bergson's (1965) élan vital, which influenced Perls (1969b: 63–4) is identical to this creative life force or Physis, which is characteristic of Gestalt therapy and derives from the legacy of Smuts (1926/1987). Perls acknowledged Smuts' idea of the energetic motive of creative evolution as a major influence in his work. Perls, Hefferline and Goodman (1951/1973) speak of creative transformation. Physis is this life force and is associated with self-actualisation, evolution, healing and creativity. It combines the biological and organismic aspect of Gestalt therapy, and its capacity for transcendence, our holistic evolution and spirituality.[6]

Impact of Perls' Ideas on the Overall Field of Counselling and Psychotherapy Theory

Definitions of counselling and psychotherapy abound, as do attempts to distinguish between the two disciplines. Although this is an interesting discussion, it lies beyond the scope of this book and therefore in this chapter we accept Nelson-Jones' (1982) arguments that attempts to distinguish between counselling and psychotherapy are never wholly successful (Clarkson and Carroll, 1993) and follow the example of Truax and Carkhuff (1967) who use the terms interchangeably.

Many of the theoretical and practical contributions made by Perls and other innovators of the period have been absorbed, as if by osmosis, throughout psychotherapy and counselling as practised today. Psychotherapists of many orientations have integrated ideas that originated with, or were popularized by, Perls and his contemporaries. Ideas that were innovatory reactions to psychoanalysis in the 1940s and early 1950s have now been so thoroughly accepted that it is hard to conceive just how radical they were at the time. A flavour of how novel Perls' contributions appeared during his lifetime (in contrast to how they appear in today's context) is given in this interview with Erving Polster:

> I . . . remember the power of seeing someone have a profound personal experience in a group of people who had not previously been intimate. That was a revelation to me. It wasn't done much then. Nowadays it's taken for granted, but then to see somebody say something that was so powerful they would cry, right there among fifteen people from the community who were not related to them, who were not necessarily even their friends, was a revelatory experience. (in Wysong and Rosenfeld, 1982: 48)

Perls' Impact upon the Development of Humanistic Psychotherapies

Clearly Perls has had an enormous impact upon the development of humanistic psychotherapy. Gestalt ideas and practices are now pervasive in most humanistic, transpersonal and existential therapies. Rowan (1988; 1992) has given a very comprehensive account of the nature and development of humanistic, existential and transpersonal psychotherapies. His books are peppered with references to Perls and Gestalt and yet they subtly but significantly underestimate the extent of Perls' influence upon many of the ideas which he discusses. For example he devotes a chapter to 'Encounter Groups as a Paradigm of Integrative Psychotherapy' (1992: 118–30) in which he itemizes the fundamental contributions of Will Schutz, Jim Elliott and Elizabeth Mintz to humanistic psychotherapy. Although he acknowledges that 'Encounter agrees with the body therapies and with Gestalt' (p. 124), he fails to explain that Schutz (and to a lesser extent Mintz) was profoundly and directly *influenced in the development* of his ideas by Fritz Perls and Gestalt. Fritz Perls and Will Schutz were trainers in residence at Esalen at the same time and before Schutz wrote most of his books. Eventually the two men fell out, but for the first year of their acquaintance Schutz sat in upon Perls' workshops and has himself described how much he admired and was influenced by Perls (in Gaines, 1979). Again Rowan quotes Schutz (1973) to illustrate the commitment to the holistic integration of the human organism, which is one of the basic beliefs of the humanistic approach, without indicating Fritz Perls' crucial role in the synthesis of body and psychotherapies in the early 1940s (Perls, 1947/

1969a) (see pp. 12 and 176). Finally Rowan includes his own list of guidelines for group participants which he says is based on an amalgamation of the principles of Schutz, Elliott and Mintz. He does not mention Perls as a source of these principles, even though the list includes awareness of the body; the here-and-now; taking responsibility; support and confrontation; and attention to habitual language, such as the use of questions rather than statements, addressing people directly and saying 'I' rather then 'it'. These are all concepts popularized by Perls before they were taken up by the authors mentioned, one of whom (Schutz) was directly influenced by Perls, while another (Mintz) has subsequently published in the *Gestalt Journal*. Of course Rowan is at liberty to quote whichever sources he wants for ideas which have now become widely disseminated but we hope that this brief discussion illustrates how Perls' direct impact upon the overall field of humanistic counselling and psychotherapy has often been subtly diminished or overlooked.

Parallels Between Perls' Ideas and Some Contemporary Psychoanalytic Concepts

In addition some of Perls' ideas have either been unconsciously assimilated into the mainstream of psychodynamic psychotherapy or been reinvented during the last two decades when psychoanalysis has found new life, particularly through the development of object relations and self psychology. This section discusses the parallels between some of Perls' ideas and certain aspects of contemporary object relations and psychodynamic theory. It explores how Perlsian ideas may have been *indirectly* assimilated into the psychodynamic and psychoanalytic approaches, as well as more obviously into humanistic approaches. It does *not* attempt to show that the psychodynamic and psychoanalytic therapists cited have been *directly* influenced by Perls, which on the whole they were not. Rather it proposes that Perls was at the same time both a part of and a major contributor to a *Zeitgeist* or cultural revolution which allowed the developments of the last twenty years: 'Gestalt therapy . . . is threatened with a form of assimilation that will continue to erode its distinctive identity. There are signs that Gestalt therapy is being absorbed, as if by osmosis, into the psychotherapeutic mainstream without recognition or acknowledgement of its contributions' (Miller, 1989: 23).

Perls' Holism and his Synthesis of Body and Psychotherapies

Perls (1947/1969a; Perls, Hefferline and Goodman, 1951/1973; Perls, 1969b; 1976) popularized the idea that the human being is a whole organism which is constantly interacting with other people and the environment in a process of creative exchange. He believed that human beings can only be understood if they are considered as a whole, in the context of their environment. A holistic attitude to people and to healing now has widespread credence. Most humanistic approaches to therapy and to health treat the whole person, not the symptom, and many medical practitioners now aspire to treat their patients holistically. There are also parallels between Perls' holistic view of the self and the object relations concept of self as a creative, flexible and self-regulating whole, which develops in the context of relations to other people: 'A person is a whole self' (Guntrip, 1973: 181).

Freudian psychoanalysis had on the whole worked with the verbal and intellectual processes of the patient. Reich in reaction placed much greater emphasis upon the physical body and muscular tensions of the patient. Perls (1947/1969a; 1948) and Perls, Hefferline and Goodman (1951/1973) amalgamated aspects of the two approaches but criticized the narrowness of both. They developed a unitary method of psychotherapy which synthesized body and psychotherapies to mirror their holistic beliefs (see pp. 33–40). This encompassing attitude, new and refreshing at the time, has since made such an impact upon the psychotherapeutic world that it is almost taken for granted; so that a psychodynamic counsellor instructs trainees to supplement listening and remembering by watching closely for the client's non-verbal communications and reactions (Jacobs, 1988) as part of her basic techniques. The importance of integrating holistic approaches in psychotherapy is now recognized within many branches of psychoanalysis: 'Although Reich fell into disrepute in the 1950s, his ideas are currently enjoying a positive re-evaluation. Many of his ideas on character armor and personality development are now seen as major contributions to psychoanalytic theory' (Bohart and Todd, 1988: 91). Perls' early and seminal positive evaluation of Reich (in the 1930s, 1940s and 1950s) is rarely if ever acknowledged.

Korb, Gorrell and Van der Riet (1989) summarize how Gestalt therapy was in many ways ahead of its time, especially regarding the holistic conception of the human being:

> In some ways the current conceptualizations of the therapeutic enterprise have caught up with Gestalt therapy. From the beginning, we have seen humans as whole organisms containing parts that function together in a more than mechanistic fashion. In 1988, the holistic point of view is being increasingly accepted as integral to body/mind theory and research. Healing is seen as one of the processes of a whole and dynamic individual. The conception of the individual as always being in a process of interacting with the environment has been incorporated into new approaches to therapy and in revisions of long-standing approaches. (p. 131)

*The Therapeutic Relationship: from Transference to
Contact and Dialogue*

In his first book *Ego, Hunger and Aggression* (1947/1969a, first published in South Africa in 1942), Perls criticized Freud's overemphasis upon the therapist's neutrality and the transferential relationship. He insisted that the therapist show herself as a human being and not as a blank screen. Perls, Hefferline and Goodman (1951/1973) proposed that the therapeutic relationship is a dialogue, where the therapist makes contact with the client in an equal exchange. Therapist and client meet person-to-person. In this dialogue or meeting, they suggested that therapists behave as full-blooded human beings, sometimes revealing their current reactions to the client, or sharing their genuine feelings and experiences with her. Therapists simultaneously accept and affirm the client's feelings as valid in their own right in the current situation, whether or not they are also transferential. Thus, if a client is angry with the therapist, the Gestalt therapist does not assume that the client is 'really' angry with her mother, father or lover, but accepts that the client *is* angry with her *now* and meets her anger with her own genuine response – perhaps an apology for the misunderstanding that has arisen between them, perhaps an angry retort. The Gestalt therapist makes contact with the angry client, person-to-person. Although Perls did sometimes talk of transference in very dismissive terms, for the main part he did not deny its existence but wanted to draw his readers' attention to the fact that psychoanalysis had until then relatively ignored the person-to-person meeting.

Until the late 1930s and early 1940s, traditional psychoanalysts believed that as far as possible the therapist should remain neutral, a blank mirror on to which the client could project her own story and past relationships. At least in theory, psychoanalysts did not share their real feelings with their patients and actually tried to reveal as little of themselves as possible – often considering that the whole psychoanalysis was threatened if the client discovered personal information about them.[7]

Perls popularized the notion (previously mooted by Horney, Sullivan, Ferenczi and Buber, amongst others) that the person-to-person relationship between two real and equal human beings in therapy is as important for healing as the transferential relationship and emphasized the need for cooperative dialogue between therapist and client. The ideas of Perls and his predecessors relating to the themes of relationship and dialogue have almost certainly *both* had an enormous impact upon the subsequent development of psychotherapy *and* been independently reinvented by other schools of therapy.

Many humanistic, existential, psychodynamic and psycho-analytic therapists/counsellors have since emphasized the real or adult relationship, while others have described several different relationships which are interwoven in the overall therapeutic relationship (Rowan, 1988; Yalom, 1980; Greenson, 1967; 1971; Greenson and Wexler, 1969; Jacobs, 1988; Clarkson, 1990). Many authors of the self psychology and object relations approaches advocate the selective use of therapist self-disclosure, as is illustrated by the following examples, which show parallels with Perls' thinking.[8] Kohut (1984) advised psychoanalysts to adopt a relaxed, easy-going and empathic manner and to make themselves emotionally available to the client. Guntrip (1973) clearly believed that the therapist should be a real person in therapy: '[The therapist must be] . . . a whole, real human being. . . and not just a professional interpreter . . . Only then can the patient find himself and become a person in his own right' (p. 66). Masterson (1981) also suggested abandoning or modifying traditional thera-peutic neutrality to confront clients with the destructiveness of some of their behaviour. Kahn (1991), an integrative psychologist, recommended that the therapist be genuine and transparent and avoid hiding behind a mask.

Assimilation of Perls' Emphasis upon the Here-and-Now

Perls (1947/1969a) criticized Freud for an overemphasis upon the past and for his 'archaeological approach'. At the time when he wrote, Perls' attitude was anathema to the psychoanalytic establish-ment. Since then some psychoanalysts have themselves made similar criticisms of Freud. Spence (1982), for example, has suggested that Freud's 'archaeological' model of therapy is inade-quate.

Perls, perhaps more than any of his contemporaries, widened professional and lay interest in the existential concept of the here-and-now and emphasized 'that the most important thing to pay attention to is whatever is going on right now, either inside the client or between the present participants' (Rowan, 1992: 119). The importance of the here-and-now interaction of client and therapist, together with awareness of present process, is now assimilated in many different humanistic, psychoanalytic and psychodynamic schools. Most humanistic and existential therapies accentuate the concept of the here-and-now. Rowan (1992) says that 'approaches that specialise in this aspect include group analysis, personal construct therapy, cognitive-behavioural therapy, neurolinguistic programming, existential analysis, person-centred therapy' (p. 119), as well as Gestalt therapy and encounter groups. The object relations approach also places considerable emphasis upon present relationships and present awareness:

> At the same time, the focus on 'here and now' interaction between client and therapist is the current trend of traditional, 'neo-Freudian' therapy as well, in all but the most hidebound centers, deriving no doubt partly from the influence and competition of Gestalt and other 'present-centered therapies', but also partly from the concurrent development of object relations theory, which may give somewhat more direct causative weight to the past, but arrives at much the same point in terms of use of the present interaction in therapy (see for example Winnicott, 1986). (Wheeler, 1991: 95–6)

Modern psychodynamic counselling theory gives equal importance to the 'present in here' and the 'present out there' as to the 'past back there' in the counselling situation (Jacobs, 1988). Research (Nicholson and Berman, 1983) suggests that therapeutic treatments which do not make extensive explorations of early childhood material are just as effective as therapies which do. This tends to support Perls' emphasis upon present awareness although, as we have pointed out (pp. 45 and 95), Perls and other Gestaltists do not ignore the past: they work with it in active and spontaneous ways by bringing the unfinished business of the past into the present situation.

While Perls has undoubtedly directly influenced many humanistic, existential and transpersonal psychotherapists and authors (e.g. Gabrielle Roth, Will Schutz, Rollo May, Sam Keen), it cannot be shown that Perls directly influenced the object relations or the psychodynamic theorists' position regarding the present. Perls' contribution was that he, more than anyone at that time, brought to the attention of a wide public the present awareness and phenomenological exploration of the existing field as therapeutic approaches. He thus helped create an atmosphere in which a wide range of future theorists inevitably integrated the significance of here-and-now process.

Perls' Emphasis upon the Existential Concepts of Choice and Responsibility

Freud's view of humanity was essentially deterministic. Primary irreducible drives determine all human behaviour. People's responses are laid down by their instinctive drives, based upon their biological inheritance. The fundamental premises of his drive theory never ceased to inform Freud's theoretical perspective, even though he later introduced a series of modifications which decreased the exclusive emphasis on drive processes as the sole determinants of human experience and behaviour. Freud believed that repression is universal and is necessitated by the fundamentally anti-social nature of human passions. We all therefore have repressed wishes. Whether we end up disturbed or relatively symptom-free depends on how our personalities regulate those repressed wishes. For Freudians that depends on the crucial formative experiences with our families in early childhood: 'Psychoanalysis holds that in truly important moments of one's life one is unwittingly held captive by the past' (Adelson and Doehrman, 1980: 100).

Perls popularized the concepts of free will and existential choice. He argued that people choose from moment to moment who and how they are, and are therefore responsible for many aspects of their life including their neurotic symptoms, the meaning they give to their experiences and the institutions they create or tolerate. Even today these remain fundamentally challenging ideas. At the time when Perls first wrote, they were radical.

While not uncritical of Perls' occasional over-insistence upon responsibility,[9] Yalom (1980) has fully acknowledged the extent and quality of Perls' contribution to the concept of responsibility as an important therapeutic theme: 'Of the proponents of an active therapist style in the approach to responsibility, none have been more vigorous or inventive than Fritz Perls' (Yalom, 1980: 246). Yalom has thoroughly explored the extensive impact of Perls' work on responsibility assumption on popular American thinking and publications, upon movements such as est, as well as upon the whole field of psychotherapy. He suggests that the concept of responsibility has caught public attention and has influenced the themes and facilitators of psychotherapy workshops (he cites Rollo May and Albert Ellis) and writers of popular psychology texts, such as Dyer (1978) and Weinberg (1978). Yalom has also reviewed the research evidence regarding whether or not responsibility awareness increases as a result of therapy and whether or not responsibility assumption is in fact significant or beneficial. He concludes: 'These data all suggest that the successful psychotherapy patient becomes more aware of personal responsibility for life' (Yalom, 1980: 266) – which conclusion indicates the important impact of Perls' popularization of the concept of personal responsibility upon the overall field of psychotherapy.

Perls' Popularization of the Phenomenological Method of Investigation

Perls (1947/1969a) integrated into the field of psychotherapy and counselling the concept of phenomenological investigation, in order to gain a true sense of the 'thing itself'. He urged therapists to set aside all their previous assumptions and to describe what they apprehend without explanation or interpretation, as a way of reaching the essence of experience.

This was in direct opposition to the well established psycho-analytic methods of free association and interpretation. Most of the analysts of the day diagnosed and analysed their clients' responses in exactly the way that Perls criticized. Far from meeting the client without previous bias, they believed it to be intrinsic to their job to have a thorough knowledge of Freud's complex theories of child development and then to apply these to the clients they treated and to explain their clients' present behaviour in terms of the past.

Thus when Perls said 'apply the description technique. . . I do not mean psychoanalyze' (1947/1969a), he was challenging the most valued methods of his profession. Perls (1947/1969a) and Perls, Hefferline and Goodman (1951/1973) reopened for discussion various questions of technique which had previously seemed settled; and thus paved the way for the plethora of different theoretical approaches which were to be developed in the 1950s and 1960s. Yontef (1991) has pointed out that some brands of psychoanalysis have now moved much closer to the current experience of the client and therapist, and in doing so have come nearer to the phenomenological approach. However he feels even recent psychoanalytic understanding of phenomenology is limited:

> But there is a limit to the phenomenological focus of even the most modern psychoanalytic therapies. They still come from the heritage of free association and interpretation, and don't expand the phenomeno-logical emphasis to include phenomenological focusing training or experimentation. Experimental phenomenology is not yet included in the expanded psychoanalytic therapies. (p. 18)

The Impact of Holism and Field Theory on Psychotherapy

Inspired by Smuts (1987) and Lewin (1935), Perls (1947/1969a) brought the perspectives of field theory to the overall field of psycho-therapy and made them known to a wider and different audience than Lewin had done. The psychoanalysis of the era appeared to delve deep into the hidden meanings of the individual's character structure, dreams and childhood memories while sometimes ignoring her contemporary social sphere. It examined symptoms and looked for explanations and solutions within the individual herself, encouraging clients to re-examine their present life to see how their unconscious feelings were colouring their present perceptions. Indeed Bohart and Todd (1988) attribute the growing popularity of psychology and psychoanalysis in the first half of this century to the fact that they were essentially conservative: problems could be defined as residing within the individual. Solutions could therefore be sought that did not require change in anyone else – in the community at large, in society or in political or educational systems.

Perls' emphasis upon wholes and the interdependence of individual and environment challenged the political status quo. He and Goodman were highly critical of the social customs, the institutions and the educational methods of the time, believing that they contributed to the creation of the modern dissociated man. If the institutions contribute to the malaise of modern man, then the institutions must be changed: 'And nothing is more clear, unfortunately, than that certain tensions and blocks cannot be freed unless there is a real environmental change offering new possibilities. If the institutions and mores were altered, many a recalcitrant symptom would vanish very suddenly' (Perls, Hefferline and Goodman, 1951/1973: 281).

Many approaches to psychotherapy now take for granted the need to consider an individual in terms of her background, and some family therapists prefer to work with the whole family system. But at the time that Perls wrote *Ego, Hunger and Aggression* (early 1940s), thinking in terms of the wider field was a radical innovation. Notions such as holism are now gaining currency under the growing understanding of chaos theory (Clarkson, 1992b).

Impact of Perls' Emphasis upon Health and Self-Actualization

Perls and his colleagues believed that human beings have a natural ability to be healthy and to evolve creatively. Why was this such an important innovation? Up until the late 1930s, psychoanalysis had been largely pessimistic, emphasizing that human drives are anti-social, dark, inhumane forces. Integration into society requires the control or suppression of these drives and thus human beings were considered to be made up of competing energies; they were in constant conflict with themselves. Human health was therefore thought to be the domination of the self by the most worthy socialized part. So when Perls (1947/1969a) suggested that human beings have an intrinsic capacity to regulate and actualize themselves, he was making a radical and dramatic break with the psychological beliefs of the day. Perls, Hefferline and Goodman (1951/1973) worked out and described the structure and dynamics of the self-regulating and self-actualizing needs in humans. This complex body of theory had an enormous influence upon the human potential movement and the humanistic psychotherapy which was to develop in the 1950s and 1960s.

Perls and his colleagues were also innovatory and influential in the way they applied their principles of human development to ordinary people. They discussed at length the ordinary healthy processes of ordinary people and their writing abounds with examples of healthy people in ordinary circumstances. Until this time psychology and psychiatry had been largely preoccupied with containing and explaining the severely disturbed, or with providing for soldiers and the victims of shell-shock and trauma. Psycho-analytic writings generally emphasized the study and description of pathological processes. The actual experience of psychoanalysis was expensive, time-consuming and intellectually demanding; so for the most part it was only available to a tiny intellectual and wealthy minority.

In this context, addressing a large part of *Ego, Hunger and Aggression* (Perls, 1947/1969a) as well as *Gestalt Therapy* (Perls, Hefferline and Goodman, 1951/1973) to the ordinary person as a self-help manual was revolutionary. The 'manuals' provide exercises which enable the ordinary person to study her current functioning and become the expert on her own psychology. For present-day readers who can get a do-it-yourself guide on anything, it is hard to imagine just how enabling this step was. Although the theoretical portions of both books are challenging, the self-help parts are relatively 'user-friendly'.

Perls' first book marks a historical turning point in the psycho-therapeutic field. It was at the same time part of, and contributory to, a general movement which challenged the stranglehold of the psychiatric profession and promoted the empowerment of individuals to help and self-actualize themselves. The publication of *Ego, Hunger and Aggression* in South Africa in 1942 for example coincided with the publication of Rogers' first book; while its publication in Britain in 1947 came at the same time as the first 'T-group' or sensitivity training held at the National Training Laboratory at Bethel, Maine in the USA, where therapy-like services were for the first time made available to non-disturbed individuals in a summer workshop.

Perls' career thereafter continued to be seminal in the popular movement to apply psychological principles of human development to ordinary people. After *Gestalt Therapy* his published works become increasingly popular in tone. Although the anti-intellectual nature of the Perlsian Gestalt of this period had some detrimental effects upon the immediate theoretical development of Gestalt (see pp. 143 and 161–2), Perls brought the concepts of personal development and psychological growth to a broad selection of lay as well as professional audiences in the USA. He travelled around America demonstrating his techniques to packed auditoriums; while at Esalen, Perls offered psychological exploration to bright, highly functioning Americans, who chose to spend their holidays in personal exploration. In the years between 1947 and 1970 the image of psychology in the Western world had expanded and changed beyond all recognition, and Perls – with many others – had played a key role in this expansion.

Summarizing this section on the assimilation of Perls' ideas in general psychotherapeutic theory, we can state that Perls and his colleagues were highly innovatory and described a number of psychotherapeutic principles and practices which have been absorbed into the general field of psychotherapy. Others are now being rediscovered by other therapists of all orientations. Miller (1989) gives a well specified example of this process:

> The other day I happened to read a pre-publication manuscript written by Dr Michael Robbins (1991), a well known analyst, on the therapy of 'primitive personalities', the borderline, narcissistic, and schizoid character types. . . The author argues in this paper that an orthodox psychoanalytic approach based on inner conflicts, mechanisms of defence, and a therapy intent on bringing unconscious forces to light does not work with such personalities. He wants to revise the traditional analytic model so that it will account for the interplay between self and other instead of limiting itself to the inner world of a single individual. He defines introjection and projection as mental constructs that are constantly made and re-made in a person's current relationships, rather than as left-over deposits fixed in the personality from early childhood. He strikes an existentialist note when he suggests that inauthenticity arises from actively distorting oneself to meet others' expectations instead of embracing the truth of one's own being. He conveys respect for the inventiveness that is lost in symptom-formation; that is, he discerns its roots in children's creative if painful contortions to keep their connection to disturbed family settings that are essential to the children's survival. He gives the patient's experience priority over the therapist's interpretations. And he refuses to reduce the relationship between therapist and patient to a mere instance of transference. *This paper sets down in the language of psychoanalytic object-relations theory virtually all the basic principles of Gestalt therapy, spelled out by Frederick and Laura Perls and Paul Goodman forty years ago.* Maybe Perls was right when he said that he had merely rediscovered them, for now it seems that they are being rediscovered by others. (p. 23, present authors' italics)

Conclusion: the Ideas are Often Greater than the Man

Fritz Perls co-created and disseminated one of the most creative approaches to psychotherapy developed this century. He was an extraordinarily perceptive and intuitive trainer and therapist. Yet many aspects of the man engender personal distaste. Fortunately, as is often the case, the ideas are greater than the man. In aesthetics, debates rage about whether a work of art is to be judged as separate from the life of the artist (Orwell, 1980). Scientists and lay people ponder upon the extent of Oppenheim's personal responsibility for Nagasaki. Similarly, we must each consider to what extent a system of psychotherapy is to be judged by the life and ethics of its inventors.

Fritz Perls was considered by many to be an inspirational genius, who 'expanded the possibilities of therapy' (Polster, 1992) and 'was brilliant in his conceptualizing both in theory and in practice' (Yontef, 1992a). This positive assessment highlights the contrast between his outstanding achievements, on the one hand, and his failings – such as his erratic development of theory, his sometimes shame-inducing contact with clients, or his unethical exploitation of group participants – on the other.

Such polarization is of course not unique to Fritz Perls, but afflicts the study of many outstanding individuals.[10] Their personal failings are often in painful juxtaposition with their gifts. Freud's contribution to the understanding of sexuality, for example, must be modified by his apparent denial of the reality of the widespread childhood sexual abuse of many of the women that he treated (Masson, 1989: 89–92). Berne saw intimacy as the goal of transactional analysis, but never appeared to achieve satisfactory and lasting loving relationships himself (Jorgensen and Jorgensen, 1984: 129). The great Protestant existentialist theologian Tillich (1973) had an underside of sado-masochistic sexuality which contrasts disconcertingly with his inspired and inspiring preachings. Jung manifested racism in his writings.[11] Like Fritz Perls, Jung also conducted sexual relationships with patients outside his marriage, and mixed their therapy with his own dream analysis. Melanie Klein, expert of the psychology and psychotherapy of the infant, analysed her own children (which is today considered unethical in the extreme), and apparently had the most appalling relationships with them (Grosskurth, 1985). It seems there are rarely great talents without great flaws. We want to stress that we are *not* trying to exonerate Perls' failings but to contextualize them, and suggest that he made an important contribution to the field of psychotherapy, whatever his failings.

At the same time there seems to be a common collective need to blemish, criticize or find fault with those who achieve more than the common lot. Often, the greater the achievement, the greater the vilification which follows the initial adulation. Even Rogers (1951; 1959), who is for many one of the finest and most exemplary of psychotherapists, has been viciously criticized, lately for his 'benevolence' (Masson, 1989: 243)! It seems that the inevitable price of achievement is other people's envy (Berke, 1989). No wonder Rollo May writes of 'the courage to create' (1975), and makes this the title of one of his finest books. Fritz Perls certainly was creative and exceptional. He had the courage to choose to be envied rather than to envy and he has attracted more than his fair share of criticisms, perhaps because he was so exceptionally public about so many aspects of himself, his work and his life. Philippson (1992) has suggested that, ironically, *within his own framework*, 'Perls had great integrity: his actions were open and consistent with his values, including sexually. We have different values!' What is outrageous today may be good practice tomorrow. And what is good practice today might be seen as restrictive or even harmful in the future.[12] The incontrovertible truths of one era often appear very mistaken in the light of history, or the developments in science and art. Fritz Perls' person, life and work have already been the subject of such vicissitudes of fortune.

For a large part of his life, the innovative ideas which Fritz Perls co-created with Laura Perls and Paul Goodman were virtually ignored, except by a few individuals who recognized their potential and were able to understand Goodman's poetic and complex prose. In the decade before his death, Perls achieved international fame. He was adulated by many. After his death, some Gestalt theoreticians acknowledged their debt to him, but many were quick to try to redress the balance of notoriety and stress the fact that Laura Perls' and Paul Goodman's role in the creation of Gestalt had been seriously underplayed. Unfortunately, in their attempts to value Laura Perls, Paul Goodman and others, this latter group have often, in their turn, unnecessarily devalued the contributions of Fritz Perls. Perhaps now it will be possible to appreciate the unique and different contributions of each of the founders of Gestalt therapy without denigrating those of the others.

It is tempting to try to formulate one summary statement about Fritz Perls, which resolves the many paradoxes of his work and life. But like Gestalt itself, the life and contribution of Fritz Perls is a whole in which many other wholes are embedded and in which polarities coexist. Whenever any one aspect of Fritz or his work is figure, the other aspects are inevitably background in the overall field. It is in the nature of wholes that we experience different facets differently at different times. Thus at one moment, the modern student may marvel at Perls' ability to synthesize many different theoretical and creative strands to form a coherent new whole. At another moment he may be disgusted by his rudeness and slovenly habits. Then he may be deeply shocked by his confrontative or unethical behaviour. Later he may admire his intuition and keen observation, and then suddenly be surprised by his tender patience. We have described those aspects of Perls and his work which seemed most important to us and shared our reactions with the reader, but finally we see Perls holistically and from a field perspective.

To paraphrase Perls himself, the scrutiny of isolated parts of the person leads only to an understanding of those isolated parts. The essence of the whole Perls can never be captured by an analysis of the parts. People's wholeness must be respected. Analytic attempts to break them, their lives and their works into bits and pieces annihilate the essence of the whole person and work that one intended to study. This book is no courtroom but a largely phenomenological account of the Fritz Perlsian legacy through the experiences of these authors at this time in this field. It is based upon Perls' own words; other people's memories, beliefs and experiences; our subjective understandings and inevitable partiality. It offers no final statement. There are as many different ways of looking at a person as there are people to do the looking. As in Kurosawa's *Rashomon* (1969), there is no ultimate truth. We invite each reader to construct his or her own unique existential meaning from the impression we have created.

Notes

1. The Lieberman, Yalom and Miles study was conceived in 1967 and published in 1973.

2. Lieberman, Yalom and Miles (1973) define a casualty as an individual who has been 'psychologically harmed by the experience [of the group encounter]. . . . not only must the group member have undergone some psychological decompensation but this must have been persistent and there must have been evidence that the group experience was the responsible agent' (pp. 6, 172).

3. Some aspects of Freudian theory regarding childhood development have, of course, since been questioned and modified by many major psychoanalysts, e.g. Klein and Kohut.

4. For example, Kepner discusses the similarity between much of what Perls wrote and the theories of Kurt Lewin and explains the very different practice of Perls and Lewin by their different foci. Lewin was a social psychologist, and what was figural for him was the social environment; while Perls was a physician and psychotherapist, and in practice the *individual* and *individual* change became most figural for him. However, his theory, like Lewin's, came from a similar lineage of Gestalt psychology and Goldstein's organismic theory (see Chapters 1 and 2).

5. Philippson's (1991) critique of Wheeler maintains that Wheeler has oversimplified the Goodman/Perls position and that in the 'creative resolution' Perls, Hefferline and Goodman (1951/1973) did not ignore the structure of ground. In

another critique of Wheeler's work, Yontef (1992b) has insisted that Perls (1947/1969a) demonstrates a clear understanding of field theory and was influenced by Wertheimer's, as well as Lewin's, field orientation.

6. 'Now, normally the élan vital, the life force, energizes by sensing, by listening, by scouting . . . this basic energy . . . these muscles are used to move about, to take from the world, to touch the world, to be in contact . . .' (Perls, 1969b: 63–4).

7. As has frequently been pointed out, there was a considerable discrepancy between Freud's apparent underestimation of the importance of the real relationship between patient and therapist and his own practice, for his case studies indicate that he was actually often self-revealing and surprisingly personal with his patients (Yalom, 1980, for example).

8. As we indicated on p. 175, we stress that we are *not* suggesting that Perls directly influenced these authors, merely indicating that there are parallels between the innovatory ideas concerning the relationship, which he popularized, and the subsequent contributions of the writers mentioned.

9. See pp. 149–50.

10. Miller (1989: 11–12) has raised similar questions in discussing Fritz Perls' legacy: 'Many notable clinicians and innovators in psychotherapy from Freud forward – Reich, Jung, Milton Erickson, R.D. Laing, to name a few striking examples – cast ambiguous shadows over the ranks of their followers. They loom before us in a blur of roles: are they scientists penetrating the secrets of human nature or religious healers? Mesmerists, sleight-of-hand experts? Charlatans? Misunderstood geniuses, cranks, or even madmen? . . . Perls in his later years left a legacy of mixed blessings.'

11. For example: 'The "Aryan" unconscious has a higher potential than the Jewish; that is both the advantage and the disadvantage of a youthfulness not yet fully weaned from barbarism' (in Masson, 1989: 140–1). He took over as editor of the *Zentralblatt* (which conformed with Nazi ideology) at the time when the Jews were being ousted, and remained editor even after confrontation of his anti-Semitic statements. He became president of an anti-Semitic society.

12. See the recent article by Woodmansey (1988) in the *British Journal of Psychotherapy*, questioning whether clients might not actually be being harmed by the *lack* of touching in many psychotherapies.

Select Bibliography of Perls' Major Writing

Books

Perls, F.S. (1947/1969a) *Ego, Hunger and Aggression*. New York: Vintage Books (first published in South Africa in 1942).

Perls, F.S. (1969b) *Gestalt Therapy Verbatim*. Moab, UT: Real People Press.

Perls, F.S. (1969c) *In and Out the Garbage Pail*. New York: Bantam Books.

Perls, F.S. (1976) *The Gestalt Approach, and Eye Witness to Therapy*. New York: Bantam (first published 1973).

Perls, F.S., Hefferline, R.F., and Goodman, P. (1951/1973) *Gestalt Therapy: Excitement and Growth in the Human Personality*. London: Penguin Books. (Originally published in New York by the Julian Press 1951; reprinted by them with new Authors' Note 1969.)

Perls, F.S., Hefferline, R.F., and Goodman, P. (1993) *Gestalt Therapy: Excitement and Growth in the Human Personality*. Highland, NY: Gestalt Journal. (Originally published 1951).

Baumgardner, P., and Perls, F.S. (1975) *Legacy from Fritz*. California: Science and Behavior Books.

Articles

Perls, F.S. (1948) 'Theory and Technique of Personality Integration', *American Journal of Psychotherapy*, 2: 565–86.

Perls, F.S. (1970) 'Four Lectures', pp. 14–38 in J. Fagan and I.L. Shepherd (eds), *Gestalt Therapy Now: Theory, Techniques, Applications*. New York: Harper Colophon.

Perls, F.S. (1978a) 'Psychiatry in a New Key', *Gestalt Journal*, 1(1): 32–53.

Perls, F.S. (1978b) 'Finding Self through Gestalt Therapy', *Gestalt Journal*, 1(1): 54–73.

Perls, F.S. (1979) 'Planned Psychotherapy', *Gestalt Journal*, 2(2): 5–23 (originally delivered at the William Alanson White Institute, New York, 1946-7).

Perls, F.S. (in press) Numerous unpublished manuscripts found in the homes of Marty Fromm and Laura Perls, to be published by the *Gestalt Journal*.

References

Adelson, J., and Doehrman, M.J. (1980) 'The Psychodynamic Approach to Adolescence', in J. Adelson (ed.), *Handbook of Adolescent Psychology*. New York: Wiley.

Albery, N. (ed.) (1992) *The Book of Visions: An Encylopaedia of Social Innovations*. London: Virgin.

American Psychiatric Association (1987) *Diagnostic and Statistical Manual of Mental Disorder: DSM III R*. Washington: American Psychiatric Association.

Baumgardner, P., and Perls, F.S. (1975) *Legacy from Fritz*. California: Science and Behavior Books.

Beisser, A.R. (1970) 'The Paradoxical Theory of Change', in J. Fagan and I. Shepherd (eds), *Gestalt Therapy Now*. Palo Alto, CA: Science and Behavior Books.

Bergin, A.E. (1971) 'The Evaluation of Therapeutic Outcomes', pp. 217–70 in S.L. Garfield and A.E. Bergin (eds), *Handbook of Psychotherapy and Behaviour Change*. New York: Wiley.

Bergson, H. (1965) *Creative Evolution*. London: Macmillan.

Berke, J. H. (1989) *The Tyranny of Malice*. London: Simon and Schuster.

Berne, E. (1970) 'Book Review', *American Journal of Psychiatry*, 126(10): 163–4.

Blanck, G., and Blanck, R. (1974) *Ego Psychology*. New York: Columbia University Press.

Bohart, A., and Todd, J. (1988) *Foundations of Clinical and Counselling Psychology*. New York: Harper Collins.

Breshgold, E. (1989) 'Resistance in Gestalt Therapy: An Historical/Theoretical Perspective', *Gestalt Journal*, 12(2): 73–102.

Brown, D., and Pedder, J. (1991) *Introduction to Psychotherapy: An Outline of Psychodynamic Principles and Practice* (2nd edn). London and New York: Tavistock/Routledge.

Buber, M. (1965) *Between Man and Man* (R. Gregor Smith, trans.). New York: Macmillan.

Buber, M. (1987) *I and Thou* (R. Gregor Smith, trans.). Edinburgh: T. and T. Clark (first published 1937).

Cavaleri, P. (1992) 'Karen Horney and Frederick Perls', *Quaderni di Gestalt*, 1: 53–9.

Clark, N., and Fraser, S.T. (1987) *The Gestalt Approach* (2nd edn). Horsham: Roffey Park Management College.

Clarkson, P. (1988) 'Gestalt Therapy: An Update', *Self and Society*, 16(2): 74–9.

Clarkson, P. (1989) *Gestalt Counselling in Action* (2nd edn). London: Sage.

Clarkson, P. (1990) 'A Multiplicity of Psychotherapeutic Relationships', *British Journal of Psychotherapy*, 7(2): 148–63.

Clarkson, P. (1991a) 'Laura Perls Memorial', *British Gestalt Journal*, 1(1): 3.

Clarkson, P. (1991b) Keynote address at British Gestalt Conference, London.

Clarkson, P. (1991c) 'Individuality and Commonality in Gestalt', *British Gestalt Journal*, 1(1): 28–37.

Clarkson, P. (1992a) 'Physis in Transactional Analysis', *ITA News*, 3: 14–19. Also published 1992 in *Transactional Analysis Journal*, 22(4): 202–9.

Clarkson, P. (1992b) '2500 Years of Gestalt (from Heraclitus to the Big Bang)', *British Gestalt Journal*, 2.

Clarkson, P., and Carroll, M. (1993) 'Counselling, Psychotherapy, Psychology and Psychiatry: The Same and Different', chapter in P. Clarkson (ed.), *On Psychotherapy*. London: Sage.

Clarkson, P., and Clayton, S. (1992) *Professional Development, Personal Development and Counselling or Psychotherapy: How to Differentiate and Negotiate Boundaries in Organisational Work*. Unpublished manuscript.

Clarkson, P., Mackewn, J., and Shaw, P. (1992) *Quantum Group Process*. Training workshop at *metanoia*, London.

Clarkson, P., and Shaw, P. (1992) 'Human Relationships at Work – The Place of Counselling Skills and Consulting Skills and Services in Organisations', *MEAD: The Journal of the Association of Management Education and Development*, 23(1): 18–29.

Corey, G. (1991) *Theory and Practice of Counselling and Psychotherapy*. Pacific Grove, California: Brooks/Cole.

Davidove, D. (1991) 'Loss of Ego Function, Conflict and Resistance', *Gestalt Journal*, 14(2): 27–43.

Delisle, G. (1988) *Balises II: A Gestalt Perspective of Personality Disorders*. Montreal: Le Centre d'Intervention Gestaltiste, Le Reflet.

Delisle, G. (1993) *Personality Disorders: A Gestalt Perspective*. Highland, NY: Gestalt Journal.

Dublin, J.E. (1977) 'Gestalt Therapy, Existential-Gestalt Therapy and/versus "Perls-ism"', pp. 124–50 in E.W.L. Smith (ed.), *The Growing Edge of Gestalt Therapy*. Secaucus, NJ: Citadel Press.

Dyer, W. (1978) *Pulling Your Own Strings*. New York: Funk and Wagnalls.

Fagan, J., and Shepherd, I.L. (eds) (1970) *Gestalt Therapy Now: Theory, Techniques, Applications*. New York: Harper Colophon.

Feder, B., and Ronall, R. (eds) (1980) *Beyond the Hot Seat: Gestalt Approaches to Group*. New York: Brunner/Mazel.

Fiedler, F.E. (1950) 'A Comparison of Therapeutic Relationships in Psychoanalytic, Nondirective and Adlerian Therapy', *Journal of Consulting Psychology*, 14: 436–45.

Frank, J.D. (1979) 'The Present Status of Outcome Studies', *Journal of Consulting and Clinical Psychology*, 47: 310–16.

Frankl, V.E. (1973) *Man's Search For Meaning*. London: Hodder and Stoughton.

Frew, J.E. (1983) 'Encouraging What is Not Figural in the Gestalt Group', *Journal for Specialists in Group Work*, 8(4): 175–81.

Friedländer, S. (1918) *Schöpferische Indifferenz*. Munich: Georg Muller.

From, I. (1981) Personal communication.

From, I. (1984) 'Reflections on Gestalt Therapy after Thirty-Two Years of Practice: A Requiem for Gestalt', *Gestalt Journal*, 7(1): 4–12.

From, I. (1991) Personal communication.

Gaines, J. (1979) *Fritz Perls Here and Now*. California: Celestial Arts.

Goldstein, K. (1939) *The Organism*. New York: American Book Company.

Goodman, P. (1947) *Communitas*. New York: Random House.

Goodman, P. (1960) *Growing Up Absurd*. New York: Random House.

Goodman, P. (1962) *Utopian Essays and Practical Proposals*. New York: Random House.

Goodman, P. (1990) 'The Drama of Awareness', in programme notes for *Stop-Light: Five Noh Plays*, performed at CHARAS Theater, New York, on 16 December 1990.

Goodman, P. (1991) *Nature Heals: Psychological Essays*. New York: Gestalt Journal (first published 1977).

Greenberg, E. (1989) 'Healing the Borderline', *Gestalt Journal*, 12(2): 11–55.

Greenberg, J.R., and Mitchell, S.A. (1983) *Object Relations in Psychoanalytic Theory*. Cambridge, MA and London: Harvard University Press.

Greenberg, L.S. (1975) 'A Task Analytic Approach to the Study of Psychotherapeutic Events', *Dissertation Abstracts International*, 37: 4647B.

Greenberg, L.S. (1979) 'Resolving Splits: The Two-Chair Technique', *Psychotherapy: Theory, Research and Practice*, 16: 310–18.

Greenberg, L.S., and Clarke, K.M. (1986) 'Differential Effects of the Gestalt Two-Chair Intervention and Problem Solving in Resolving Decisional Conflict', *Journal of Counselling Psychology*, 33(1): 11–15.

Greenberg, L.S., and Rice, L.N. (1984) *Patterns of Change: Intensive Analysis of Psychotherapy Process*. New York: Guilford Press.

Greenson, R.R. (1967) *The Technique and Practice of Psychoanalysis*, vol. 1. New York: International Universities Press.

Greenson, R.R. (1971) 'The "Real" Relationship between the Patient and the Psychoanalyst', pp. 425–40 in R.R. Greenson (ed.), *Explorations in Psychoanalysis* (1978). New York: International Universities Press.

Greenson, R.R., and Wexler, M. (1969) 'The Nontransference Relationship in the Psychoanalytic Situation', pp. 359–86 in R.R. Greenson (ed.), *Explorations in Psychoanalysis* (1978). New York: International Universities Press.

Grosskurth, P. (1985) *Melanie Klein: Her World and Her Work*. London: Maresfield Library.

Guerriere, D. (1980) 'Physis, Sophia, Psyche', pp. 86–134 in J. Sallis and K. Maly (eds), *Heraclitean Fragments: A Companion Volume to the Heidegger/Fink Seminar on Heraclitus*. Alabama: University of Alabama Press.

Guntrip, H. (1973) *Psychoanalytic Theory, Therapy and the Self*. New York: Basic Books.

Hall, R. (1977) 'A Schema of the Gestalt Concept of the Organismic Flow and its Disturbance', pp. 53–7 in E.W.L. Smith (ed.), *The Growing Edge of Gestalt Therapy*. Secaucus, NJ: Citadel Press.

Harman, R. (1984) 'Recent Developments in Gestalt Group Therapy', *International Journal of Group Psychotherapy*, 34(3): 473–83.

Heidegger, M. (1962) *Being and Time* (J. Macquarrie and E. Robinson, trans.). New York: Harper and Row.

Henle, M. (1978) 'Gestalt Psychology and Gestalt Therapy', *Journal of History of the Behavioral Sciences*, 14: 23–32.

Hill, C.E., Carter, J.A., and O'Farrell, M.K. (1983) 'A Case Study of the Process and Outcome of Time-Limited Counselling', *Journal of Counselling Psychology*, 30(1): 3–18.

Horney, K. (1937) *The Neurotic Personality of Our Times*. New York: Norton.

Horney, K. (1939) *New Ways in Psychoanalysis*. New York: Norton.

Humphrey, K. (1986) 'Laura Perls: A Biographical Sketch', *Gestalt Journal*, 9(1): 5–11.

Husserl, E. (1931) *Ideas: General Introduction to Pure Phenomenology*, vol. 1. New York: Macmillan.

Husserl, E. (1968) *The Idea of Phenomenology*. The Hague: Nijhoff.

Hycner, R. H. (1985) 'Dialogical Gestalt Therapy: An Initial Proposal', *Gestalt Journal*, 8(1): 23–49.

Hycner, R.H. (1991) 'The I–Thou Relationship and Gestalt Therapy', *Gestalt Journal*, 13(1): 42–54.

Jacobs, L. (1978) *I–Thou Relation in Gestalt Therapy*. Doctoral dissertation, California School of Professional Psychology, Los Angeles.

Jacobs, L. (1989) 'Dialogue in Gestalt Theory and Therapy', *Gestalt Journal*, 12(1): 25–68.

Jacobs, M. (1988) *Psychodynamic Counselling in Action*. London: Sage Publications.

Jorgensen, E. W., and Jorgensen, H. I. (1984) *Eric Berne, Master Gamesman: A Transactional Biography*. New York: Grove Press.

Jung, C.G. (1968) 'Archetypes of the Collective Unconscious', pp. 3–41 in Sir H. Read, M. Fordham, G. Adler and W. McGuire (eds), *The Collected Works of C.G. Jung*, vol. 9, part I (2nd edn) (R.F.C. Hull, trans.). London: Routledge and Kegan Paul (first published 1954).

Kahn, M. (1991) *Between Therapist and Client: The New Relationship*. New York: W.H. Freeman.

Kempler, W. (1973) *Principles of Gestalt Family Therapy: A Gestalt Experiential Book*. Norway: Nordahls.

Kepner, E. (1980) 'Gestalt Group Process', pp. 5–24 in B. Feder and R. Ronall (eds), *Beyond the Hot Seat*. New York: Brunner/Mazel.

Kepner, J.I. (1987) *Body Process: A Gestalt Approach to Working with the Body in Psychotherapy*. New York: Gardner.

Kernberg, O. (1976) *Object Relations Theory and Clinical Psychoanalysis*. New York: Jason Aronson.

Kierkegaard, S. (1939) *The Point of View for My Work as An Author* (W. Lowrie, trans.). New York: Oxford University Press (first published 1845).

Kierkegaard, S. (1941) *Concluding Scientific Postscript* (W. Lowrie and D.F. Swenson, trans.). Princeton, NJ: Princeton University Press (first published 1846).

Kierkegaard, S. (1944) *The Concept of Dread* (W. Lowrie, trans.). Princeton, NJ: Princeton University Press (first published 1844).

Klein, M. (1964) *Contributions to Psychoanalysis, 1921–1945*. New York: McGraw-Hill.

Klein, M. (1975) *Envy and Gratitude and other works, 1946–1963*. New York: Delaccotte Press.

Koffka, K. (1935) *Principles of Gestalt Psychology*. New York: Harcourt, Brace and World.

Köhler, W. (1969) *The Task of Gestalt Psychology*. Princeton, NJ: Princeton University Press.

Köhler, W. (1970) *Gestalt Psychology: An Introduction to New Concepts in Modern Psychology*. New York: Liveright (first published 1947).

Kohut, H. (1971) *The Analysis of the Self*. New York: International Universities Press.

Kohut, H. (1977) *The Restoration of the Self*. New York: International Universities Press.

Kohut, H. (1984) *How Does Psychoanalysis Cure?* Chicago: University of Chicago Press.

Kohut, H., and Wolf, S. (1978) 'The Disorders of the Self and Their Treatment: An Outline', *International Journal of Psycho-Analysis*, 59: 413–24.

Korb, M.P., Gorrell, J., and Van der Riet, V. (1989) *Gestalt Therapy: Practice and Theory* (2nd edn). New York: Pergamon Press.

Kovel, J. (1976) *A Complete Guide to Therapy*. London: Penguin (reprinted 1991).

Kurosawa, A. (1969) *Rashomon: A Film by Akira Kurosawa from the Film Script by Akiro Kurosawa and Shinobu Hashimoto*. New York: Grove Press.

Landman, J.T., and Dawes, R.M. (1982) 'Smith and Glass' Conclusions Stand Up Under Scrutiny', *The American Psychologist*, 37: 504–16.

Latner, J. (1974) *The Gestalt Therapy Book*. New York: Bantam Books.

Lewin, K. (1926) 'Vorsatz, Wille and Bedürfnis (Intention, Will and Need)', *Psychologische Forschung*, 7: 440–7.

Lewin, K. (1935) *A Dynamic Theory of Personality*. New York: McGraw-Hill.

Lewin, K. (1952) *Field Theory in Social Science: Selected Theoretical Papers*. London: Tavistock (first published 1951).

Lieberman, M.A., Yalom, I.D., and Miles, M.B. (1973) *Encounter Groups: First Facts*. New York: Basic Books.

Lowen, A. (1975) *Bioenergetics*. New York: Coward, McCann and Geoghegan.

Luborsky, L., Singer, B., and Luborsky, L. (1975) 'Comparative Studies of Psychotherapies: Is It True that "Everybody has Won and All Must Have Prizes"?', *Archives of General Psychiatry*, 32: 995–1008.

Mackewn, J. (1991) 'Transference and Countertransference: A Gestalt Perspective'. Unpublished paper delivered at *metanoia*, 1991.

McLeod, L.T. (1991) *The Self in Gestalt Therapy Theory*. Unpublished master's thesis, Antioch University, London.

Mahler, J.S., Pine, F., and Bergman, A. (1975) *The Psychological Birth of the Human Infant*. New York: Basic Books.

Marcel, G. (1952) *The Metaphysical Journal* (B. Wall, trans.). London: Rockliff Publishing Corporation (first published 1927).

Maslow, A. (1954) *Maturation and Personality*. New York: Harper and Row.

Maslow, A. (1968) *Toward a Psychology of Being*. New York: Van Nostrand.

Masson, J. (1989) *Against Therapy*. London: Collins.

Masterson, J.F. (1976) *Psychotherapy of the Borderline Adult: A Developmental Approach*. New York: Brunner/Mazel.

Masterson, J. F. (1981) *The Narcissistic and Borderline Disorders: An Integrated Developmental Approach*. New York: Brunner/Mazel.

Masterson, J.F. (1983) *Countertransference and Psychotherapeutic Technique*. New York: Brunner/Mazel.

May, R. (1950) *The Meaning of Anxiety*. New York: Norton.

May, R. (1975) *The Courage to Create*. New York: Bantam Books.

Merleau-Ponty, M. (1962) *Phenomenology of Perception* (C. Smith, trans.). London: Routledge and Kegan Paul.

Miller, M. V. (1989) 'Introduction to *Gestalt Therapy Verbatim*', *Gestalt Journal*, 12(1): 5–24.

Moreno, J. L. (1934) *Who Shall Survive?* New York: Nervous and Mental Disease Publishing.

Moreno, J. L. (1964) *Psychodrama*, vol. 1 (rev. edn). New York: Beacon House (first published 1946).

Naranjo, C. (1982) 'Gestalt Conference Talk 1981', *Gestalt Journal*, 5(1): 3–19.

Nelson-Jones, R. (1982) *The Theory and Practice of Counselling*. London: Holt, Rinehart and Winston.

Nevis, E. (1987) *Organizational Consulting: A Gestalt Approach*. New York: Gardner Press.

Nevis, E. (1992) Personal communication.

Nicholson, R.A., and Berman, J.S. (1983) 'Is Follow-Up Necessary in Evaluating Psychotherapy?', *Psychological Bulletin*, 93: 261–78.

Ornstein, R.E. (1972) *The Psychology of Consciousness*. San Francisco: W.H. Freeman.

Orwell, G. (1980) 'Benefit of Clergy: Some Notes on Salvador Dali', pp. 640–6 in *Collected Essays, Journalism and Letters of George Orwell 1944–1945*. London: Secker and Warburg.

Ovsiankina, M. (1928) 'Die Wiederaufnahme von Interbrochenen Handlungen', *Psychologische Forschung*, 2: 302–89.

Parlett, M. (1992) 'Field Theory'. Plenary lecture at European Gestalt Conference, Paris.

Parlett, M., and Page, F. (1990) 'Gestalt Therapy', pp. 175–98 in W. Dryden (ed.), *Individual Therapy in Britain*. Milton Keynes: Open University Press.

Perls, F.S. (1947/1969a) *Ego, Hunger and Aggression*. New York: Vintage Books (first published in South Africa in 1942).

Perls, F.S. (1948) 'Theory and Technique of Personality Integration', *American Journal of Psychotherapy*, 2: 565–86.

Perls, F.S. (1969b) *Gestalt Therapy Verbatim*. Moab, UT: Real People Press.

Perls, F.S. (1969c) *In and Out the Garbage Pail*. New York: Bantam Books.

Perls, F.S. (1970) 'Four Lectures', pp. 14–38 in J. Fagan and I.L. Shepherd (eds), *Gestalt Therapy Now: Theory, Techniques, Applications*. New York: Harper Colophon.

Perls, F.S. (1976) *The Gestalt Approach, and Eye Witness to Therapy*. New York: Bantam (first published 1973).

Perls, F.S. (1978a) 'Psychiatry in a New Key', *Gestalt Journal*, 1(1): 32–53.

Perls, F.S. (1978b) 'Finding Self through Gestalt Therapy', *Gestalt Journal*, 1(1): 54–73.

Perls, F.S. (1979) 'Planned Psychotherapy', *Gestalt Journal*, 2(2): 5–23 (originally delivered at the William Alanson White Institute, New York, 1946–7).

Perls, F.S., Hefferline, R.F., and Goodman, P. (1973) *Gestalt Therapy: Excitement and Growth in the Human Personality*. London: Penguin Books. (Originally published in New York by Julian Press in 1951; reprinted by them with new Authors' Note 1969).

Perls, F.S., Hefferline, R.F., and Goodman, P. (1993) *Gestalt Therapy: Excitement and Growth in the Human Personality*. Highland, NY: Gestalt Journal (first published 1951).

Perls, L. (1991) *Living at the Boundary*. Highland, NY: Gestalt Journal Publications.

Perls, L. (1992) 'Concepts and Misconceptions of Gestalt Therapy', *Journal of Humanistic Psychology*, 32(3): 50–6 (first published 1978).

Perls, R. (1992) Personal communication.

Philippson, P. (1991) 'Book Review: *Gestalt Reconsidered* by Gordon Wheeler', *British Gestalt Journal*, 1(2): 103–6.

Philippson, P. (1992) Personal communication in response to authors' questionnaire.

Polster, E. (1985) 'Imprisoned in the Present', *Gestalt Journal*, 8(1): 5–22.

Polster, E. (1987) *Every Person's Life is Worth a Novel*. New York: W.W. Norton.

Polster, E. (1989) Personal communication.

Polster, E. (1991) 'Response to "Loss of Ego Functions, Conflict and Resistance"', *Gestalt Journal*, 14(2): 45–65.

Polster, E. (1992) Personal communication.

Polster, E., and Polster, M. (1974) *Gestalt Therapy Integrated: Contours of Theory and Practice*. New York: Vintage Books.

Posner, R. (1991) Personal communication in response to authors' questionnaire.

Reich, W. (1945) *Character Analysis*. New York: Orgone Institute Press (first published 1933).

Reich, W. (1952) *The Sexual Revolution*. London: Vision Press (first published 1936).

Reich, W. (1968) *The Function of the Orgasm*. London: Panther Books (first published 1942).

Resnick, R.W. (1984) 'Gestalt Therapy East and West: Bi-Coastal Dialogue, Debate or Debacle?', *Gestalt Journal*, 7(1): 13–32.

Ribiero, J.P. (1985) *Gestalt-Terapie: Refazendo Um Caminho*. Sao Paulo: Summus.

Robbins, M. (1991) 'The Therapy of Primitive Personalities'. Unpublished manuscript.

Rogers, C.R. (1951) *Client-Centred Therapy: Its Current Practice, Implications and Theory*. Boston: Houghton Mifflin.

Rogers, C.R. (1959) 'A Theory of Therapy, Personality and Interpersonal Relationships, as Developed in the Client-Centred Framework', pp. 184–256 in S. Koch (ed.), *Psychology: A Study of a Science*, vol. 3. New York: McGraw-Hill.

Rolf, I. (1977) *Structural Integration: The Re-Creation of the Balanced Human Body*. New York: Viking Press.

Rooth, G. (1987) 'Gestalt Therapy', pp. 291–3 in R. Gregory (ed.), *The Oxford Companion to the Mind*. Oxford: Oxford University Press.

Rosenblatt, D. (1991) 'An Interview with Laura Perls', *Gestalt Journal*, 14(1): 7–26 (interview 1982).

Rowan, J. (1988) *Ordinary Ecstasy*. London: Routledge (first published 1976).

Rowan, J. (1992) *Breakthroughs and Integration in Psychotherapy*. London: Whurr.

Rutter, P. (1990) *Sex in the Forbidden Zone: When Men in Power – Therapists, Doctors, Clergy, Teachers and Others – Betray Women's Trust*. London: Unwin (first published 1989).

Saner, R. (1989) 'Culture Bias of Gestalt Therapy: Made in the USA', *Gestalt Journal*, 12(2): 57–73.

Sartre, J.P. (1938) *Nausea*. Harmondsworth, Middlesex: Penguin.

Sartre, J.P. (1958) *Being and Nothingness* (H.E. Barnes, trans.). London: Methuen (first published 1943).

Schoen, S. (1993) *Presence of Mind: Literary and Philosophical Roots of a Wise Psychotherapy*. Highland, NY: Gestalt Journal.

Schutz, W. (1967) *Joy: Expanding Human Awareness*. London: Souvenir Press.

Schutz, W. (1973) *Elements of Encounter*. Big Sur: Joy Press.

Serlin, I.A. (1992) 'Tribute to Laura Perls', *Journal of Humanistic Psychology*, 32(3): 57–66.

Shearman, C. (1993) 'An Integrative Approach to Working with Harmful Behaviours'. Unpublished manuscript.

Shepard, M. (1975) *Fritz*. New York: Bantam.

Sherrill, R. Jr (1974) *Figure/Ground: Gestalt Therapy/Gestalt Psychology Relationship*. Unpublished doctoral thesis, the Union Graduate School.

Simkin, J. (1974) *Gestalt Therapy Mini-Lectures*. Milbrae, CA: Celestial Arts.

Smith, E.W.L. (ed.) (1977) *The Growing Edge of Gestalt Therapy*. Secaucus, NJ: Citadel Press.

Smith, M.L., Glass, G.V., and Miller, T.I. (1980) *The Benefits of Psychotherapy*. Baltimore, MD: Johns Hopkins University Press.

Smuts, J.C. (1987) *Holism and Evolution*. Cape Town, SA: N & S Press (first published 1926).

Spence, D.P. (1982) *Narrative Truth and Historical Truth: Meaning and Interpretation in Psychoanalysis*. New York: Norton.

Spinelli, E. (1989) *The Interpersonal World: An Introduction to Phenomenological Psychology*. London: Sage.

Stevens, B. (1970). *Don't Push the River (It Flows by Itself)*. Lafayette, CA: Real People Press.

Stevens, J.O. (ed.) (1975) *Gestalt Is*. Moab, UT: Real People Press.

Stevens, J.O. (1989) *Awareness*. London: Eden Grove (first published 1971).

Stoehr, T. (in press) *Paul Goodman's Contribution to Gestalt Therapy*. Cleveland, OH: Institute of Cleveland Press.

Sullivan, H.S. (1953) *The Interpersonal Theory of Psychiatry*. New York: Norton.

Sullivan, H.S. (1962) *Schizophrenia as a Human Process*. New York: Norton.

Sullivan, H.S. (1964) *The Fusion of Psychiatry and Social Science*. New York: Norton.

Tillich, H. (1973) *From Time to Time*. New York: Stein and Day.

Tobin, S.A. (1982) 'Self Disorders, Gestalt Therapy and Self Psychology', *Gestalt Journal*, 5(2): 3–44.

Truax, C.R., and Carkhuff, R.R. (1967) *Toward Effective Counseling and Psychotherapy*. Chicago: Aldine.

Tubbs, W. (1972) 'Beyond Perls', *Journal of Humanistic Psychology*, 12: 5.

van Deurzen-Smith, E. (1988) *Existential Counselling in Practice*. London: Sage.

Watts, A.W. (1951) *Psychotherapy East and West*. New York: Pantheon.

Watts, A.W. (1957) *The Way of Zen*. London: Thames and Hudson.

Weinberg, G. (1978) *Self-Creation*. New York: Avon.

Wertheimer, M. (1925) 'Gestalt Theory', pp. 1–11 in W.D. Ellis (ed.), *A Sourcebook of Gestalt Psychology* (1938). London: Routledge and Kegan Paul.

Wertheimer, M. (1938) 'The General Theoretical Situation', pp. 12–16 in W.D. Ellis (ed.), *A Sourcebook of Gestalt Psychology* (1938). London: Routledge and Kegan Paul.

Wertheimer, M. (1944) 'Gestalt Theory', *Social Research*, 11(1): 78–99.

Wertheimer, M. (1959) *Productive Thinking* (2nd edn). New York: Harper and Row (first published 1945).

Wheeler, G. (1991) *Gestalt Reconsidered: A New Approach to Contact and Resistance*. New York: Gardner.

Winnicott, D.W. (1958) *Through Paediatrics to Psycho-analysis*. London: Hogarth Press.

Winnicott, D.W. (1965) *The Maturational Process and the Facilitating Environment*. New York: International Universities Press.

Winnicott, D.W. (1986) *Home is Where We Start From*. London: Penguin Books.

Woodmansey, A.C. (1988) 'Are Psychotherapists Out of Touch?', *British Journal of Psychotherapy*, (5)1: 57–65.

Wysong, J. (1992) Personal communication.

Wysong, J., and Rosenfeld, E. (1982) *An Oral History of Gestalt Therapy:*

Interviews with Laura Perls, Isadore From, Erving Polster, Miriam Polster.
Highland, NY: Gestalt Journal.

Yalom, I. (1980) *Existential Psychotherapy.* New York: Basic Books.

Yalom, I. (1985) *The Theory and Practice of Group Psychotherapy* (3rd edn). New York: Basic Books (first published 1970).

Yalom, I. (1989) *Love's Executioner and Other Tales of Psychotherapy.* London: Penguin.

Yontef, G.M. (1980) 'Gestalt Therapy: A Dialogic Method'. Unpublished manuscript.

Yontef, G.M. (1982) 'Gestalt Therapy: Its Inheritance from Gestalt Psychology', *Gestalt Therapy*, 4(1/2): 23–39.

Yontef, G.M. (1987) 'Gestalt Therapy 1986: A Polemic', *Gestalt Journal*, 10(1): 41–68.

Yontef, G.M. (1988) 'Assimilating Diagnostic and Psychoanalytic Perspectives into Gestalt Therapy', *Gestalt Journal*, 11(1): 5–32.

Yontef, G.M. (1991) 'Recent Trends in Gestalt Therapy in the United States and What We Need to Learn from Them', *British Gestalt Journal*, 1(1): 5–20.

Yontef, G.M. (1992a) Personal communication in response to author's questionnaire.

Yontef, G.M. (1992b) 'Considering *Gestalt Reconsidered*: A Review in Depth', *Gestalt Journal*, 15(1): 95–118.

Yontef, G.M. (1992c) *Awareness, Process and Dialogue: Essays on Gestalt Therapy.* Highland, NY: Gestalt Journal.

Zeigarnik, B. (1927) 'Uber das Behalten von Erledigten und Unerledigten Handlungen', *Psychologische Forschung*, 9: 1–85.

Zinker, J. (1978) *Creative Process in Gestalt Therapy.* New York: Vintage Books (first published 1977).

Zinker, J. (1980) 'The Development Process of a Gestalt Therapy Group', pp. 55–77 in B. Feder and R. Ronall (eds), *Beyond the Hot Seat.* New York: Brunner/Mazel.

Index

Index compiled by Mary Norris